Booth's House of Lords

PLOTTED ON WINDSOR'S UNEQUAL-AREA-EXPEDIENT PROJECTION

RELIABLE SOURCES

100 Years at the National Press Club

Centennial Edition

RELIABLE
SOURCES

100 Years at the National Press Club

Centennial Edition

Turner®
Publishing Company

Nashville, Tennessee • Paducah, Kentucky

TURNER PUBLISHING COMPANY

Nashville, Tennessee

www.turnerpublishing.com

ISBN: 978-1-68162-379-5
Library of Congress Control Number: 2007940975

Photo this page: The National Press Club occupies the top two floors of this 14-story office building at 14th and F Streets, NW, Washington, D.C. Equipped with state-of-the-art communications, the building is open 24 hours a day. It shares a city block with the National Theatre, shops and offices and the J.W. Marriott Hotel. It has its own postal zip code–20045. Opened in 1927, it was renovated in 1985. Tenants are only an elevator ride away to the National Press Club's forum of national and international leaders.

TABLE OF CONTENTS

Gil Klein

New National Press Club presidents soon realize they stand on the shoulders of their predecessors, who for 100 years have volunteered their time to build, maintain and expand the Club. It has been a remarkable achievement.

And anyone who writes a history of the National Press Club realizes how much debt is owed to previous chroniclers. The Club's lore has been passed down from generation to generation, updated every couple of decades with a new book. To prepare myself to be Club president in 1994, I read every one of those books to gain an appreciation for the job I was undertaking.

The 20th Anniversary Yearbook in 1928 was the first to capture the Club's founding saga. Twenty years later, "Dateline: Washington" expanded the history through World War II and placed the Club in the context of Washington journalism. What was most remarkable about that book was its authors. Chapters were written by legendary *New York Times* bureau chief Arthur Krock; Bruce Catton, who went on to write a best-selling Civil War narrative history; and Fletcher Kneble, who later wrote several popular novels. For the Club's 50th birthday, it produced "Shrdlu," a title that every newspaper reporter in 1958 would understand but few journalists would in the 21st century. As typesetters keyed in copy on the old Linotype machines in the 1950s, they would sometimes make errors. To note where the errors were, they would run their hand down the left side of the keyboard that would type "shrdlu."

This book draws heavily from "Reliable Sources," the history produced a decade ago through the effort of 1997 President Richard Sammon of *Congressional Quarterly*. That book had been written haphazardly over more than a decade before Sammon organized a final effort to get it out in time for the Club's 90th birthday. For this book, we not only updated the history since 1997, but we went back through all of the old histories to make sure we are presenting the full flavor of the Club's lore. It is substantially a different book, but we retained the title "Reliable Sources," not only because we thought it was a good title but also because this book's foundation rests on its immediate predecessor.

Working on this book has been a cadre of devoted Club members.

John Cosgrove has been a member since the 1940s and was one of the authors of "Shrdlu." He served as president in 1961 when he worked for Broadcasting Publications, and the account of President John Kennedy attending Cosgrove's inauguration is included here. Cosgrove's service to this book was invaluable. He can look at a picture from a half century ago and identify everyone in it. He remembers details of decades-old events and can pick out factual errors in copy that no one else would catch.

David Hess was Club president in 1985 when he was White House correspondent for Knight-Ridder Newspapers. As a Board member, he worked on the gargantuan task of reconstructing the National Press Building, and as president, he not only presided at ceremonies rededicating the building but also finished the agreement that merged the Washington Press Club and the National Press Club, burying the enmity between women and men journalists.

Ken Dalecki served on the Club's Board of Governors when he worked for *Kiplinger Washington Editors* and has been active in the Club for years, serving as chairman of several committees and on the National Press Building Corp. board.

Sylvia Smith of the *Fort Wayne (Ind.) Journal Gazette* has been secretary of the Club since 2000. She has been an integral part of the many of the changes in the Club during the past few years, and she employed her fine copy editing skills in service to this book.

Christina Zamon, the Club's archivist, holds a master's degree in history and a master's degree in library science from the University of Maryland, and she is accredited through the Academy of Certified Archivists. But most important for the book is that she kept a cheerful yet professional demeanor while finding information and photographs, even as she was responding to all of the other requests for help in the year leading up to the Club's centennial.

All of these people came into the Archives on Saturdays and labored during their evenings and vacations to plan, research and write this book, to cull through photographs and write captions, and to edit each other's copy. That is the kind of loyalty the National Press Club engenders.

Gil Klein
Media General News Service
Club President, 1994
Editor of *Reliable Sources: 100 Years at the National Press Club*

John Cosgrove

Ken Dalecki

David Hess

Sylvia Smith

Christina Zamon

Llewellyn King

Journalists by their nature are not joiners. They are neither club people nor members of boards or fraternal organizations.

These cats, these men and women of the Fourth Estate, walk alone. Except, that is, when it comes to the National Press Club.

The National Press Club is not the world's only press club, but it is the largest, best known and the most durable. Since 1908, it has overcome the pervasive individualism of journalists to provide them a professional organization, a sanctuary and a refuge. It is a place where the tired editor, the weary foreign correspondent and the bruised reporter can come in from the cold. Come in to warm at the fires of camaraderie; to be soothed by conviviality; and to talk and talk and talk to people who know exactly what is being talked about.

When the National Press Club was founded in 1908, news was transmitted by telegraph, and the Linotype (the technological marvel that revolutionized the production of newspapers) had been invented fewer than 20 years earlier. Afternoon newspapers dominated journalism, and many cities had half a dozen newspapers; some had many more. The newsmagazine, the glossy magazine, newsletters, radio and television were still in the future.

At that time, ours was a profession with no formal rules of entry; no training; hardly a college graduate; and only the ability to do the job, learned on the job, counted.

Like boxing, it was often a way out of the ghetto, a way for a bright boy to leave the manual work that had sustained his father.

They were a rough-hewn lot. They ranged from the just adequate to those who have yet to see a peer, such as H.L. Mencken. Writing counted, and speed was often a physical function – as in running back to the office.

Today we are trained and educated, yet surprisingly similar to the journalists at the time of the Club's founding. We are good, and we are bad; some write like angels, others are simply craftsmen.

For 50 years the National Press Club was a professional organization and a crucible of ideas. But it was also a drinking club. As late as the 1960s, it was still a drinking club with the patrons often three deep at the bar. Lore and law contributed to this. Strong drink and journalism were a tradition, and government policy abetted drinking at the Press Club. The National Press Club served during Prohibition, and for nearly four decades afterward it was the only place where you could get a drink on Sunday. Its two famous bars were, for nearly 40 years, the only places in Washington, D.C., where it was legal to stand up and walk around with a drink.

The law changed, society changed, journalists changed, but the Club continues to thrive. It thrives because it is an adaptive institution, correcting for the sins of the past, such as racial segregation and the exclusion of women, while striving, like the news business itself, toward the future.

The National Press Club of 2008 is a different place from the Club I joined in 1966; and yet it is the same place. It is multi-faceted; it is about journalism, about journalists, about fraternity, about the past and for the future.

The work binds us, so we remain unchanged at our core, while always changing. We venerate our little traditions; from voting in person for Club leaders to the lovely, touching but unsentimental memorial gatherings for those who have left us.

The tradition of speeches from the most important podium in the free world continues unabated. A verbal shot across the ballroom of the Club is heard around the world instantly. Newsmaker events give us news and give those who cannot afford the paraphernalia of public relations and press agents a ready avenue to the media.

The first members of the Club would not recognize the state-of-the-art electronics in the library, the Broadcast Operations Center, or the gym. But they would know the feel of the place, the love of words, the sanctity of news, the hatred of cant, the mistrust of power, the loathing of corruption and the rest of the panoply of evils that are the targets of the journalist's calling.

They would know all of these. And they would applaud and approve that their work and their Club are alive, well and as special as they have ever been in Washington, D.C.

Llewellyn King
Publisher, King Publishing Group

California Gov. Arnold Schwarzenegger proudly shows the NPC windbreaker given to him in appreciation for his Feb. 26, 2007, appearance before a sold-out luncheon. The former Mr. Universe got an extra-large. (Photo by Christy Bowe)

CHAPTER ONE

THE WORLD'S FORUM

*"This room really is the sanctum sanctorum of American journalism. It's the Westminster
Hall, it's Delphi, the Mecca, the Wailing Wall, everybody in this country having anything
to do with the news business, this is the only hallowed place I know of that's absolutely
bursting with irreverence."*
— Eric Sevareid of CBS News, speaking at the National Press Club, Nov. 16, 1977

It's 1:00 p.m. on Monday, Feb. 26, 2007, in the 100th year of the National Press Club as
it careens towards its centennial celebration.

In the ballroom, Gov. Arnold Schwarzenegger of California holds court. The luncheon
features not just a former boffo movie star turned boffo politician, but also two Kennedys
— Eunice and her daughter Maria Shriver, Schwarzenegger's wife. Club President Jerry
Zremski of the *Buffalo News* has his hands full just organizing who will sit at the head
table. The ballroom is sold out; the balcony jammed with people. At least 30 television
cameras line the back of the room; six send the governor's speech out live.

Schwarzenegger castigates Washington politicians — from the president to the lowest
House back bencher — for pointless divisiveness and partisanship that stops anything from
passing.

"How come Republicans and Democrats out here don't schmooze with each other?" he
asks. "You can't catch a socially transmitted disease by sitting down with people who hold
ideas different from yours."

For the last question, Zremski phrases it in hopes of drawing out Schwarzenegger's
classic movie line.

"We've enjoyed having you here at the NPC today. And if we were to invite you again
in a year or so, will you be back?"

"I'll be back," says the Terminator with the classic snarl in his voice.

But that isn't the only news being made in the Club that lunch time.

In the conference rooms, the Newsmaker Committee hosts NASA scientist James
Hansen, one of the most prominent global warming investigators. He calls for a morato-
rium on building new coal-fired power plants.

"Until we have that clean coal power plant, we should not be building them," Hansen
says. "It is as clear as a bell."

In the Associated Press report of the story, a National Mining Association spokesman
calls Hansen's proposal "unreasonable, to put it charitably."

All morning the conference rooms, First Amendment Lounge and Holeman Lounge are
filled with groups vying for the media's attention. They have names such as "Take Back the
Power," "X-treme Eating," "Ecumenical Delegation," and "What Could Kill You."

The State Department holds a small luncheon in the Winners' Room. The Close Up
Foundation, which brings high school kids to learn about Washington, has breakfast in the
Lisagor Room.

Upstairs in the Reliable Source Bar and Grill, restaurant manager Mesfin Mekonen
seats members at tables for the buffet lunch. Once an Ethiopian prince, Mekonen has been
a favorite of members since he was hired by the Club after the fall of Ethiopian Emperor
Haile Selassie in 1974.

In the Eric Friedheim National Journalism Library, Director Tom Glad e-mails this
week's *Record* that tells members about the Schwarzenegger luncheon and everything
else going on in the Club this week. Researcher Barbara Van Woerkom helps members

Reliable Source Restaurant Manager Mesfin Mekonen presents menus to Frank Greve and Lisa Zagaroli, both of McClatchy newspapers. (Photo by Christy Bowe)

find some tidbit of information for a story. In the library's classroom, a group huddles over the computers, taking a class called "Blog for Your Business."

On the fourth floor in the new National Press Club Broadcast Center, Tiina Kreek makes final technical plans for a press conference the next day. It will feature Jim Press, president of Toyota North America, announcing from the studio that Blue Springs, Miss., 10 miles outside of Tupelo, will be the next site of a Toyota plant in the United States. Beaming live from the Club, Press's image will appear on screens in a Blue Springs high school auditorium with a two-way audio hookup. Back in the studio, CNBC, Bloomberg, CNN and ABC will do their own interviews.

In the business office, Membership Director Julie Schoo compiles a list of 37 new members to be presented to the Club's board that evening after the Membership Committee scrutinizes their credentials. The list shows the diversity of membership and the news media in the early 21st century.

Membership is divided into three basic categories: Active members are journalists. Affiliates are former journalists, members of foreign embassies and press officers in the U.S. government. Associates are news sources.

Among the active members joining this day are Edwin Chen of Bloomberg Business News, Marilyn Thompson of the *Los Angeles Times*, Diego Gilardoni of Swiss Public Television, El Paid bureau chief Antonio Cano, Eli Clifton of the Inter Press Service, and Tracey Schmidt of *Time* magazine.

Included among the new affiliate members are Ambassador Ali Suleiman Aujali of Libya; Karim Haggag, Egyptian embassy press officer; Mattias Sundholm, the European Union's deputy spokesman; and Laurie Ahern, associate director of Mental Disability Rights International.

And among those joining as associate members are political consultant Sascha Burns; Leonie L. Campbell, communications manager of the Asian American Justice Center; and David Castelveter, vice president for communications of the Air Transport Association of America.

Trying to expand its national reach, the Club is pushing for more out-of-town members, and this night's list includes John Caylor, CEO and editor of the Emerald Coast Times Publishing Co. in Panama City, Fla.; Jean Folkerts, dean of the University of North Carolina school of journalism; New York-based Todd Purdum, national editor of *Vanity Fair*; Wil Simon of the California Space Authority; and Roland Adams, Dartmouth University's director of media relations.

In the evening, Book Committee member John Clark introduces political pollster and adviser Frank Luntz to talk about his new book *Words That Work: It's Not What You Say, It's What People Hear.* Luntz predicts that former North Carolina Sen. John Edwards would win the 2008 Iowa caucus.

With the German Wine Society filling the Fourth Estate Dining Room and the Washington Independent Writers in the Zenger Room, the Club's Board of Governors moves its meeting to the conference room in the Broadcast Center. Since its founding, the Club has been run by journalists. The board has 15 members. Twelve of them must be journalists elected by active members only. Two are elected by associate and affiliate members, but they cannot vote in board decisions. The immediate past president is an ex officio member.

The topic this night is crucial to the Club's future. With General Manager John Bloom retiring in July, the board has to pick a replacement. Tonight it is presented with two finalists recommended by the search committee headed by former President Tammy Lytle of the *Orlando Sentinel*. Within weeks, the board would select Bill McCarren, a longtime member and a journalism business entrepreneur.

People coming out of the wine society dinner stop to examine the newspaper mats in the lobby. These relics of newspaper front pages had been collected beginning in the earliest days of the Club. Like so many people passing by, they cannot help but touch the indented lettering and wonder at the decades-old headlines. The past of those newspaper mats meets the future of blogs and two-way satellite press conferences in the century-old National Press Club, where news is breaking sometimes simultaneously in different rooms and journalists often wrestle with the future of their craft.

Former Soviet President Mikhail S. Gorbachev took questions from a capacity crowd on Oct. 25, 1996. (Photo by Marshall Cohen)

Washington Post publisher Philip Graham once described journalism as the "first rough draft of history." During its first 100 years, the NPC provided much of the raw material for that rough draft through its luncheon speakers and newsmaker programs. Since 1932, presidents, foreign leaders, top government officials, candidates for high office and business, military, sports, entertainment and cultural leaders have made news while speaking at the Club. The ebb and flow of historical tides through the Great Depression, World War II, the Cold War, the demise of the Soviet Union and the rise of a global economy and international terrorism is reflected in the rostrum of NPC guests. Swirling within these grand themes are many subplots: fads, scandals, individual triumphs and myriad burning issues of the day.

From its earliest days, the Club attracted newsmakers. On Oct. 3, 1909, explorer Frederick A. Cook made his claim for being the first man to reach the North Pole, an assertion soon challenged at the Club by Navy Commodore Robert E. Peary. On May 16, 1916, President Woodrow Wilson came to the Club to warn that U.S. involvement in the war in Europe was imminent.

President-elect Franklin D. Roosevelt was the first VIP formally invited to address a Club assembly, inaugurating the speakers program on Nov. 22, 1932. Most of the Club's major speakers deliver luncheon addresses, but Roosevelt attended a dinner in his honor at the invitation of the Entertainment Committee. Shortly thereafter, the Club established the Speakers Committee, which exists to this day, and appointed Ernest Lindley of *Newsweek* as its first chairman. By 1934, Club luncheons were attracting speakers of national prominence, including filmmaker Cecil B. DeMille, Securities and Exchange Commission Chairman Joseph P. Kennedy, author Upton Sinclair and Secretary of State Cordell Hull.

Remarks were off the record in the luncheons' early years, but that proved impractical as the program grew in prominence and with the advent of recordings and radio coverage.

In just a few years, the luncheons had become a Club tradition and a national landmark.

"I urge continuity in the press club luncheons, which have become a very valuable asset to the club," 1939 Club President Arthur Hachten of the International News Service wrote in his annual report. "We have held 24 of them this year, practically an average of one every two weeks. They have been splendidly patronized by the membership and have contributed substantially to the interest in the club…. Many members have told me that these luncheons give them a new appreciation of their membership and attached a new value to it."

A seat in the ballroom and a full hot meal cost about 75 cents in the late 1930s, and members and guests often numbered from 300 to 400. Although prices have risen with inflation, luncheons remain one of the best deals in town. Few venues offer a good meal with a bird's eye view to history.

One of those historic eras was the late 1980s and early 1990s as the Soviet Union imploded, freeing Eastern Europe and creating nearly a dozen new countries. In July 1988, three years after Mikhail Gorbachev took office, Soviet military advisor Marshal Sergei Akhromeyev told an astounded Club audience that Poland and Hungary were free to go their own ways.

The next year, just seven days after the fall of the Berlin Wall, Polish Solidarity Leader Lech Walesa declared to a packed ballroom, "The Iron Curtain is no more. We have fought, and we have won." But he tempered his victory declaration by soberly saying, "I call it a house of cards…. If we want real victory, we have to lay solid foundations under this house of cards by pouring economic concrete."

Lothar de Maziere, the first and only freely elected president of East Germany, presented the Club with a chunk of the Berlin Wall. Vaclav Havel, the poet and playwright president of Czechoslovakia, warned of the growing tensions in Yugoslavia that could lead to civil war.

Boris Yeltsin's speech in June 1991 electrified the Club.

Fresh from victory as the first popularly elected president of Russia, Yeltsin arrived in Washington to take his place among the world's leaders. Large and imposing, yet unaccustomed to the glare of the television lights, Yeltsin appeared nervous as he looked out at the expectant crowd in the ballroom.

"There will be no turning back from the path Russia has chosen," Yeltsin said in a speech that would last only five minutes. Then he took question after question from an

Polish democracy leader Lech Walesa declares the Cold War's demise at a Nov. 6, 1989, packed-house luncheon. (Photo by John Metelsky)

Boris Yeltsin and member Paul D'Armiento flash the thumbs-up sign, June 20, 1991. (Photo by John Metelsky)

NPC member Don Bishop, left, checks in with President Vaclav Havel of Czeckoslovakia and Shirley Temple Black, U.S. ambassador to Czechoslovakia. (Photo by Marshall H. Cohen)

Popular luncheon speaker H. Ross Perot is greeted by George Embrey of the Columbus Dispatch for a March 18, 1992, appearance as Club President Kay Kahler looks on. (Photo by John Metelsky)

insatiably curious audience, responding to queries ranging from the future of the Soviet Union to his own religious beliefs. His interpreter struggled to keep up, frantically jotting notes when Yeltsin's answers ran several minutes.

"I shall never be the advocate of slow, half-hearted change, because along that path the system will take revenge on us," he said.

Slow, half-hearted change is usually not what top speakers at the Club want. Take H. Ross Perot. When he spoke early in 1992, his speech inspired more than 10,000 people to order the audiotape from the Club library. In a short time he was an independent candidate for president and would be the spoiler in the campaign that elected Bill Clinton president.

Dr. Martin Luther King, Jr. told a crowded luncheon in 1962 that "the Negro race must work passionately and unrelentingly for first-class citizenship, but we must never use second-class methods to gain it." The speech was a major policy statement for his Southern Christian Leadership Conference, which he said "seeks to implement the just law by appealing to the conscience of the great decent majority."

Both Ronald Reagan and Jimmy Carter announced their candidacies for president from the Club's podium. Soviet Premier Nikita Khrushchev's appearance was such a spectacular event that it is detailed in chapters three and four.

Fidel Castro, fresh from his victory over dictator Fulgencio Batista in 1959, told Club President William H. Lawrence of the New York Times that he had no dictatorial ambitions of his own. After that, no high level Cuban leader

From one president to another: NPC President Joe Slevin presents President Ronald Reagan with his honorary membership card in 1981. (Photo by Stan Jennings)

NPC President William H. Lawrence prepares to introduce Soviet Premier Nikita Khrushchev on Oct. 9, 1959. (Photo by Benjamin E. Forte)

Dressed in his trademark combat fatigues, Cuba's Fidel Castro confers prior to his address to the Club in 1959 with Club member Peter Edson of NEA Services, left, and Club President William H. Lawrence of the New York Times, right. (Photo by UPI)

Black Muslim leader Louis Farrakhan raises hands to quiet the crowd while his bodyguards look on. (Photo by Stan Jennings)

TV and still photographers line the back of the ballroom for Farrakhan's speech. (Photo by Stan Jennings)

Palestine Liberation Organization Chairman Yasser Arafat is greeted by Club President Clayton Boyce and Vice President Gil Klein, right, before his speech to discuss the Israeli-Palestinian accord of Sept. 14, 1993. (Photo by Marshall Cohen)

was allowed into Washington until 1994, when Cuban National Assembly President Ricardo Alarcon faced down hecklers at the club who had infiltrated the audience to denounce Castro's totalitarian government.

For years, Palestinian Liberation Organization President Yasser Arafat was denied a visa to come to Washington to accept the Club's invitation to speak. When he finally was permitted to come to Washington in 1993 to sign a peace agreement with Israeli Prime Minister Yitzhak Rabin, he made a point to appear at the Club. In one of the fastest ticket sell-outs in Club history, his speech was announced on a Friday and he spoke to a full house on Monday. He called for moral and economic support for Palestinians and a swift implementation of the agreement.

In 1984 a storm of opposition erupted when Nation of Islam leader Louis Farrakhan was invited to speak despite his racist and anti-Semitic remarks. Farrakhan did not moderate his views during his sold-out appearance, and Club President John Fogarty of the *San Francisco Chronicle* said in a *Record* statement that "I am proud to be president of an organization whose members and officers have the courage not to turn away from controversy."

Farrakhan returned in 1986 for a news conference where his body guards frisked re-

Minnesota governor and ex-wrestler Jesse Ventura talks about what it is like being an independent chief executive at a Feb. 22, 1999, luncheon. (Photo by Christy Bowe)

Former British Prime Minister Margaret Thatcher gives her world view at a luncheon on June 26, 1996. (Photo by Marshall Cohen)

Former Chairman of The Joint Chiefs of Staff and future Secretary of State Colin Powell presents NPC President Larry Lipman with a little red wagon as a token of Powell's Alliance for Youth project during a luncheon on May 17, 1999. (Photo by Marshall Cohen)

At a 1994 luncheon, actor Robert Redford said the best way for the public to protest violence in films is to shun violent movies. (Photo by Marshall Cohen)

Actress Elizabeth Taylor drew an enthusiastic capacity crowd when she spoke in 1987. (Photo by Stan Jennings)

porters entering the room. For that, the Club banned him for five years and adopted rules making explicit its authority over security.

At least once, what was most significant about a speech was not what was said but what was not said. As is detailed in chapter three, Secretary of State Dean Acheson's speech in January 1950 omitted the Korean Peninsula from the American security perimeter. Some historians believe that omission may have encouraged the North Koreans to invade South Korea six months later.

Sell-outs are not rare; usually several speakers a year draw a capacity crowd. Among those sharing the distinction are actress Elizabeth Taylor, Microsoft founder Bill Gates, Pentagon Chief of Staff Colin Powell, Sen. Hillary Rodham Clinton, former British Prime Minister Margaret Thatcher, actors Tom Hanks, Robert Redford and Christopher Reeve, House Speaker Newt Gingrich, *Harry Potter* series author J.K. Rowling (who had an entire class of fifth graders hanging over the balcony rail) and Jesse "The Body" Ventura, the former wrestling star turned Minnesota governor who attracted 35 television cameras.

※◎※

Apart from the luncheon series is the Newsmaker program. It began with the name Morning Newsmakers, and reporters could eat Danish and drink coffee as they listened to speakers in a more informal gathering. The initial purpose was to have lesser-known speakers who could not draw a luncheon crowd. The luncheons were the front-page news, while the newsmakers were the inside items. But in recent years, as reporters find it more difficult to take two hours out of their days for a luncheon and as high-powered speakers want a faster, more flexible venue, the Newsmaker program has attracted many front-page events of its own. And Newsmakers happen at all times of the day. They are more akin to a standard press conference than the luncheon. The Club host tries to keep a semblance of order as reporters ask questions.

Afghanistan President Hamid Karzai makes a point with Newsmaker chairman Peter Hickman at an overflow Feb. 27, 2003, event. (Photo by Christy Bowe)

A stalwart of the Newsmaker program was Peter Hickman, who by mid-2007 had handled more than 950 of them since 1992 when he hosted Salim A. Salim, secretary general of the Organization for African Unity. The Newsmaker program has hosted 140 heads of state or heads of government since 1992. Twice it has hosted all three heads of the Baltic republics at once.

Hickman remembers a Newsmaker with Yasser Arafat in 1996. Adding to the intensity of the event were Arafat's two aides who quarreled with each other in Arabic as Hickman tried to keep the proceedings in order in English.

Morning Newsmaker sessions have become increasingly central to professional programming at the Club. Yasser Arafat, president of the Palestine National Authority, was featured speaker on March 4, 1997. On the right is Hasan Abdul Rahman, Palestinian representative to the United States. On left is Hanan Ashwari, Minister of Education for the Palestine National Authority. In back is Peter Hickman, vice-chairman of the Morning Newsmaker Committee. This Newsmaker session was the first to be carried live by the Club on the Internet in addition to conventional broadcasting.

Perhaps the fastest arrangement of a Newsmaker came in 2005, he said, when he got a call in the morning from the ambassador from the Kyrgyz Republic, one of the former Soviet states. The ambassador's president had just been overthrown, and the ambassador would like a Newsmaker to talk to the press. When? That afternoon. It happened.

Usually Scottish political figures don't draw a huge crowd for a Newsmaker, Hickman said, but when the speaker was actor Sean Connery, a vocal proponent of Scottish nationalism, the room was packed with more than 300 people. As he walked into the Club, Connery noticed the international flags in the lobby. No Scottish flag? Connery asked. Those are reserved for sovereign countries, Hickman told him. Within days, a Scottish flag arrived in the Club's mail.

Actor Sean Connery drew a large crowd to a Newsmaker presentation in 2001, when he spoke in favor of an independent Scotland. (Photo by Christy Bowe)

A Club tradition is to have luncheon speakers sign what is know as the "Gold Book." Few venues anywhere in the world have such a collection of distinguished autographs. As of 2007, the Club had several thousand signatures in 26 Gold Books, all but the current one kept under lock and key in the Club's archives.

The names proffer a parade of historic figures, including presidents dating back to Theodore Roosevelt; military leaders such as John J. Pershing and Omar Bradley; celebrities from as far back as Will Rogers, Charlie Chaplin, Mary Pickford and Douglas Fairbanks; foreign leaders from around the globe; authors from Leo Tolstoy to Gore Vidal and Tom Clancy; and leaders in sports, religion, business and countless other endeavors.

Many names are illegible, including those of King Abjullah of Jordan, actress Dolly Parton, astronaut Neil Armstrong, South African leader Desmond Tutu, cyclist Lance Armstrong, Defense Secretary Donald Rumsfeld,

Gov. Mark Warner, of Virginia, compares hand injuries with NPC member John Fales prior to the governor's July 6, 2005 talk about the role of the National Guard. (Photo by Marshall Cohen)

actor Charlton Heston, U.N. Secretary General Kofi Annan and actor Tony Curtis, and former Secretary of State Henry Kissinger, who wrote that his pending speech in 2002 was "A demonstration of suicidal impulses."

Other speakers have penned brief comments. Consumer activist Ralph Nader, an 11-time speaker, commended the Club in 2004 for its "boldness." Dan Glickman, who made appearances first as Agriculture Secretary and then as president of the Motion Picture Association of America, wrote, "Thanks for allowing me to make the transition from soybeans to Spielberg." Virginia Gov. Mark Warner apologized for his "bad handwriting." He had a broken hand when he signed the Gold Book in 2005. Comedian Bob Newhart penned "what a hoot again" for his second appearance at the Club. Cartoonist Jim Davis drew a sketch of a burping Garfield, noting that "Oh, and my cat loved the lunch!" Actress Rachel Welch drew a big pair of lips along with "HI THERE." Former Education Secretary Bill Bennett, a six-time speaker, called the luncheon program "the

Garfield cartoonist Jim Davis introduces NPC Archivist Christina Zamon to the famous cat during an April 30, 2004, luncheon. (Photo by Laura Falacienski)

Below: Folksinger and social activist Pete Seeger strums on his banjo for NPC President Doug Harbrecht and a luncheon audience on Feb. 10, 1998. (Photo by Marshall Cohen)

best podium in America!" *USA Today* founder Al Neuharth signed under "From one S.O.B. to the many in NPC." Chef Julia Child wished the Club "Bon Appetit," and O.J. Simpson prosecutor Marsha Clarke asked, "What the *hell* am I doing here?" When author Tom Wolfe spoke at the Club in 1998, he noted that "When I worked at the *Post*, I never managed to reach the 13th floor stratosphere. I like it." Irving Berlin, Jerome Kern, John Philip Sousa and Winton Marsalis sketched scales of their music with their signatures, and folk singer Pete Seeger drew a banjo.

The Club hosts about 70 luncheons a year. Membership on the Speakers Committee is a coveted assignment. Speakers are selected based on their newsworthiness and name recognition. The job of the committee's chair is to fend off unworthy speakers while luring the big names. During committee meetings, members throw out the names of potential speakers. Votes are taken on recommendations to pass to the Club president, who holds final authority on whom to invite. Committee members assigned to handle a luncheon are charged with acting as liaison with the speaker and his or her staff, drafting a press release and speaker introduction with research help from the Club library, inviting a spectrum of Club members to the head table and greeting the guests upon their arrival at the 14th Street entrance to the National Press Building. Their "reward" is getting to sit next to the guest during the half-hour luncheon before the speech.

The Club relies on the prestige of its forum to draw speakers who often command hefty fees in other venues. Speakers get a chance to give an uninterrupted speech that at the least will be broadcast nationally by C-SPAN and XM Satellite Radio. The head table is made up of journalists interested in their topic. And speakers will be asked questions in an orderly fashion. If they have news to make, they will get it out here.

An invitation to speak can neither be bought nor paid for. The only compensation, aside from delivering a message, is a free meal, an NPC coffee mug and a framed certificate of appreciation signed by the Club president. For many years, speakers – almost always men – were given an NPC necktie after their speech as a token of appreciation. That came to an end when women became regular guests in the 1970s. Club presidents found themselves in the awkward position of giving ties to such speakers as feminists Germaine Greer and Gloria Steinem. When presented with her NPC tie, Steinem offered to don a man's jacket, too and "confirm your worst suspicions." The selection of souvenir gifts was expanded to include a scarf, paperweight, windbreaker and the current standard, a coffee mug.

When he spoke in February 2007, Schwarzenegger said all he wanted was "one of those windbreakers that you give to speakers when they talk here." Schwarzenegger remembered receiving a jacket when he first spoke at the Club in the early 1990s as chairman of President George H.W. Bush's Council on Physical Fitness and Sports. Although the Club stopped giving windbreakers years before, Melinda Cooke, assistant to the Club president, rushed to the front desk and requisitioned the only extra-large windbreaker in stock.

VIP speakers are accustomed to generous perks at other venues. When comedian Jerry Lewis spoke in 1995, his aides asked that the Club provide a limousine to pick him up when he arrived in Washington. NPC President Monroe "Bud" Karmin of Bloomberg Business News informed them that the Club did not provide such services but that he would be glad to fetch Lewis in his well-worn Honda Civic. Lewis made other arrangements.

Some controversies involving speakers never get public attention. In 1985, Indian Prime Minister Rajiv Gandhi was scheduled to speak. But his embassy said the speech would be scrubbed if the Club

Feminist icon Gloria Steinem, editor of Ms. *magazine, spoke at the club on Jan. 24, 1972. She is shown here with Katharine Graham,* The Washington Post *publisher, at left. (Photo by Martin Kuhn)*

Can you identify these famous signatures of Club Speakers?

1. Henry Kissinger 2. Lance Armstrong 3. Charlton Heston 4. Donald Rumsfeld 5. B.B. King 6. Desmond Tutu 7. Neil Armstrong 8. Elizabeth Taylor 9. Colin Powell 10. Dolly Parton

Top: Indira Gandhi at the Club on Nov. 5, 1971. Bottom: Indira and Rajiv Gandhi, mother and son, are at the head table with Club President Vivian Vahlberg on July 30, 1982. Both Indian prime ministers were later assassinated. (Photos by Stan Jennings)

Egyptian President Hosni Mubarak is welcomed to the Club by President David Hess on March 13, 1985. (Photo by Marshall Cohen)

did not cancel a scheduled Newsmaker appearance by a critic of India's policies in the disputed territory of Punjab. NPC President David Hess of Knight-Ridder refused to back down. The Morning Newsmaker was held, and Gandhi went ahead with the luncheon as if nothing had happened.

Ever wonder why the Club has had so few Chinese government officials as luncheon speakers? The last one was foreign minister Wu Xuegian in 1988. A piece of cloth about four-by-six-feet is the reason. Many foreign embassies have officials who are members of the Club, and their embassies often donate their national banner as part of the Club's flag display at the base of the grand staircase. China has refused to allow its officials to speak at the Club so long as the Taiwanese flag is part of the display, even though the flag of the People's Republic of China is represented. China considers Taiwan a renegade province.

Other controversies do get public attention. The U.S. occupation of Iraq fostered several protests. Protesters unfurled an "End the War" banner from the ballroom balcony during a speech by Secretary of Defense Donald Rumsfeld in 2003. Shouting protesters had to be escorted out during speeches by Ambassador L. Paul Bremer, who was the U.S. administrator in Iraq, and by Sen. Hillary Rodham Clinton, who had voted for the war.

Journalists are trained not to show emotion during news events. So it always irked many Club members that audiences listening to the luncheons on television or radio would hear applause during a speech. They feared that listeners and viewers would assume that journalists were indicating their approval of the speaker's remarks instead of knowing they were hearing the enthusiasm of guests often invited by the speaker. In recent years, Club presidents have made the somewhat awkward announcement at the beginning of each speech that any applause the audience hears does not necessarily come from journalists.

The reach of NPC luncheons has come a long way since the days when reporters scribbled notes in a pad. First there were radio and then TV broadcasts of selected events. In 1980 the Club began its affiliation with the newly formed C-SPAN cable network.

"On Jan. 2, 1980, we covered our first National Press Club luncheon with Paul Volker, and we haven't missed any since," said C-SPAN founder Brian Lamb. "It's a rare opportunity in society on a national basis for an individual to get up and give a full speech on their terms – not anyone else's terms."

Lamb, the Club's 2002 Fourth Estate Award winner and an honorary NPC member, thanked the Club in a 2004 speech "for everything you've done for C-SPAN." The sentiment was mutual. The public affairs network Lamb founded reaches nearly 90 million listeners and makes available for sale to the public tapes and DVDs of some 1,600 NPC events.

National Public Radio also broadcast all NPC luncheons until Aug. 19, 2005. NPR member stations continue to broadcast luncheons selectively. On July 14, 2006, with Vice President Dick Cheney at the podium, XM Satellite Radio started broadcasting NPC luncheons nationwide.

C-SPAN has broadcast every Club luncheon since January, 1980. Here C-SPAN founder Brian Lamb, center, is greeted by Club President Sheila Cherry, right, and Vice President Rick Dunham to mark the 25th anniversary of the broadcasts.

Security is something the Club deals with regularly. The facilities are well known to the Secret Service. Several days before a high-profile visit, agents do a "walk through" with Club officials, rehearsing every step of an upcoming visit. Guests requiring extra security often enter the building through a back entrance, come up to a different floor and use a stairway that leads directly to the Holeman Lounge, which is often used for pre-luncheon receptions. Precautions may include draping windows. Three or four riflemen are posted on the roof during a presidential or vice presidential visit. Before the use of secure cell phone communications, the Secret Service used a special portable landline telephone plugged into a phone jack in the manager's office, which is used as a "command center."

United Nations Secretary General Kofi Annan, left, and Llewellyn King of King Publishing share a light moment before Annan's address on Jan. 24, 1997. (Photo by Marshall Cohen)

On the day of a visit by the president, vice president or a visiting head of state needing extra security, bomb-sniffing dogs sweep through the Club and offices on the 12th floor. Agents monitor hallways and stairwells, and all movement is stopped while the VIP moves from the building entrance to the Club, and from the Club to the exit. Details can include dietary requests. Preparations for an appearance by Vice President Dick Cheney included removing the labels on water bottles to avoid any commercial use.

On rare occasions, luncheons involving especially newsworthy guests booked at the last minute have been held off-site because the Club's facilities were in use. The nearby Willard Hotel was used for a speech by Israeli Prime Minister Benjamin Netanyahu, and the Hotel Washington was used for United Nations Secretary General Kofi Annan and General Motors President Roger Smith.

Once, the Club hosted two luncheons simultaneously. Wall Street guru Peter Lynch was lined up to speak on Oct. 7, 1994, as the culmination of a Club-sponsored financial writers' conference. More than 350 people were signed up. Then Club President Gil Klein of the Media General News Service got a call from the South African embassy. Nelson Mandela, one of the heroes of the late 20th cen-

South Africa President Nelson Mandela admires his NPC mug after his Oct. 7, 1994 speech to a sell-out audience. (Photo by Marshall Cohen)

tury, would be in town for his first visit as president. He would like to speak at the Club – on Oct. 5. No, he couldn't do breakfast, and he couldn't do dinner. It had to be lunch. Klein said yes, not quite sure how it would be done. He huddled with Director of Operations John Bloom who arranged to move the Lynch luncheon to the Hotel Washington, where Vice President Bud Karmin of Bloomberg Business News presided, and brought Mandela into the ballroom for what turned out to be the biggest luncheon of the year. More than 750 people attended both luncheons, and both speakers made news.

The most newsworthy portion of a luncheon often comes in the question-and-answer segment at the end of the program. Some VIPs, including First Lady Nancy Reagan, reject Club invitations because the Club will not forgo the Q&A portion of the program. Questions are submitted in writing during the luncheon on cards sent to the podium from the audience or from on-line submissions made through the Club's Web site. The luncheon host, usually the Club president, selects what questions to ask.

Guests are asked to keep their remarks to about 20 minutes to leave time for Q&A. This guideline is sometimes ignored, either inadvertently or as a filibuster technique. Vice President Al Gore left no time for Q&A while speaking about the information superhighway in 1993. At the other extreme, Israeli Prime Minister Benjamin Netanyahu invited guests to ask questions without ever giving a speech. The loquacious Netanyahu had no trouble filling the hour with expansive answers to questions about the turmoil in the Middle East. Samuel Pierce Jr., President Reagan's secretary of housing and urban development, presented a different challenge in 1983. His speech was not long, and his answers to questions were little more than "yes" and "no." Club President John Fogarty of the *San Francisco Chronicle* may have asked a record number of questions to get through the hour.

Israeli Prime Minister Benjamin Netanyahu drew a crowd at the Club on July 10, 1996. (Photo by Marshall Cohen)

Speakers are the headliners at luncheons, but there was one luncheon at which the head table received a standing ovation. Gen. Paul Tibbets, who flew the B-29 Superfortress *Enola Gay* on its atomic bomb mission over Hiroshima, spoke at a luncheon marking the 50th anniversary of Japan's surrender in World War II. Club President Bud Karmin of Bloomberg Business News read brief sketches of the wartime service of nine members, all veterans of the war in the Pacific. Four were former Club presidents: Don Larrabee, Frank Holeman, Warren Rogers Jr. and John Cosgrove. Two members, Joe Laitin and Edgar A. Poe, had witnessed the Japanese surrender aboard the battleship *Missouri* in Tokyo Harbor. Others were members Ed Prina and Shirley Povich. Also at the table was Adm. John Harllee, who witnessed the attack on Pearl Harbor. All said they were grateful that the atomic bomb had forced Japan into surrender. Many members of the audience had moist eyes as they stood to applaud the veterans.

President Gerald Ford catches up on old times with his former press secretary, Ron Nessen, right, and Bob Schieffer of CBS News at Ford's last of many appearances at the Club on July 17, 2003, during his foundation's annual journalism awards luncheon. (Photo by Marshall Cohen)

Gerald R. Ford had a special relationship with the Club. He gave luncheon speeches before, during and after his presidency and holds the record for 15 addresses. Hugh Sidey of *Time* described Ford as the only president he knew

Canadian Prime Minister Jean Chretien prepares to sign guest book, held by Kate Goggin, executive assistant to the Club president, on April 9, 1997. (Photo by Art Garrison)

Head waiter Andrew Price presents comic George Carlin with a birthday cake during his luncheon appearance on May 13, 1999 as Club President Larry Lipman looks on. (Photo by Christy Bowe)

who genuinely liked reporters. Starting in 1988, the Gerald R. Ford Foundation presented its annual journalism awards for coverage of the presidency and defense issues at a Club luncheon. For 13 years, Ford personally presented the awards. "Over the years I've taken my journalistic arrows," Ford said during his 1998 speech, but added, "they've been outweighed, far, far outweighed, I must say. And it's never affected the wonderful friendships that I've enjoyed with so many people in this room and throughout the press corps." During his last visit to the Club in 2003, Ford delighted in tributes presented by journalists who covered his administration. Bob Woodward of the *Washington Post* recounted his negative reaction to Ford's pardoning of Nixon, a sentiment that was shared by much of the nation at the time. "I had it wrong," Woodward told Ford. "In fact it was the right thing to do to get on with the nation's business."

When Canadian Prime Minister Jean Chretien came to speak in 1998, his advance staff wanted the NPC seal taken down from behind the podium. They said the green leaves in the seal would look like horns sprouting from Chretien's head. The Club did not buckle, and the seal stayed in its customary place. The backdrop later was changed to a more television-friendly blue screen with National Press Club repeated in white lettering.

Actor Christopher Reeve makes a plea for spinal cord injury research during a Dec. 1, 1999, luncheon. Logistics for his appearance were a special challenge for the Club. (Photo by Christy Bowe)

By 2007, Andrew Price had served hundreds of VIPs during his 40 years with the Club's wait staff. He takes care of the luncheon head tables, providing guests with special NPC silver flatware. President Ford came to recognize Price during his many visits to the Club and once jokingly admonished him for offering a plate of chocolate desserts. "You're a bad boy," Ford said with a smile. Actor Tony Curtis warned, "Don't take those cookies," when Price started to pass the dessert plate. Orchestra leader Benny Goodman, at a Club jazz event, asked Price for a shot of Scotch, and singer Roberta Flack once requested a glass of Hennessy cognac. They got what they wanted.

Actor Christopher Reeve, paralyzed from the neck down in an equestrian accident, required special handling when he spoke about spinal cord research in a packed ballroom in 1999. Because he was highly prone to infections, no one was allowed to touch the former *Superman* star. He was kept in relative isolation until he was wheeled onto a specially built dais. Club President Larry Lipman of the *Palm Beach Post* was the only person with him at the head table.

The future of the journalism business is often the topic, especially in recent years as the Internet challenges both newspapers and broadcast news. In 1993, author Michael Crichton told the Club the American news media were "a dinosaur on the way to extinction," and predicted it would be gone in a decade. Not mincing any words, he said the news media "produce a product of very poor quality. Their information is not reliable, there's too much chrome and glitz, its door rattles, it breaks down almost immediately and is sold without a warranty. It's flashy but it is basically junk, and people have begun to stop buying it."

CNN founder Ted Turner gives a raspberry response to a question from President Gil Klein on Sept. 27, 1994. (Photo by Art Garrison)

Author Tom Wolfe offered these observations about television news in 1998: "The highest rank in television news is someone who does not have to leave the building, namely the anchorman or woman. And the more you have to leave the building the lower your status. So right there, it's all turned around." The same year, Internet scoopster Matt Drudge told the Club that "now, with a modem, anyone can follow the world and report on the world with no middle man, no big brother. And I guess this changes everything." CNN founder Ted Turner told the Club in 2006, "When you can send the same information electronically, and people can get it instantaneously, it's over for newspapers, unfortunately."

But in 2005, retired *Washington Post* executive editor Ben Bradley discounted predictions of the demise of newspapers. They have a future, he said, because "you can't take the computer to the john with you."

As Eric Sevareid said, "… absolutely bursting with irreverence."

Eric Sevareid addresses the then all male audience at the Press Club in 1961. Club President John Cosgrove is on his left. At the head table that day were CBS foreign correspondents, who were all in Washington for their year-end summaries. (Photo by Benjamin E. Forte)

Left: President Lyndon Johnson was a surprise guest at the inaugural of Club President Al Cromley of the Daily Oklahoman. Here the two presidents check copy coming off a wire service teletype machine outside the Main Lounge.

Below: South Africa President F.W. deKlerk in 1991 with Club President Kay Kahler. (Photo by Stan Jennings)

Martha Stewart, editor of Martha Stewart Living Magazine, during Q&A conducted by President Sonja Hillgren at Nov. 12, 1996, luncheon. (Photo by Art Garrison)

Bindi Irwin, 8-year-old daughter of the late Australian "Crocodile Hunter" Steve Irwin, wowed a lunch audience Jan. 19, 2007, with her enthusiasm for carrying on her father's work. Accompanied by her mother Terri, Bindi is the youngest person to address a luncheon audience. (Photo by Carl Ericson)

Vice President George Bush visited the Press Club on Oct. 9, 1981. (Photo by John Metelsky)

Club member Richard G. Thomas chats with Independent Presidential Candidate Ross Perot on April 25, 1995. (Photo by John Metelsky)

Famed journalist Walter Lippman listens to his introduction by NPC President William Lawrence on Sept. 23, 1959. (Photo by News Associates)

Sen. John F. Kennedy vowed to conduct a vigorous presidency when he spoke as a candidate at a luncheon on Jan. 14, 1960.

Journalist Roger Mudd, left, greets former White House press secretary James Brady, who had been wounded during an assassination attempt against President Reagan, when Brady spoke at the Club in 1989. (Photo by Marshall H. Cohen)

Country music star Dolly Parton posing with NPC President Jack Cushman, had the podium removed during her March 23, 2000, luncheon address so that guests could "see the whole package." (Photo by John Metelsky)

Itzhak Perlman spoke through his violin on Jan. 22, 1997. (Photo by Marshall Cohen)

Actress Whoopi Goldberg addresses the National Press Club on April 7, 1997 (Photo by Christy Bowe)

Actress Goldie Hawn enjoys her Club visit with President Dick Ryan in a Dec. 10, 2001, appearance. (Photo by Christy Bowe)

Acress Angelina Jolie, Goodwill Ambassador for the U.N. Refugee Agency, ponders a question about tsunami aid during a March 8, 2005, luncheon. (Photo by Marshall Cohen)

Club President Don Larrabee, right, had a hard time getting a crowd to listen to Georgia Gov. Jimmy Carter in 1973. The next year, Carter announced his presidential candidacy at the Club and went on to victory in 1976. (Photo by John Metelsky)

Former Vice President Walter Mondale was luncheon speaker on March 9, 1982. (Photo by John Metelsky)

Speed-reading and quick analysis are required to sort and ask questions at Club luncheons. Vice President Clyde LaMotte shuffles questions while John Love, director of the President's energy office answers the previous query. (Photo by Stan Jennings)

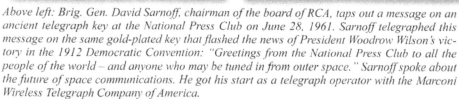

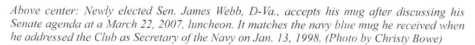

Above left: Brig. Gen. David Sarnoff, chairman of the board of RCA, taps out a message on an ancient telegraph key at the National Press Club on June 28, 1961. Sarnoff telegraphed this message on the same gold-plated key that flashed the news of President Woodrow Wilson's victory in the 1912 Democratic Convention: "Greetings from the National Press Club to all the people of the world – and anyone who may be tuned in from outer space." Sarnoff spoke about the future of space communications. He got his start as a telegraph operator with the Marconi Wireless Telegraph Company of America.

Above center: Newly elected Sen. James Webb, D-Va., accepts his mug after discussing his Senate agenda at a March 22, 2007, luncheon. It matches the navy blue mug he received when he addressed the Club as Secretary of the Navy on Jan. 13, 1998. (Photo by Christy Bowe)

Above right: The Dalai Lama with veteran NPC Record editor and photographer John Metelsky in 1993.

Right: Placido Domingo, general director of The Washington Opera, addressed the Club in his tenor's voice at a luncheon on Nov. 10, 2004. (Photo by Marshall Cohen)

Canadian Prime Minister Pierre Elliot Trudeau took questions from Club President Robert Farrell in 1977 at a quickly arranged news conference in the old ballroom. (Photo by Stan Jennings)

Secretary of Transportation Elizabeth Dole was the first speaker in the newly renovated ballroom on Feb. 13, 1984. (Photo by Stan Jennings)

Richmond Mayor and former Virginia Gov. Douglas Wilder and actor Ben Vereen clink NPC mugs after a Feb. 7, 2006, luncheon about the National Slavery Museum. (Photo by Marshall Cohen)

Actors Paul Newman and Joanne Woodward were in the audience to hear author Gore Vidal speak in 1994. (Photo by Christy Bowe)

NPC President Peter Holmes of the Washington Times *(left) chats with former President Gerald Ford (center) and House Minority Leader Robert Michel, Dec. 6, 1989. (Photo by John Metelsky)*

President Clinton is welcomed to the Club on March 11, 1997, by Club President Richard T. Sammon, along with former CBS anchorman Walter Cronkite, a 50-year Club member. (Photo by Marshall H. Cohen)

Egyptian President Anwar Sadat lights up as NPC President Frank Aukofer poises a question during Sadat's Feb. 6, 1978, luncheon. (Photo by John Metelsky)

Senate Democratic Leader Tom Daschle and House Minority Leader Richard A. Gephardt make points during a joint address on Jan. 30, 1997.

Left: Actress Ashley Judd, global ambassador for Youth AIDS, plays coy at an NPC dinner event on June 22, 2005. (Photo by Christy Bowe)

Below left: Boxers Muhammad Ali and Ken Norton show off for the cameras before a National Press Club luncheon on August 27, 1976. (Photo by Stan Jennings)

Below: Multi-time Tour de France winner and cancer survivor Lance Armstrong was greeted by Washington area cyclists during his Dec. 17, 2003, luncheon. (Photo by Christy Bowe)

Far left: Tennis legend Arthur Ashe poses with NPC member Eleanor Clift of Newsweek in May 1992. (Photo by Marshall H. Cohen)

Left: Actor Gary Sinise makes a plea for helping disabled veterans during a Jan. 26, 2007, luncheon. (Photo by Christy Bowe)

Fred Rogers of Mr. Rogers' Neighborhood entertains the audience in 1990 with his friend, Owl. (Photo by John Metelsky)

Comic Victor Borge goes crackers at a May 17, 1993, luncheon. (Photo by Marshall H. Cohen)

Above: Actress Audrey Hepburn signs the famed "Gold Book" before her address April 7, 1989. (Photo by Stan Jennings)

Above right: NPC President Warren Rogers of the Chicago Tribune-New York News Syndicate queries actress Ingrid Bergman. (Photo by U.S. News Service)

Right: National Press Club, Sept. 22, 1995. Luncheon speaker Gen. Paul Tibbets, pilot of the Enola Gay. Left to right: Past NPC President Don Larrabee, NPC member Joseph Laitin, NPC member John Harllee, NPC member Edgar A. Poe, NPC member Edgar Prina, luncheon speaker Gen. Paul Tibbets, past NPC President Frank Holeman, past NPC President John Cosgrove, and Shirley Povich. (NPC photo by John Metelsky)

Piano-playing satirist and Club member Mark Russell regales an NPC audience on Aug. 11, 1998, in one of his many Club appearances. (Photo by Art Garrison)

Actor and chairman of the President's Council on Physical Fitness and Sports, Arnold Schwarzenegger has Andrew Klein, son of member Gil Klein, and friend Brian Arnold, doing push-ups at a May 1, 1992 appearance. (Photo by Marshall Cohen)

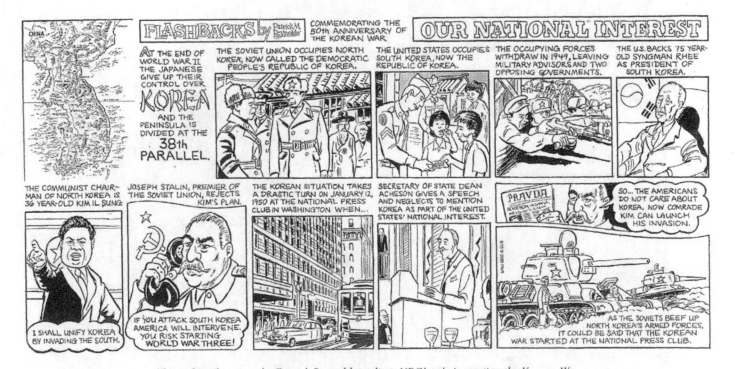

This political cartoon by Patrick Reynolds outlines NPC's role in starting the Korean War.

Graham B. Nichol, a flamboyant police reporter for the Washington Times, *gathered 32 fellow journalists on March 12, 1908, to found the National Press Club.*

CHAPTER TWO

AT THE CREATION

Indeed, the National Press Club membership probably lugged around enough secret in-formation to have helped the Axis powers win the war if they could have gotten hold of it."
— Lyle Wilson in "Dateline: Washington"

On a cold, wet and windy day near the end of February 1908, Graham Bright Nichol, a police and city hall reporter for the *Washington Times*, hobbled on crutches to the corner of 14th and F streets. He had just turned 33 years old, but he made his way around Washington on one leg after the other leg had been broken in an accident and amputated when he was 30. Tall, broad shouldered with a shock of red hair, he was called "Nick" by his friends. He was well known among Washington reporters for generosity, good spirits in spite of his infirmity, and a fondness for poker.

At that corner, next to the Ebbitt Hotel and not 10 feet from the northwest corner of the present National Press Building, Nichol ran into James Hay Jr., also a reporter for the *Washington Times*, who was the son of a House member from Virginia and who later made a name for himself as a short story writer for the *Saturday Evening Post*.

Jamming his five-gallon hat to his head against the wind, Nichol roared in his Big Bertha voice:

"I'm getting damned tired of having to hunt a stuffy, ill-ventilated little hall room in a cheap boarding house every time I want to play a game of poker! Hell's bells! Why don't

Turn of the century newspaper houses. Known as "Newspaper Row" in its day, this street was a bustle of commerce in the heart of the nation's capital. It was on this street where the National Press Club was founded in 1908 on 1205 F St. and later relocated to the corner of this street, which in this photograph shows the Old Ebbitt Hotel at far right.

we get up a press club? A place where the fellows can take a drink or turn a card when they feel like it?"

His teeth chattering from the cold, Hay replied, "How? And where?"

"I don't know, and I don't give a damn where," Nichol said. "But all the same, we're going to have a club."

≈⊚ ⊚≈

Washington in 1908 was in the throes of optimism that dominated America at the turn of the century. The United States emerged from the Spanish-American War as a rising world power. Theodore Roosevelt neared the end of his energetic second term spanned by the Progressive Era of government reform. He had breathed vitality into the job of chief executive, wresting power from Congress and generating lively newspaper copy. Millionaires flocked to Washington and built mansions along Massachusetts Avenue. A grand Beaux Arts railroad station had just opened near the Capitol. The first House office building (Cannon) was completed in December 1907, and the first Senate office building (Russell) was under construction. A magnificent new Willard Hotel with its "Peacock Alley" and "Round Robin bar" had opened where the old hotel had stood for decades. Just getting started was a new plan to transform the Mall and official Washington to make a grand world capital.

Yet in many ways, Washington was still a sleepy, Southern city. The metropolitan area had yet to expand to the borders of the District of Columbia. A thousand residents still made their living as farmers. Public relations officers and press aides didn't exist. Even the president had no person responsible for press relations. The State, War and Navy departments were all in one building – the French Second Empire behemoth next to the White House now known as the Eisenhower Executive Office Building that houses just part of the White House staff. In 1908, the attorney general appointed the first "special agents," the genesis of what would become the FBI. Congressional staffs were tiny. Other than committee chairs, senators and House members could hire one personal

An artist's sketch from an 1873 Harper's Magazine shows the original "Newspaper Row" on 14th Street between E and F Streets, NW. The present National Press Building stands on a site once occupied by the Ebbitt Hotel, shown in the top left corner. Reporters filed their stories to hometown papers from the Western Union building, shown at the right, where the J.W. Marriott Hotel now stands.

staff member, and until the first House and Senate office buildings were completed, they had no office space. The federal budget was $621 million, and the city's life waxed and waned with the comings and goings of Congress. The city was still small enough for men and women, mostly of career-government families, to walk casually along the sidewalks and pause to talk to acquaintances. It was segregated, with many African Americans living in shanties in the alleys behind large, white-occupied houses.

In journalism, William Randolph Hearst and Joseph Pulitzer had transformed newspapers into political and economic powerhouses. Journalism was in transition, leaving behind its hard-scrabble roots to fancy itself as more professional. The first school of journalism was opened at the University of Missouri in 1908. That same year launched the *Christian Science Monitor*, which promised its readers a more thoughtful and accurate accounting of the world than was available in much of the popular press. Newspapers were plentiful – and profitable. Washington boasted four daily papers – the *Post,* the *Times*, the *Evening Star* and the *Herald.* The *Post* was on E Street between 13th and 14th streets, and the *Star* was a couple blocks down Pennsylvania Avenue. Beginning with the Civil War, a "Newspaper Row" grew around the intersection of 14th and F streets as reporters from out-of-town newspapers found offices in the two-story brick and shingle buildings across the street from the old Willard Hotel where they could find politicians and administration officials relaxing in the hotel's bars and parlors. Those offices became a de facto press club as correspondents dropped in on each other and gathered for drinks. Reporters took the street car to the Capitol, walked to the White House and all of the federal agencies, wrote their copy on new-fangled machines called typewriters, and rushed their copy to the Western Union office at the corner of 14th and E streets to be wired to their home office. As late as 1898, as many as 60 of the most important newspapers in America maintained their offices in the dingy and by then dilapidated buildings. Even as correspondents moved to better accommodations as the century turned, they stayed close to 14th and F streets.

In their off hours, reporters and editors congregated at Gerstenburg's, known to the correspondents as "The University of Gerstenburg," a public house on E Street that was noted for its crowded mahogany bar and the odor of Limburger cheese. Just a few doors down E Street, on the other side of the *Post* building, stood Shoomakers, a low-ceilinged, dark bar room that dated to the days of Henry Clay and Daniel Webster. Reporters knew

Looking east on F Street in 1906 from 14th Street. The tall building on the left is the Sun Building, built by the Baltimore Sun in the 1880s as the city's first high rise.

they would find not only like-minded colleagues at these establishments but also a few members of Congress who ambled down from the Capitol.

These were comfortable establishments that reporters enjoyed. But they had one major failing. The bars in Washington closed at midnight. Writers and editors for morning papers often worked until midnight and had no place to find food, drink and companionship when they finished. In these establishments, someone was always plotting to form a press club.

No formal club developed until a group of correspondents during the Lincoln administration formed the "Bold Buccaneers." It lasted only a short while. In 1867, nearly 50 correspondents in the Capitol press gallery organized the Washington Correspondents Club. Its first and only president was William Lawrence Gobright of the Associated Press. Incensed that the Washington Correspondents Club was restricted to Capitol Hill reporters, newsmen employed by the local papers in Georgetown and Washington founded a rival organization called The Press Club. John C. Proctor of the *National Republican* was its first and only president.

Both clubs failed largely because they had no headquarters and collected no dues. For 16 years, journalists made do with the local drinking establishments until 1883 when the Washington Press Club was organized by Frank Truesdall, a correspondent for the *Baltimore American*. The club operated out of the back of the newspaper's quarters at 1410 Pennsylvania Ave., but from the beginning some members complained that confidences murmured in the club mysteriously appeared in the pages of the *American* the next day. Truesdall found that members did not honor their tabs or pay their dues, and that club was dead by 1887.

A gentle breeze graces a still F Street sidewalk of the Hooe Iron Building.

In 1885, another club was formed that would survive to become one of the most elite journalism organizations in the country. Ben Perley Pore, who grew up in Washington during the John Quincy Adams administration, gathered a select group of 40 newspapermen to create the Gridiron Club. While it never had a clubhouse or served as a regular gathering place for members, it became the Skull and Bones Society for Washington journalists. It survives to this day, known mostly for its once-a-year, white-tie dinner where invitations are highly sought after, and members roast and toast the president of the United States and the upper crust of Washington's political establishment.

The "common" newspapermen persisted in their pursuit of a club, and in 1891 organized the National Capital Press Club. It took over the quarters at the corner of 14th and E streets of the defunct Sports Club, which had been created by a few congressmen. It soon had more than 100 members and appeared to be on its way to permanency. Its annual dinners competed in glamour with the Gridiron Club. But credit was extended to members, and few bothered to settle their accounts at the end of the month. Facing mounting debt, the club arranged a benefit and brought in a trainload of entertainers from New York. The show raised $7,000, but so many tabs were signed that the proceeds were eaten up – or swigged down. The club folded in 1894, its bar, china, silver and plush late-Victorian furnishings sold at auction.

And that's where things stood when Graham Nichol met James Hay at the corner of 14th and F streets that blustery day in February 1908.

After exclaiming, "I don't know, and I don't give a damn where," Nichol made his way that night to the Number One Police Station on 12th Street a short distance south of Pennsylvania Avenue. It was the loafing ground and pseudo-club of the city's police reporters and their friends. His talk of starting "a press club, located in a few upstairs rooms somewhere" met with instant enthusiasm. All said they were tired of lounging in police headquarters and lunchrooms. "A few upstairs rooms" sounded luxurious.

Someone asked, how much would it cost? Nichol guessed $10 per man – if enough men could be found. Grabbing a sheet of copy paper, he put himself down for the first $10. The others followed suit – a major investment, considering a reporter worked for $15 to $18 a week, and a city editor made the princely sum of $25. These were, after all, chronically broke men who worked long hours for a pittance yet believed themselves to be gentlemen craftsmen in the thick of the political arena. Nichol soon collected a purse of $300.

From there, events moved quickly. On March 12, 1908, at 4:30 p.m., 32 newsmen assembled at the Washington Chamber of Commerce. They elected Nichol chairman of the meeting. J. Russell Young of the *Evening Star* and others told of previous failed efforts to found press clubs in Washington and described successful clubs in other cities. They decided a press club was entirely feasible and adjourned to meet on March 29 in the F Street parlor of the Willard Hotel.

At that meeting, Nichol laid down the basic concept of the Club. It "shall forever be emphatically a newspaperman's club, with the management exclusively in the hands of newspapermen, and with all the officers elected, and all the policies formed by men actively engaged in earning their livings by the pen, the pencil or the artist's brush."

In its constitution adopted that day, the Club pledged to promote social enjoyment among its members, cultivate literary taste, encourage friendly intercourse among newspapermen and those with whom they are thrown in contact in pursuit of their vocation, aid members in distress and foster ethical standards in the profession.

CHAPTER TWO

The corner of Pennsylvania Avenue and 14th Street with the new high-rise Willard Hotel as it looked shortly before the Club's founding. The old Washington Post Building was flanked by bars frequented by journalists before they had their own Club. (Photo courtesy of the Library of Congress)

That it was a "men's club" was not unusual by 1908 standards. In the late 19th and early 20th centuries, men of all social conditions organized civic, charitable, religious, college and professional associations to provide havens in a fast-changing world. By 1910, America had about 400 fraternal organizations with a membership of more than 9 million.

Young made the motion that would ensure the success of the Club. Granting credit to club members would be forbidden, he proposed. Food, drink and anything else must be paid for in cash. The ensuing debate was hot. Some prospective members said it was beneath the dignity of gentlemen to be denied credit. The word of a member of the press should be sufficient for any Club management, they said. But Young stood firm and won a majority. Many say it is the only reason the Club survived its early days. Not until the early 1990s did the Club's Board of Governors vote to allow members to sign a chit for food and beverage.

At the same meeting, Nichol calculated that the Club could be operated on a yearly budget of $6,000 and predicted an $8,000 income for the first year. He proved to be an optimist.

Although the Club was his brainchild, Nichol refused its presidency. William P. Spurgeon, managing editor of the *Washington Post*, was elected the first National Press Club president. Charles Willoughby, also of the *Post*, was appointed chairman of the committee to find a site for the Club. A tall Southerner of immense courtesy and geniality, Willoughby was influential in the Washington real estate market.

His committee settled on renting two floors above a jeweler's shop at 1205 F St. With $300 to buy second-hand furniture but no money to hire movers, Club members hauled everything themselves. Legend has it that some burly D.C. policemen pitched in to help. The chief of police heaved at the cumbersome piano. Somehow they muscled an enormous bar up the stairs.

"No steeper or longer stairs ever led to a press club," James Hay wrote. "And to reach the card room on the third floor, it was necessary to take a journey that well might have disheartened an Alpine goat."

So fast did the founders work that on May 2, 1908, the National Press Club opened its doors to an immediate brisk business. The Capitol press galleries adjourned to 1205 F St., and every newspaperman downtown who could get away was there. On May 18 the Club held its official housewarming. Several members of Congress showed up, as did the British and Japanese ambassadors. Buffalo Bill Cody regaled the crowd with tales of taking Sitting Bull to see President Grover Cleveland.

"Every square foot of the Club's space was crowded that housewarming night," Hay wrote. "The card room was packed to capacity. So was 'the lounge,' a sort of anteroom to the bar. And, incidentally, so was the bar. By nine o'clock everybody was talking, the orchestra was playing, nobody was listening, the cash register fell far behind the bar service."

Watching over the Club was its own little "god" – a Billiken, described as a clay "squat, smiling, comic figure" with oriental eyes – that served as a good-luck piece. As Scott Hart wrote in the 1948 "Dateline: Washington" history, the Club attracted to these small quarters "the great of the government, of the stage, of the prize ring, the wrestling ring, of education and literature who found they could talk freely there with people who wrote about them. And they could unbend completely in the company of men who were born with a built-in disregard for such matters."

The Club's tenure at 1205 F Street St. lasted only a year, but that was long enough to inspire legends. One was of the fire. On Dec. 23, 1908, someone tossed a lit cigarette into a wastebasket. Flames erupted. Normally a seltzer bottle would be enough to extinguish the blaze, but this being the Christmas season, the seltzer supply was depleted. The flames spread, and President Spurgeon called the fire department. Firemen doused the flames, and water rained down on the jewelry store below, where the proprietor, Mr. G. Goldsmith, stood protecting his wares with an umbrella. Despite the flames, smoke, firemen and water, the poker game never stopped. One Club historian 40 years later called it "the eternal poker game which continues 24 hours a day, six days a week in its hurtle into eternity."

A statue of a little god known as the Billiken held a position of prominence in the original clubhouse. Carried with great honor to the second clubhouse, it was lost in a subsequent move. A reproduction now presides over the Truman Lounge.

Not the fire but success caused the Club to move as membership outgrew the quarters. On March 1, 1909, the Club rented space on the second and third floors of the historic Rhodes Tavern above Afleck's Drug Store. It was at the corner of 15th and F streets across the street from the Treasury Building, right on the Inaugural Day parade route. Even before the Club moved in, it augmented its treasury by renting the rooms to financier John Hayes Hammond for the princely sum of $5,000 so that he and his friends could watch President William Howard Taft's inaugural parade on March 4.

That gave the Club cash to spend when it threw its second house-warming party on March 20. Two of the city's tallest policemen led a procession from the old quarters, stepping to the beat of a Neapolitan string quartet. Members carried torch lights. Four members carried the Billiken on a platform raised high over their heads. Behind them came 100 members, "pencil shovers," as the Club's "20th Anniversary Yearbook" called them, carrying beer steins, billiard cue sticks, records and other paraphernalia. "Little Fat God Moves," headlined one newspaper the next morning.

Many U.S. presidents passed by historic Rhodes Tavern, the second home (1909-1914) of the National Press Club at 15th and F streets. President Ronald Reagan and Mrs. Reagan are shown here on inauguration day in 1981. The tavern was torn down in 1984.

With $1,900 set aside for decorations and remodeling, the new clubhouse created an aura of intimacy and coziness that members lamented losing long after moving into more august quarters. It had a common room dominated by a fireplace, and the walls were decorated with front-page fiber matrices or "mats" used for the rotary press to print newspapers. The mats were stained, lacquered and imbedded in the walls. One of them from an 1876 Dakota Territory newspaper described the Battle of Little Bighorn. The new setting was informal, a place where members and their guests sat and talked in small groups around the fireplace.

Into this intimate space came many of the big names of the day. Arctic explorer Robert E. Peary told of his expedition to the North Pole. Wild West legends "Bat" Masterson and "Seth" Bullock swapped tales. Industrialist Andrew Carnegie promoted his ideas about an international league to enforce peace. The legendary actress Sarah Bernhardt expressed her indebtedness to the American public and press. Victor Herbert played his cello. On Jan. 31, 1910, William Howard Taft hoisted his 300 pounds up the stairs to become the first president to visit the Club. Bartender Frank Matera served him a glass of water and received the rosebud Taft wore in his lapel. The president's one complaint about his office, he said, was that "nobody drops in."

In his talk to the members, Taft described a far different Washington from 2008:

"It is a great pleasure to me to walk along the street, look into windows and pass by a great many people who don't know who I am, and at times to meet a fellow who looks once at me and then passes on without any further curiosity, and another fellow who looks twice, nudges his friend and then, with that degree of reverence that we feel for high officials, says, 'Hello, Taft!'"

1910 Board of Governors

The rotund president became a regular Club visitor during the rest of his term.

In the evening of Nov. 19, 1910, former President Theodore Roosevelt stopped by the Club. Roosevelt was "full of good humor and bubbling enthusiasm," according to the 1928 "Yearbook." He talked of his recent African safari. A lion sprang at him three times, TR said, forcing him to spring aside each time. "The next morning," he said, "I saw a commotion among the birds. Lifting my glasses to my eyes, I discovered it was caused by the self-same lion practicing short jumps." Politics was in the air that night, but Roosevelt was mum about challenging his old friend and protégé Taft for the 1912 Republican nomination.

By 1914, the Club was booming. Its membership included some of the biggest names in Washington journalism. They hosted key legislators and members of the administration for such antics as a debate: "Resolved, that whiskers are a greater detriment to man than bald heads." House Speaker Nicholas Longworth led the pro-bald side, while former Speaker "Uncle Joe" Cannon took up the cause for whiskers.

It was time to move to even larger quarters. On March 6, 1914, the Club moved into the Riggs Building, later known as the Albee Building, at the corner of 15th and G streets.

The big game hunter, fresh from jungle adventure, gets ready to go gunning for the biggest game of all! Theodore Roosevelt, unhappy with Taft, before the Bull Moose campaign of 1912, as Cliff Berryman of the Washington Evening Star *figured it.*

"Ah, those quarters atop the Riggs Building! Didn't they look palatial that day, with their wainscoting of newspaper mats, their big fireplaces, their reading rooms, card rooms, smoking rooms and the like?" the 1928 "Yearbook" gushed. "And when our four gnomes, 'Constant Reader,' 'Old Subscriber,' 'Vox Populi' and 'Pro Bono Publico,' smiled indulgently down from their places above the fireplace, didn't we have that 'grand and glorious feeling?'" And on the mantel ledge was the inscrutable Billikin. Shortly after moving in, the Club established a roof garden restaurant that gave diners a panoramic view of the White House, Washington Monument and the Virginia countryside.

Woodrow Wilson was a special friend of the Club. Even before becoming president, he was an associate member based on his reputation as an author. As governor of New Jersey, Wilson showed up for one of the Club's "hobby nights" and recited a limerick. Shortly after he was elected president, he attended the Club's spelling bee that pitted senators and House members against journalists. (The politicians won.) But Wilson is most remembered for his appearance on March 20, 1914, for the housewarming of the Club's new quarters in the Albee Building.

Under the subhead "President Wilson Bares His Soul," the 1928 "Yearbook" described the event:

"Mr. Wilson said that he must be some kind of fraud if people think him a cold and removed person with a thinking machine inside capable of adjustment to circumstances and not subject to the winds of affection and emotion. 'If I were to interpret myself I would say that my constant embarrassment is to restrain the emotions inside me. You may not believe it, but sometimes I feel like a fire from a far from extinct volcano, and if the lava does not seem to spill over it is because you are not high enough to see into the basin.'"

Roof Garden at the Albee-Riggs Building. (Photo by Harris & Ewing)

He described things he lacked time to do as president – such as read a good detective mystery. He said he sometimes felt like buying an assortment of beards, rouge and coloring and master the art of disguise to get away from the White House, to go out as an ordinary citizen and have a jolly good time. "If I were free, I would come not infrequently to these rooms," he said.

One could hardly imagine a modern-day president saying he wished he could spend more time schmoozing with reporters.

Wilson's remarks had been off the record. But Club members pressed the president to let them quote him. He relented, and the next day front page headlines from coast to coast gave the nation the picture of the president that he had given his fellow Club members.

With such connections to the Wilson administration, it was not surprising that Secretary of State William Jennings Bryan made the first transcontinental telephone call for the Bell Telephone Co., on Jan. 26, 1915, from the Club's lounge.

World War 1 brought many changes. After so many years of peace, war came as a shock to the city. Even before America's entry in 1917, the war brought a new buzz of activity to Washington and the Club. Club historian Homer Dodge described scene:

"Turbaned Indian rubbed elbows with kilted Scots Highlander and blue-bloused French officers courteously jostled the gorgeously garbed Beraglieri, while more drab soldiers of English and American regiments lent contrast."

German diplomats stopped showing up, and even Club members of German heritage faced tough times. One of the charter members, German-born A.D. Jacobson, who for many years served as an editor at the *Postital* and wrote a syndicated column on European aristocracy, was sent to an internment camp. Members appeared in military uniform. A few joined a volunteer cavalry troop at Fort Meyer in Arlington, Va., and straggled back to the Club saddle sore and weary after a day of drill.

When America entered the war in 1917, a service flag with 51 stars designating members serving in the armed services flew over the Albee Building, and the Club played a new role in wartime news censorship. In a controversial move, President Woodrow Wilson formed the Committee on Public Information to be the central source for war news. Members of the press staffed the committee in an old brick mansion on Jackson Place. Each day, government departments issued announcements to reporters.

George Creel, who had worked on Wilson's re-election campaign in 1916, directed the committee, which was created on April 14, 1917. Generals and admirals asked that more than 100 topics be kept secret. Creel whittled their list down to 18. He then took those to the Club and asked members what they thought.

"The temper of the gathering, hostile at first, grew more friendly as understandings were reached, and at the end there was an agreement that the plan merited a fair trial," Creel wrote in "Dateline: Washington." The 18 requests – asking news organizations not to print troop movements, base locations, ship sailings and coastal defenses – were printed on 6-by-12 inch cards and distributed to every Washington correspondent and to every newspaper in the country. No censorship board was created. "Their enforcement is a matter for the press itself." Washington correspondents, Creel said, "leaned over backwards in their observance of the card's requests."

Club members who had fought in the Great War returned to found their own American Legion post on Nov. 19, 1919, a year after the signing of the armistice ending the First World War. Post 20 was also known as The Pershing Post or the Black Jack Post in honor of Gen. John J. "Black Jack" Pershing, commander of the Allied Expeditionary Force and an associate Club member. As chief of staff of the War Department and into his retirement years, Pershing's name was listed on Club rolls in 1920 and 1924.

Pershing was not the only celebrity in Post 20 during those early days. Included in the membership were Theodore Roosevelt Jr., Vice President Charles G. Dawes and Gen. John A. Lejeune, for whom the Marine Corps Camp Lejeune was named. When Marshal Ferdinand Foch, the French hero of WWI came to Washington, Post 20 feted him at the Club with Pershing making the primary remarks.

Post 20 remains active in the 21st century, nearly 90 years after its founding.

After the war came Prohibition, which began in the District of Columbia at midnight on June 30, 1919. For a Club founded on the basis of its bar, the moment was suitably observed. "On the Day of Judgment, the Club placed on sale its cellar, which was not mean," Dodge wrote. "As the hours passed, it became apparent that the Club would be left in illegal possession of ardent and spirituous liquors. Quite early, beer was free on tap. With supply and deadline converging, prices of champagnes and fine brandies, old wines and proud whiskies dwindled steadily toward midnight, when on the dirging stroke, all that was left was set out on tables … for the having of anyone with the desire and strength to grasp them."

But Prohibition did not drain the Club completely. Later that year, the Prince of Wales, who later became King Edward VIII, arrived for a reception. Club President Earl Godwin received guests with the prince, who was known to enjoy Scotch. One of the Club's stewards obtained a good selection and generously sampled it during the reception. As the reception line drew thin, the steward sidled up behind the prince, jabbed him so hard with his elbow that the prince nearly fell over, and in a thick stage whisper said, "Have a little drink, prince?" After his Club visit, the prince was quoted in the London press as saying he was sorry he had not been a newspaperman.

Most everyone, including many members, expected the Club would ignore Prohibition or find a way to circumvent the law. But the Board of Governors insisted that the law be scrupulously enforced. Bootlegging waiters were discharged, and members bringing their own liquor to the Club were disciplined. But with so much booze flowing in Washington, such rigorous enforcement was hard to maintain. One of the smallest rooms in the Club became known as the Turf Club, where some members stored their hooch in an

President Warren G. Harding, an active member of the Club, casts his ballot in the Club election held Dec. 15, 1921. Left to right: William J. Donaldson, House Press Gallery; Theodore Tiller, Washington Times; Paul Mixter, Detroit Free Press; Edward Coffin, American Red Cross; the President; Robert B. Armstrong, Los Angeles Times.

assortment of jars and bottles. "Among members (of the Turf Club) as well as guests were distinguished legislators, holders of high office, jurists," Dodge wrote. "Many a man whose name meant much in the world was known to point a wee finger at the ceiling."

But the loss of bar receipts during Prohibition and a drop in membership following the war pressed the Club's finances to a point where rent payment for the Albee Building fell behind. The bank owning the building threatened to evict the Club. But Club President Earl Godwin of the *Washington Times* knew how to play hardball, too. He asked the bank, "How would you like to see printed in newspapers across the country that you evicted the president of the United States?" President Wilson was a member. The bank granted more time, and the back rent was paid.

⚮ ⚮

Club membership and finances rebounded in the 1920s as Washington became the center of diplomacy, first during debate on the Versailles Treaty and then when President Warren Harding summoned world leaders to the Conference on the Limitation of Armaments. Correspondents from all over the world arrived. Most were given temporary Club privileges as well as writing rooms, typewriters, cable rooms and other equipment.

One British correspondent, Willmot Lewis of *The Times of London*, stayed and became a Club fixture for 30 years, serving on the Board of Governors. During the war he had been a press officer for Gen. Pershing, which gave Lewis unparalleled entrée to Americans. The urbane Lewis dated Baltimorean Wallis Warfield, who later became Wallis Simpson and then the Duchess of Windsor. Lewis married Ethel Noyes, whose father ran the *Washington Star* and the Associated Press. Apart from his post at the *Times*, he also held an unofficial title of "Ambassador Incognito" for the British government. It is said he gathered most of his news from other reporters in the Club's card room, and it was there in 1931 that he was notified he would be knighted. Sir Willmot dined at the Club on the day he died in 1950.

President Warren G. Harding, who had been publisher of the Marion (Ohio) *Star*, became an active Club member and voted in its elections. The 1920 presidential election pitted two Ohio publishers against each other. The Democratic nominee was James M. Cox, who owned the paper in Dayton. During Harding's "front porch" campaign in Marion, a group of reporters assigned to cover him created a makeshift club known as "The Order of the Elephant" to play cards in their off hours. After Harding was inaugurated, the "order" continued its game at the Press Club and invited Harding to join. Much to their surprise, he came. According to Club legend, he won $1.80. Several times afterward, Harding showed up at the Club, sometimes unannounced. He was convulsed by the Club's debate – Fat vs. Lean Men – and the Club feted him on his birthday on March 4, 1922. Harding was at the Club to witness an elaborate radio hookup arranged by the Naval Air Station with the *Detroit News*. As the president listened, all that could be heard was clicks and buzzes until suddenly a wrathful voice came out of the speaker in full, volume, "The goddamned thing won't work."

Attendance at Club events in the 1920s said a lot about its stature, the relationship between the press and official Washington and perhaps the lack of entertainment in the nation's capital. That Fat vs. Lean debate that convulsed Harding was between two fat House members and two rangy senators with the speaker of the House as the moderator. A songwriters' night in 1924 drew Irving Berlin, John Philip Sousa and Victor Herbert, among others, who not only performed but wrote a few bars of their favorite songs in the Club's guest book. Berlin surprised the Club by admitting that though he could write songs, he could not perform them. Gen. Pershing arrived to watch the first movies of the ex-Kaiser. When in 1925 the Club held a ceremony to burn a $5,000 mortgage it had taken out to pay for its move to the Albee Building, the man holding the match was Treasury Secretary Andrew Mellon, one of the richest men in the country. Looking on were House Speaker Nicholas Longworth, the attorney general and the secretary of agriculture. At another event, humorist Will Rogers performed and liked the Club so much he became a member. And on June 11, 1927, the Club held a reception for the then most famous man in the world – aviator Charles Lindbergh. The Club was way too small for such an event, and Club President Louis Ludlow of the *Columbus Dispatch* arranged to use the auditorium at the U.S. Chamber of Commerce.

The Club was outgrowing its Albee Building home, and it was time to think about moving. Burning the Club's mortgage paved the way for bigger dreams: Club member James William Bryan's plan for a permanent home for the National Press Club perched atop the largest private office building in the city and filled with journalists looking for a central place to gather. That story is so audacious that it is described in chapter seven. On Feb. 4, 1928 – only 20 years after the Club was founded – the Club's new building was dedicated by President Calvin Coolidge. The Billiken having been lost, the procession to the new building was led by "Princess Alice," an Alaskan native totem "liberated" by Club members outside a Fairbanks saloon during a visit by President Harding in 1923. (See the Princess Alice story on page 57).

Princess Alice was named for Alice Roosevelt Longworth, Theodore Roosevelt's daughter and wife of House Speaker Nicholas Longworth. It was she who nearly destroyed the Club's inauguration of Eugene "Red" Leggett of the *Detroit Free Press* in 1931. Nicholas Longworth was to engage "Cactus Jack" Garner, the Democratic minority leader, in a mock debate that was to be carried over a national NBC Radio hookup. But Alice Longworth put a stop to it, saying it would be undignified for her husband. When all seemed lost, down a side aisle came "a gum-chewing gentleman in a sack suit," according to the Club's 1932 yearbook. He climbed on the stage, twisted his unruly forelock, looked around, chuckled and bellowed into the microphone: "Folks, if you ever want to see anything funny, just take a couple hundred newspapermen and dress 'em up. They look downright comical." Will Rogers saved the day, and the broadcast went on the air.

RECEPTION 2253
by
National Press Club
to
COL. CHARLES A. LINDBERGH, M. N. G.
in the Auditorium of the
Chamber of Commerce of the United States
Connecticut Avenue and H Street
Washington, D. C.
SATURDAY, JUNE 11TH, 1927 AT 9:30 P. M.

Admit One   H Street Entrance

A ticket to a Club reception for aviation hero Charles Lindbergh shortly after his trans-Atlantic flight.

President Calvin Coolidge reviews plans for the new press building on Sept. 15, 1925.

President Coolidge laying corner stone of new building, April 8, 1926.

President Herbert Hoover dropped in on the Jan. 23, 1932, inaugural of Bascom Timmons of the *Houston Chronicle*. Theodore Joslin, a Club member and secretary to Hoover, recalled later in his book, "Hoover Off the Record," that the president was reluctant to accept the Club's invitation. The plight of the Depression weighed heavily on him. He was working to improve the banking situation and was expecting an important report that night.

"Oh, alright," he finally relented to Joslin. "I will go. But I can only stay a very short time." On the way to the Club, Hoover reminded Joslin they could stay just 10 minutes. But after the formalities, Hoover settled in to watch the show. A Secret Service agent signaled Joslin to nudge the president. It was time to go.

"We haven't been here long, have we?" the president asked. "Only a few minutes," Joslin replied. "I'm glad of that," Hoover whispered. "This is good. Let's stay a while longer. I don't think it will make much difference."

The Secret Service agent insisted that they go. The president "will be sore" if he doesn't get back. "Sore nothing," Joslin retorted. "The president for once is having a good time. It's the nearest thing to a night out I have ever known him to have. You fellows get out of sight and stay out of sight. Now beat it."

Hoover was soundly trounced by Franklin Roosevelt in the next election, but whiling away an evening at the Club was never an issue. Roosevelt's election – and the end of Prohibition – ushered in a new era for the nation and the Club. A speech by President-elect Roosevelt inaugurated the Club's regular speakers series that continues to this day. The Club threw a black-tie dinner in his honor in 1933 for its Silver Jubilee. A rare picture shows Roosevelt standing in carefully concealed leg braces to receive his credentials as a "cub reporter" from Club President Raymond Brandt of the *St. Louis Post-Dispatch*. Roosevelt was back early the next year to watch a Club-produced skit spoofing regimentation under the New Deal's National Recovery Act.

As World War II raged in Europe, the Club became a platform for V.I.P. refugees from countries defeated by Hitler's Germany. Czechoslovakia's ambassador spoke in March 1939; Wilhelm Munthe de Morgenstierne of Norway in April 1940; Hendrick Kauffman of Denmark in May 1940; and Constantin Fotich of Yugoslavia in April 1941.

Newly elected President Roosevelt was honored by the Press Club in 1933 in the depths of the Great Depression. On the president's left is Club President Raymond P. Brandt of the St. Louis Post-Dispatch.

FDR receives Club membership card from President Raymond Brandt prior to black tie dinner in 1933. Former President Theodore Tiller of the Washington Times *bears witness. Note President Roosevelt's leg braces fastened to his shoes...authority and grace despite pain.*

It was a quiet Sunday in December 1941. The Redskins were playing their last game of the season at Griffith Stadium. The weather was warm enough for a round of golf. Shortly after 2:35 p.m., President Roosevelt's press secretary, Steve Early, picked up his phone and arranged a simultaneous conference call to all three wire services.

"This is Steve Early at the White House," he said with as much composure as he could muster. "At 7:35 a.m. Hawaiian time, the Japanese bombed Pearl Harbor. The attacks are continuing and – No, I don't know how many are dead."

In a moment, everything changed.

Generals, admirals and government officials by the score were paged at Griffith Stadium. Caddies raced around golf courses to pick up players. Cars screeched to a halt on the highways as the news was broadcast on car radios. Reporters rushed to work and to the Club. Within 30 minutes the Club began to fill up. By some telepathy the idea seemed to spread that reporters should go there. By early Sunday evening, the crowd had grown to presidential election-night size, Lyle Wilson, UPI's bureau manager, wrote in "Dateline: Washington." Newsmen caught in the storm of crisis sought one another's company, one another's information and opinions, and perhaps one another's comfort in the easygoing headquarters where they were accustomed to finding these things.

Des Moines Register *matrice reporting Dec. 7, 1941, bombing of Pearl Harbor (from NPC collection).*

"The capital press corps took on its biggest job in World War II," Wilson wrote. "For some, the job would be to learn what it is to die. For others, it would be to suffer despair, discomfort and great fear to send the story back. For those who stayed in Washington, the job was to cover the biggest story up to now, to cover it under the rules of censorship, sometimes under the galls of officious stupidity, always under pressure of edition time."

Even before the United States entered the war, agencies began to censor news as more and more public officials began to speak in whispers, enjoining reporters not to report all they knew. In early 1941, the Navy asked for secrecy about the repair of British warships in American shipyards. Soon other agencies, including the Weather Service and Maritime Commission, asked reporters not to reveal information.

The reverberations in the National Press Club were loud and discordant. Frustration was fed by bewilderment and confusion, even outright anger. Just what did the government want, and where would it end?

The government's Office of Censorship was established just days after the Japanese attack on Pearl Harbor. Once again a journalist, Byron Price of the AP, ran the office, which had powers to approve as well as to stop any story for publication regardless of the agency or department it referred to, with the exception of the White House.

It drew up a code to classify the categories of information, which in the interest of national security ought not to be published. It appealed to the press to observe the code and hired a staff of fewer than a dozen experienced reporters to answer questions in borderline cases. They were instructed to deal only with facts and not opinions.

"Price hated censorship," Wilson wrote, "but he administered it as a voluntary system, with an implacable determination that it should work .... If it were all added up, I would venture that Price forced muddleheaded military, naval and civilian personnel to disgorge more information than he ever specifically suppressed."

Some Club members were instrumental in breaking down the suspicion that military leaders held for reporters. With the Navy in disarray following Pearl Harbor and early defeats in the Pacific, Club member Neely Bull, who was related by marriage to the chief of naval operations, Admiral Ernest J. King, convinced the gruff officer that he should meet quietly with some leading reporters. The meetings began at Bull's house, and King learned not only how to get along with the press but also how to use it to his advantage. Not until after the war did anyone outside of this circle learn it had existed.

Many of Washington's veteran reporters made it a point to know many things that could never be printed. "Indeed, the National Press Club membership probably lugged around enough secret information to have helped the Axis powers to win the war, if they could have gotten hold of it," Wilson wrote. "All things considered, I don't think it is an overstatement to say that the press corps and Byron Price's Office of Censorship together eventually pretty much educated the government's military agencies in Washington in how to get their war reported."

Censoring news during World War II was one thing. But limiting Scotch and cigarettes really had the Club buzzing. Scotch became so rare that for a while it was served only to members. By the spring of 1945, cigarettes were in such short supply that sales were limited first to members, and then to one hour a week and finally to one pack apiece. Members didn't want to stand in line for such rationing. They developed a system that assigned a number to each chair in the lounge. The member would get his pack in order of that number. Exact change was required.

The Club's weekly canteen became its most notable contribution to the war effort. It began on a sodden late fall Saturday in 1942 with an impromptu reception for seamen on liberty from the H.M.S. *Essex*. They were brought to the Club by some hospitable members and told to drink all the beer they could hold. Free beer and hotdogs for Allied

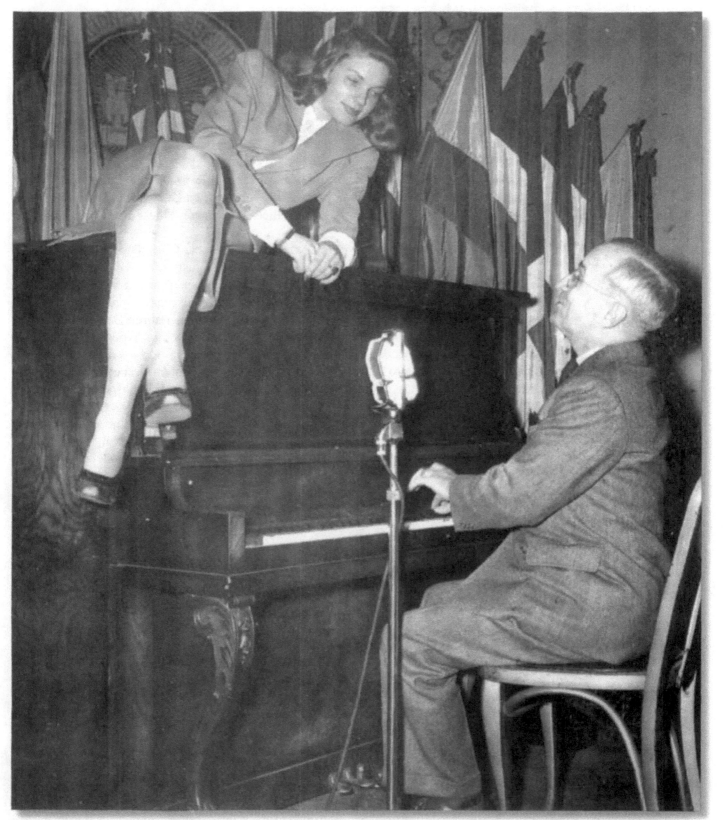

Vice President Harry S Truman tickles the ivories as actress Lauren Bacall entertains WW II servicemen at Saturday canteen on Feb. 10, 1945.

troops quickly became a phenomenal success. By Christmas, the canteens were a regular Saturday afternoon feature sponsored by the Club's American Legion Post 20. As many as 700 servicemen showed up every week for 30 weeks a year (the event was curtailed in the summers) until the end of the war. Beer flowed by the barrel, and hotdogs were piled high. GIs shouted conversation on oceans of boogie-woogie music played by military bands. Politicians, Cabinet members, admirals and generals showed up, but they were allowed to speak for no more than two minutes. On one Saturday, the entire Supreme Court showed up. Frankfurters for Justice Felix Frankfurter, as one wag noted. More to the soldiers' delight, Earl Carroll's Follies girls performed.

Now and then a reporter covering a European battle or stuck on a remote Pacific Island would be asked, "Say, Mack, they still got those canteens running back there at the National Press Club?" One member called the canteen "the burp heard round the world."

As a senator, Harry Truman was a regular visitor to the Club. During the brief time he was vice president, he attended one of the canteens. Just before he was inaugurated as vice president, he told his wife, Bess, he wouldn't get in any trouble because the NPC was an all-men's club. Truman was an accomplished pianist and sat down at an upright piano to play for the troops. When the movie actress Lauren Bacall showed up, Truman invited her to join him as 500 servicemen roared their approval. She was hoisted atop the piano as the vice president played. When the picture of the sultry, long-legged Bacall looking down into Truman's eyes appeared in newspapers the next morning, Mrs. Truman was not amused. And when Truman's daughter, Margaret, spoke at the Club nearly 50 years later, she still wasn't amused.

But the picture became one of the most famous taken at the Club, and the room where the piano now sits is known as the Truman Lounge. Anyone looking closely at the piano and the picture of it from 1945 will notice that the woodwork is not the same. Apparently so many people climbed up on it for pictures that the original cabinet had to be replaced. But the guts of the piano are original, and Victor Borge other famous people have tickled the ivories.

How famous was the Club?

In the renowned 1939 movie, "Mr. Smith Goes to Washington" – winner of 10 Academy Awards – an irate Jimmy Stewart chases a newsman known as "Nosey" into the National Press Club to denounce the entire press corps after an unflattering report about him appeared in a newspaper.

"Why don't you tell the truth for a change?" Smith yells at the reporters.

Retorts one, "Why, we're the only ones who can afford to be honest in what we tell the voters. We don't have to be re-elected like politicians."

In the 1945 war movie "Objective, Burma!" – starring Errol Flynn and nominated for three Academy Awards – a war correspondent named Mark Williams and played by Henry Hall is stuck in a jungle with a platoon of GIs. As they talk about where they would most want to be, Williams says, "At the National Press Club bar, sipping a bourbon and water."

Ballroom, 1928.

The Members' Lounge, in 1927, later renamed the Frank Holeman Lounge.

When the war ended, the Club found itself in good financial condition, according to post-war Club President Frank Holeman, and it was the Scotch that did it. "In 1939, immediately before the war, somebody persuaded the Board of Governors to buy a boatload of Hanky Bannister's Scotch," Holeman said. "The Club was one of the few places in Washington you could get honest bourbon and Scotch throughout the war at a reasonable price. So we came out of the war with $40,000 in profits, and it was all put away in treasury bonds at the Riggs Bank. We used to go over there once a year and look at them. They would mature, and we would replace them. We were living fat, dumb and happy. It was just rolling on its own."

New York Mayor Fiorella LaGuardia, center, watches the cook at a 1938 NPC Club barbeque.

Secretary of State Dean Anderson, left, talks with 1949 NPC President John O'Brien of the Philadelphia Inquirer and Sen. Tom Connally, right. (Photo by Yapfoto)

Wives await husbands in west lounge in the 1920s.

Did President George Stimpson of the Houston Post know he was looking at the next pope (Pope Pius XII) during a Club luncheon in October 1936? Eugene Cardinal Pacelli, Vatican secretary of state, said coming to the Press Club was "the only exception which I have made in my plans for a private and personal visit to this great and powerful nation."

King Peter of Yugoslavia, left, chats with Club President Clifford Prevost of the Detroit Free Press during 1942 luncheon. (Photo by J. Baylor Roberts)

President Franklin D. Roosevelt and Vice President Garner, center, are featured guests at the Newsmen's Picnic on May 22, 1937. Sen. Tom Connally is on far left.

The lobby of the Press Club, 1941.

PRINCESS ALICE

Outside the president's office on the second floor of the National Press Club stands a seven-foot wooden totem that comes with a story as unusual as its appearance.

In 1923, Warren Harding became the first president to visit Alaska. A group of report-ers went with him, and one night in Fairbanks a few of them became intrigued by this humanoid figure formed of pieces of black spruce that stood outside Miner's Home Saloon. Many might say it is ugly, but these reporters—Steven Early of the Associated Press, George Holmes of the International News Service, Bob Barry of the *Philadelphia Ledger,* Bob Norton of the *Boston Post* and Carter Field of the *Boston Herald,* decided it would look swell in the National Press Club.

The account is rather murky as to how they acquired said to-tem. One story says, "the romantic NPCers seized the chance to rescue a lanky lady in distress" at 2 a.m. It got packed away with the report-ers' belongings as the entourage left Alaska. The totem made it back to Washington, but Warren Harding did not. He died in San Francisco. The totem may have been stowed away aboard his funeral train.

Displayed in the clubhouse in the Albee Building, the figure was dubbed "Princess Alice" after Alice Roosevelt Longworth, the daughter of Theodore Roosevelt and wife of House Speaker Nicholas Longworth, a longtime Club member. Alice Longworth was a grand dame of Washington society until her death in 1961. She was well known for her eccentric character, and President Roosevelt once commented, "I can either be president or I can control Alice. I can't do both."

The totem was such an integral

Former presidents Clayton Boyce, left, and Al Cromley, right, admire Princess Alice outside the Club president's office.

part of the Club that when the time came to move from the Albee Building to the new clubhouse atop the National Press Building, Princess Alice was hoisted by Club President Fred Essary and led the parade.

President John F. Kennedy receives membership card No. 2973 from NPC President John P. Cosgrove of Broadcasting Publications, during inaugural progam at the Club, January 28, 1961.

CHAPTER THREE

IN THE SADDLE OF THE CENTURY

"...This musty, noisy, disorderly joint is by all odds the best and most vitally important Club in the world."

– Bill Lewis (Sir Willmot) of the *London Times*

The years immediately following World War II found the Club growing in membership, expanding its activities and becoming more important as the premier press center in what had become the capital of the free world. But in the post-war years the Club was challenged in many ways. Coming into the 1950s, it was still an all-white, all-male organization run by print journalists. All those things would be challenged in the next 20 years.

The Club leadership decided in 1946 to renovate a section of the Club's quarters to accommodate female guests of members, women reporters and members of the Women's National Press Club. Since its early days, the Club had always had some social arrangements for the wives, daughters and other female guests of members. Female reporters were not admitted unless they were wives of Club members. During World War II, the board allowed use of the ladies' dining room to women reporters like May Craig of the Portland (Maine) *Press Herald* and Esther Van Wagoner Tufty of the Michigan News Bureau because they worked in the press building. But these privileges were withdrawn shortly after the war. It was rumored that the wife of a powerful board member overheard a waiting newswoman complain bitterly about fat housewives coming to lunch at the Club after shopping at the downtown department store, Garfinkel's. For a complete account of women and the National Press Club, see chapter 4.

Newspapers correspondents were skeptical of radio reporters. The National Press Club was established by newspapermen, and even after Congress voted to create the radio gallery in 1939, the Club refused to admit broadcast correspondents as voting members. They could join and pay dues as associate members, but any reporter who made most of his income as a broadcast reporter was not considered a journalist worthy of active membership. Even as newspaper publishers saw the value of buying radio stations, newspaper correspondents dismissed broadcast news "as fleeting as the airwaves that carried it," according to Washington press corps historian Donald Ritchie in his book, "Reporting from Washington."

As late as 1945, the Club's membership voted down an amendment to admit broadcast reporters as active members. But two years later, the plight of Ted Koop changed everything.

Japan's Emperor Akihito, then His Imperial Highness the Crown Prince Akihito, visited on Sept. 11, 1953. The crown prince, center, sits with Club President Ted Koop, right, and Japanese Ambassador Eikichi Araki. "Through the press of the United States, I wish to express my sincere appreciation for the warm welcome extended to me both by the government and the people of this country," said the 20-year old crown prince in his remarks.

The traditional ASCAP luncheon with songwriters, hosted by President Ted Koop in March 1953. Standing from left: Harry Akst, Deems Taylor, Joan Whitney, Koop, and Leroy Anderson. Kneeling: Sol Taishoff, Editor and Publisher, singer Eddie Fisher, and Hoagy "Stardust" Carmichael.

Fred Perkins of Scripps Howard checks wire copy from AP and UPI teletypes outside the Club ballroom.

Koop was a popular member of the Club who worked for *National Geographic* when he was elected to the Board of Governors in 1947, first for a one-year term and then re-elected for a three-year term. But shortly after that election, Koop took a job as head of CBS Radio News. That meant he was no longer an active member and could not serve on the board. He was forced to resign.

His departure spurred the Club to re-examine the issue. A special committee headed by past President Charles O. Gridley of the *Denver Post* proposed on April 20, 1948, an amendment to the Club's constitution to admit as active members "those whose principal work involved the gathering, writing or editing of news for dissemination by radio, television or facsimile." The Club had finally recognized the broadcast age.

In 1953, Koop was elected as the first broadcast journalist to be Club president. His administration is noted for another milestone in Club history. He let the contract to air condition the main dining room, lounge and ballroom.

❧ ❧

"McCarthyism" has become synonymous with the lowest form of communist witch hunting. But Sen. Joseph McCarthy of Wisconsin was a regular glad-hander around the Club, especially in the early years as he courted Washington correspondents after his election to the Senate in 1946.

"He was a guy who liked to hang out at the bar," said press corps historian Ritchie. "He leaked information to reporters all the time. As long as you weren't one of the targets of his investigation, everything was fine."

McCarthy presented wheels of Wisconsin cheese and cases of Wisconsin beer to the Club, Ritchie wrote. He cooked dinner for a group of newswomen. He helped reporters find apartments in Washington's post-war housing shortage. He invited reporters to put their feet up on his desk while they chatted. He solicited reporters' opinions and introduced amendments they suggested. He gave out the phone numbers of the bars where he could be reached late at night and promised to return all calls. He joined reporters' poker games.

At a Club outing known as the "Freakness" races at the Charles Town, W.Va., race track in June 1949, McCarthy came in last in a horse race but first in a race astride a mule, Ritchie wrote.

"There were members of the Club who supported McCarthy as well as those who opposed him," Ritchie said. "The fact that he was out there riding in the Freakness race indicates how hard he tried to win reporters. But he also tried to intimidate reporters into giving him good press. In the end, his relationship with the press corps became very frigid."

The Club now honors the journalist who brought McCarthy down, Edward R. Murrow of CBS News, with a room named for him.

＊＊＊

Some historians say the National Press Club played a role in starting the Korean War. But it wasn't anything said or done at the Club. It was what was NOT said at a significant luncheon held on Jan. 12, 1950. Secretary of State Dean Acheson outlined an American "defense perimeter" in the Far East that included Japan, Okinawa and the Philippines but left out Korea and Taiwan. Just the week before, President Harry Truman had announced that the United States would not become involved in any altercation between mainland Chinese communists and nationalists on Taiwan.

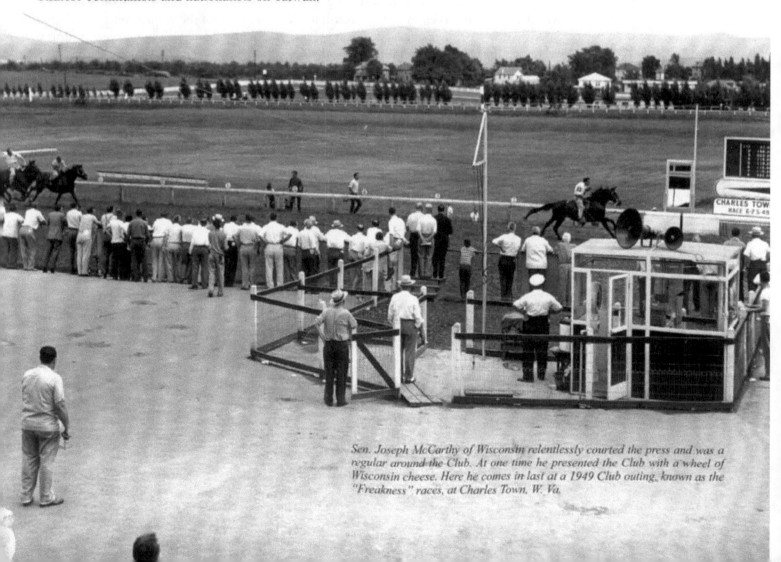

Sen. Joseph McCarthy of Wisconsin relentlessly courted the press and was a regular around the Club. At one time he presented the Club with a wheel of Wisconsin cheese. Here he comes in last at a 1949 Club outing, known as the "Freakness" races, at Charles Town, W. Va.

"There has been a lot of speculation that Acheson's statement was the final catalyst that induced Soviet Premier Joseph Stalin to arm the North Koreans with some modern weapons to attack South Korea," said Korean War historian Bevin Alexander. "A lot of history flowed out of that talk."

Truman immediately revoked the defense perimeter statement, sent U.S. troops to South Korea and the American Navy to defend Taiwan. The Korean War never really ended – hostilities halted with an armistice but no peace treaty.

More than a half century later, the Club again figured into the Korean situation. In 1994, Korean statesman Kim Dae Jung spoke at the Club just as a crisis on North Korea's nuclear capability accelerated with saber rattling in Washington and Pyongyang.

Kim proposed three things to ease the tension – President Bill Clinton should invite North Korean leader Kim Il Sung to visit Washington, former President Jimmy Carter should be named a special envoy to North Korea, and the Club should invite Kim Il Sung to speak.

NPC President Gil Klein of the Media General News Service recounted to the audience the role the Club may have had in starting the war and said, "If we could have a role in ending the conflict in Korea by having Kim Il Sung speak here, we would be pleased to do that."

Despite loud objections from the South Korean ambassador, the invitation was issued. Kim Il Sung turned it down, and he died soon afterward. But as Kim Dae Jung suggested, Carter was appointed a special envoy to North Korea, and the nuclear situation was defused—for a while. Kim Dae Jung went on to become the president of South Korea and won a Nobel Peace Prize for his efforts to end the Korean conflict.

He wrote to Klein: "Had Kim Il Sung died before President Carter's visit, the entire free world would have been in great confusion and anxiety about the future course of United States-North Korean disputes. In that sense, the National Press Club made a great contribution toward a peaceful resolution of the disputes."

Louis Lautier broke the NPC color line in 1955. (Photo by Leo Martinez)

One of the Club's first tests in the changing mores of the times was admitting African Americans. At the end of World War II, no major private club in the city allowed blacks as members. And no African Americans were employed by main stream media as Washington correspondents. The few black journalists in Washington worked for the black press, and none was accredited by the congressional press galleries.

But the black press was the leading advocate for reform in race relations and the only source of news about African Americans in many cities. Washington correspondents for black newspapers complained that few federal officials would even talk to them. Not until February 1944 was a black reporter – Harry McAlpin, who wrote for the only daily black newspaper, the *Atlanta Daily World*, and the weekly *Chicago Defender* – allowed into the White House press corps. President Roosevelt greeted him at a press conference in the Oval Office, according to Washington press corps historian Ritchie. "I'm glad to see you, McAlpin, and very happy to have you here," the president said.

Irritated that white reporters did not cover news of interest to African Americans, Louis Lautier, who wrote for the *Atlanta Daily World* and the National Negro Press Association, had to stand in line for a seat in the congressional visitors' galleries to watch a debate. He fought for and won admittance into the press gallery in 1947. Most of Lautier's reporting exposed "the injustices and absurdities of racial segregation in the nation's capital and the federal government," Ritchie said.

Lautier broke the racial barrier at the National Press Club, but it did not come without a fight. As late as the early 1940s, the Club had refused to serve a black judge brought for lunch by self-described journalist I.F. Stone, a Club member. When Stone posted a petition of outrage on the Club's bulletin board, only one other member, Win Booth of the *National Geographic*, signed it. Stone resigned in protest.

But by the mid 1950s, following the Supreme Court's Brown v. Board of Education decision, minds were changing.

The story is best told by Frank Holeman, who was a reporter for the *New York Daily News* and the Club's vice president in 1955 when Lautier applied for admission, in a 16-page account he wrote for the Club's archives in 1988.

Holeman said he was approached by Club member Alden Todd of the Federated Press in December 1954 and asked if he would support Lautier's admission. Holeman said he would but asked Todd to wait until after the Club's elections to propose him so that the issue would not be embroiled in Club politics. He promised Todd he would poll the membership committee and the Board of Governors after the election and would report back on Lautier's chances.

True to his word, Holeman told Todd that he believed a Lautier would be accepted by the membership committee and approved by a bare majority of the Club's 12-member Board.

The Main Lounge of the National Press Club circa the early 1950s was a home away from home for many members. The lounge was re-named the Holeman Lounge in 1996 to honor Frank Holeman, who can be seen standing in the center of the room. (Photo by George Tames)

Lautier's application was co-signed by three Club members who held high-ranking positions in the Washington press corps – Lee Nichols of the United Press and two columnists, Drew Pearson and Marquis Childs.

Lautier "is a highly intelligent, respected journalist who will make a good member of the Club," Pearson wrote in his column at the time. "When people get to know him, they will like him."

On Jan. 10, 1955, the Board voted six to four with one abstention to admit Lautier. For almost any other membership application, that would be enough. But the Club's bylaws required that the names of prospective new members be posted for 15 days. If a protest was signed by more than 10 active members, the membership application could be turned down. In the 47-year history of the Club to that point, only one membership had been denied after the board's approval – Italian dictator Benito Mussolini in 1928.

A petition signed by more than 10 members was filed against Lautier. It was carefully worded not to mention race but challenged Lautier's professional qualifications and character.

"To say that 'all hell broke loose!' is to understate the case," Holeman wrote. "Members quickly chose sides, applauding the Board's decision or condemning it in the strongest terms possible. Angry arguments raged through the day and long into the night in the bar, the dining room, the card room and elsewhere. There were even occasional fistfights."

Opponents of Lautier included two highly respected past presidents, Bascom Timmons, who was head of a large news bureau that represented the *Houston Chronicle* and many other papers in the West and the South, and Paul Wooton of the *New Orleans Times-Picayune* and secretary of both the White House Correspondents Association and Business Magazine Writers.

But the fight broke down by age, not geograpy, Holeman said. Older members tended to oppose the application, whether they came from the North or South, while younger members approved it. Holeman himself was a North Carolina native.

Lautier didn't help his cause by writing two columns expressing his rage and condemning two Club members by name – Jerry Greene of the *New York Daily News* and George Durno of the International News Service. The columns were circulated among Club members.

The stage was set for an explosive general membership meeting scheduled for Jan. 21. Many Board members feared a rancorous public meeting would earn the Club terrible international press and embarrass and damage the careers of members both pro and con.

Holeman said he went to Timmons and Wooton with a proposition: If a majority of the members accepted Lautier as a member, would they go along? Both said they would. Holeman proposed a secret vote of the membership, similar to a Club election. The Board of Governors agreed that they would abide by the outcome of the vote.

The election was set for Feb. 4, and the rancorous membership meeting was avoided.

"The epic struggle began a new phase," Holeman wrote. "Each side made plans to get out its maximum vote. This meant organizing a network of like-minded members who would actively campaign for their side, buttonholing co-workers and telephoning friends."

A total of 658 active members voted, by far the largest turnout for any Club election, before or since. Big name journalists, some who hadn't been seen around the Club in months or years, showed up: Columnist Walter Lippman, *National Geographic* publisher Gilbert Grosvenor, *New York Times* columnist Arthur Krock and David Lawrence, publisher of *U.S. News and World Report*. Campaign workers for and against Lautier stood in the corridor leading to the Main Lounge checking voters against lists of their supporters. As the day went on, they went to the phones to call missing troops.

After the polls closed at 8 p.m., members gathered in the taproom as poll workers counted votes. "Beer and liquor flowed freely," Holeman wrote. "Voices got louder and louder. Bets were made. Some opponents of Lautier announced they would resign immediately if he became a member. His vocal supporters retorted, 'good riddance.'"

When Paul McGahan of the *Philadelphia Inquirer* entered to announce the tally, the taproom went silent.

"The vote in this election was Yes – 377; No – 281," McGahan announced. "It took a second or two for the hushed crowd in the bar to realize the meaning of the numbers. Then pandemonium erupted: shouts, curses, excited conversation. One of the men who worked hard against Mr. Lautier, Lorenzo Martin of the *Louisville Times*, burst into tears."

And then it was over. Only one member of the Club resigned over the issue, and he was not a journalist.

"We will never know for certain what would have happened if the referendum had gone the other way," Holeman wrote. "Perhaps members in favor of integration then would have split off and formed a new organization. If the original Club survived, no doubt it would eventually have become integrated under mounting pressure from the profession, the community and the courts."

With the election of the first black journalist to membership, I.F. Stone reapplied for admission in 1956, fifteen years after the Club refused to serve his black guest. Stone, a self-proclaimed leftist radical in the age of McCarthyism, had been investigated by the House Un-American Activities Committee and was one of the journalists whose name appeared on the de facto "blacklist." The Board of Governors refused to reinstate Stone to membership. Stone took the decision personally, proclaiming bitterly that he had been "blackballed."

"I opposed Mr. Stone's reinstatement," Holeman said more than 30 years later. "I felt that reinstating Mr. Stone at that time would surely reignite the fires of dissension in the Club which we were desperately trying to put out after the bitter battle over Mr. Lautier's membership."

By the early 1980s, the controversy surrounding Stone was largely forgotten, and some Club members felt that Stone had not received the recognition he deserved. Club members honored him twice in 1981 and 1988 with a luncheon and a reception and made him an honorary member, reserved only for a select few. Izzy Stone died in 1989, but his portrait remained in the Fourth Estate dining room.

Journalist I.F. Stone talked about free speech and democracy at a March 24, 1988, luncheon.

Former President Hoover, a longtime Club supporter and dues-paying member, made his last visit to the Club at a luncheon on March 10, 1954. He had been a member since May 11, 1921, and he drew a crowd of 494 members and guests to hear him speak.

In 1956, Egypt's seizure of the Suez Canal precipitated an international crisis that reverberated at the Club. Speaking that year were Israeli Foreign Minister Golda Meir, Egyptian Foreign Minister Mahmoud Fawzi and Indian Prime Minister Jawaharlal Nehru.

John V. Horner of the *Washington Star* led the Club through its 50th anniversary jubilee year in 1958. More than 850 members and guests gathered for the Jubilee Dinner on April 12. Suddenly the band broke off its song and swung into "I'm Just Wild About Harry" as former President Harry Truman entered the room to a standing ovation. His eyes filled with tears as he addressed the crowd. He said he never "fussed" with reporters, opting instead to direct his presidential barbs at the editors and publishers. He couldn't resist adding, "I could always tell what editors and publishers were thinking about when you asked me questions."

At the head table were 13 surviving charter members of the original 192. John Russell Young, the same charter member who insisted on a cash-only policy when the Club was created, spoke for the other 12 about the milestones in the Club's history. He made sure to mention the generosity of the brewery agent who told the members in the early days, "I have a lot of confidence in you boys."

Former President Hoover during his last visit to the NPC on March 10, 1954.

A *Newsweek* article titled, "The Most Famous Journalistic Hangout," commemorated the anniversary.

"The National Press Club was founded, old-time Washington newsmen say, 'to give reporters a place to gamble without being bothered by police or their wives,'" the article said. "But this week, as the nation's most famous journalistic hangout celebrated its 50th birthday, the Club was behaving with all of the decorum befitting middle age.

"Not in years has a waiter been dangled from the Club's 13th floor windows in its own National Press Building in downtown Washington; no recent reports of spittoons being hurled at the old Willard Hotel across 14th Street. Fading, too, is the ever-ready spirit of the member who, as he was carried out on a stretcher after a heart attack, called out to the bartender: 'How about one for the road?'

"Today, the Club is a focus of newspaper activity in the news capital of the world, an unofficial clearinghouse for interminable shoptalk, and itself a prime news source," *Newsweek* said.

At a luncheon on Jan. 14, 1959, Dwight D. Eisenhower became the seventh president to be a member of the National Press Club. Although he had addressed the Club in 1948 when he was army chief of staff, this appearance was his first in six years as president.

Club President John Horner of the *Washington Star* presented Eisenhower with his membership card, telling the president that the board elected him after "having agreed that you are well qualified as a source of news." Eisenhower replied, "I understand – possibly erroneously, but I hope it's true – that members of the press deal gently with other members. So I hope the possession of this card gives me a certain immunity that up to this moment has not been mine."

President Dwight D. Eisenhower received his membership card on Jan. 14, 1959, from Club President John V. Horner of the Evening Star. *Eisenhower joked that his membership in the Club should lead to better coverage of his administration in the press.*

Premier Nikita Khrushchev, center, in the Club's East Lounge, Sept. 27, 1959, after his coast-to-coast tour with U. N. Ambassador Henry Cabot Lodge. This informal gathering, prior to news conference in ballroom, was arranged by the Soviet Embassy. From left with back to camera: Walter Ridder, John Cauley, Lew Shollenberger, Soviet Ambassador Mikhail Menshikov, unidentified speaking with Andrei Gromyko, unidentified Soviet official, John Cosgrove, Ernie Barcella, Ed Edstrom, backs of Joe Dear and Bryson Rash. Soviet interpreter Oleg Troyanovsky, right of Khrushchev. After the news conference the premier and his party went to Andrews Field for a non-stop flight to Moscow.

But the biggest luncheon in 1959 – and perhaps in the entire Club history – was the appearance of Soviet Premier Nikita Khrushchev on Sept. 16 as he began his famous tour of the United States. Interest was so intense that Club President William Lawrence of the *New York Times* worked out an elaborate plan of whom would be admitted, where they would sit or stand, and how wire services could instantly transmit the news.

Khrushchev refused to speak at the Club unless women journalists were admitted, as is detailed in chapter 4, and the event officially was a joint effort of the National Press Club, the Women's National Press Club, and the Overseas Press Club.

The ballroom was filled with 490 people having lunch, including 40 Soviet correspondents, plus many more in the balcony. Congressional press gallery superintendents, State Department security officers and a Metropolitan policeman were stationed at the balcony to check credentials. A pool of eight photographers was allowed to shoot pictures of Khrushchev as Lawrence introduced him and then had to depart from the front of the rostrum. Specially constructed stands at the far end of the room served for still and newsreel photographers, who were limited to five companies. Club waiters were assigned to carry film to couriers waiting outside the ballroom. For television, CBS News handled the pool for the other networks with three cameras positioned around the room. Radio correspondents had their own assignments.

In his speech, Khrushchev spoke of ending the Cold War, bringing peace to a divided Germany and finding a way to disarm each country's nuclear forces.

"The best and most dependable way of making war impossible is to put all states, without exception, in a position in which they will have no means of waging war, or, in other words, to solve the disarmament problem," he said. "The Cold War must be helped to disappear as quickly as possible."

President Lawrence asked Khrushchev to explain what he meant by saying, "We will bury you," at a recent diplomatic reception. The remark had been widely publicized in the U.S. media and was interpreted as a hostile threat to destroy the United States.

"My life would be too short to bury every one of you if this should occur to me," Khrushchev quipped.

He said he was not referring to a physical burial but of the progress of human development. As feudalism gave way to capitalism, capitalism will be replaced by communism, he said.

"The new and progressive will win," he said. "The old and moribund will die."

Actress Maureen O'Hara chats with Vice President Richard Nixon during the inaugural party for Club President Ed Edstrom of Hearst Newspapers, second from left, in January 1960. Chief Justice Earl Warren, left, swore in Edstrom to be Club president.

In 1960, Chief Justice Earl Warren, actress Maureen O'Hara, Vice President Richard Nixon and entertainer Bob Hope headlined the January inauguration of NPC President Ed Edstrom of Hearst Newspapers. Justice Warren swore in Edstrom in what would have been a routine ceremony except for one intentional "hitch." Mae Smith, "undisputed ruler of Club records," stepped up to the platform to inform the audience that Edstrom had an outstanding indebtedness to the Club of 10 cents. Edstrom said he was out of dimes – out of dollars, too – and the call went out, "Is there a Rockefeller in the house?"

Nixon chimed in and produced the necessary dime, noting, "Just to keep the record straight, I borrowed it from Jack Kennedy!" Later Bob Hope would add to the barbs, saying of Nixon: "They're so sure he's going to be president that they're now building a log cabin he was born in."

President William Lawrence beams with approval as Vice President Richard Nixon accompanies Jack Benny during the Club's Third Annual President's Black Tie Ball in November 1959. "The best show ever held in Washington," was the way one enthusiast described the program arranged by Broadcast Music, Inc.

French President Charles de Gaulle's address at a 1960 Saturday luncheon was broadcast live by NBC. Club President Edstrom was not a public speaker and was always uneasy handling a luncheon. The idea of playing host to the great de Gaulle, who was at the height of his imperious power, terrified him.

Edstrom acquitted himself well and after escorting de Gaulle to his limousine, returned to the Club. Bryson Rash, the 1963 Club president, takes up the tale.

"Shaking just a bit, Ed quickly ducked into the member's bar and ordered a double Scotch on the rocks to steady himself," Rash said. "In those days, there was a small restroom to the left of the long bar. Just as Edstrom lifted the drink to calm his nerves, someone bolted from the men's room and shouted in frustration, 'Ed, there aren't any towels in the men's room!'"

So much for the glory of the Club presidency.

Sen. John F. Kennedy also spoke to the Club in 1960, the year he ran for president. He told members that a president "should reopen the channels of communication between the world of thought and the seat of power.

"The question is, what do the times, and the people, demand for the next four years in the White House?" he said. "They demand a vigorous proponent of the national interest, not a passive broker for conflicting private interests. They demand a man capable of acting as commander-in-chief of the grand alliance, not merely a bookkeeper who feels that his work is done when the numbers on the balance sheet come out even. They demand that he be the head of a responsible party, not rise so far above politics as to be invisible; a man who will formulate and fight for legislative policies, not be a casual bystander to the legislative process."

Kennedy was one of the Club's greatest presidential friends. One week after his own inauguration, he paid tribute to the Club by being among the few presidents to participate in an NPC inaugural. As John Cosgrove, who worked for Broadcasting Publications when he was inaugurated Jan. 28, 1961, still quips after 46 years, "I went to Kennedy's inaugural, it was only right that he returned the favor."

"Mr. Kennedy's surprise visit electrified the East Lounge," Cosgrove said. The new NPC president did not know that Kennedy would appear until late in the afternoon before the ceremony. Kennedy's press secretary, Pierre Salinger, stopped by in the afternoon to pay the president's $90 initiation fee as an associate member and revealed to Cosgrove that Kennedy intended to make an appearance. He asked Cosgrove to keep the presidential visit under wraps.

"We had a pre-arranged signal – a long ring on the East Lounge phone when the president left the White House," Cosgrove said. "That meant Pierre and I would have time to leave the East Lounge where inaugural ceremonies were underway and arrive at the 14th Street entrance to greet Kennedy.

"Unfortunately, the presidential limousine made better time than anticipated, and when we reached the street lobby, the president was there, pacing in front of the elevators. Smilingly, he inquired, 'where have you been?'"

After Cosgrove presented the president with his membership card, No. 2973, Kennedy praised the Club for sticking to its rules and having "the decency to charge me the initiation fee and dues." Many other memberships had come his way since becoming president, Kennedy explained, often without mention of any cost.

"The president's appearance in the East Lounge was brief," Cosgrove said, "but he did manage to greet head-table guests who included House Speaker Sam Rayburn and Chief Justice Earl Warren. He had to leave before the swearing-in ceremonies, and in departing, looked at me directly and said, 'I'm sorry I can't stay any longer, but be sure to keep your hand on the Bible.'"

That comment was in reference to his own inauguration when someone watching it on television claimed Kennedy's hand was not on the Bible when he took the oath, Cosgrove said.

A startling story about the Club's role in the 1962 Cuban missile crisis emerged when the Soviet archives were opened following the fall of the Soviet Union. The following comes from a 1998 Associated Press account.

"The Russians viewed the American media as a wonderful source of what was really going on," said Timothy Naftali, a Yale University professor and co-author with Russian historian Aleksandr Fursenko of the missile-crisis history, "One Hell of a Gamble." "They understood the difference between American journalists and their own."

As tensions rose after the discovery of Soviet missiles in Cuba in October 1962, the Soviets looked for signs of how President Kennedy would respond.

Administration officials such as Defense Secretary Robert McNamara and Undersecretary of State George Ball held background briefings with top reporters and columnists. The Soviets went to great lengths to make contact with reporters they had cultivated over the years.

Disturbing news reached Moscow from Johnny Prokov, a bartender at the National Press Club and émigré from Lithuania, who voiced strongly anti-Soviet views. Prokov overheard one journalist tell another that he was going to fly south "to cover the operation to capture Cuba." Prokov passed the information to Anatoly Gorsky, correspondent for the Soviet news agency TASS, who also was a KGB officer. The information was quickly dispatched to the Kremlin, which ordered Soviet agents to find out more.

Warren Rogers of the *New York Herald Tribune* (and 1970 Club president), told Naftali and Fursenko that one of his Soviet acquaintances came up to him the next morning as he parked his car.

"What do you think of the situation?" Rogers recalled the Russian asking.

"I think it is extremely grim," Rogers replied.

"Do you think Kennedy means what he says?" the Soviet official asked.

"You're damn straight he does," said Rogers.

The Russians took this answer as confirmation of the story heard by Prokov. An American invasion of Cuba was imminent.

However, Naftali and Fursenko wrote, what Prokov overheard was a discussion of a Pentagon list of reporters who would be taken along IF the decision was to invade. No such decision was ever made.

But Soviet Premier Nikita Khrushchev decided to pull the missiles out of Cuba rather than risk armed confrontation with the United States.

In 1963, Bryson Rash was sworn in as president. He was a correspondent and broadcaster for *WRC, WRC-TV* and *NBC*. With all that broadcasting background, he had to do something special for his inaugural. Most Club presidents are print journalists, and for years each one produced a mock edition of his newspaper to be distributed during the celebration. Perhaps the most memorable of these was the faux *National Geographic* with the bare-breasted native girl on the cover produced for the inauguration of Windsor Booth in 1966. But for Rash, his broadcasting company did what it did best – produce a LP album with the title, "Is Frank Lloyd Wright? Is Anna May Wong? Is Bryson Rash?"

Heard were *NBC* anchor David Brinkley and correspondents Richard Harkness and Robert McCormick as well as *WRC*'s "Joy Boys," Willard Scott and Ed Walker.

"This record is expected to serve as a reminder to the membership of the National Press Club of the perils of an election system which permits a Bryson Rash administration to rise to power," the record promises. "It is in this spirit of reform that the veil of secrecy has been lifted to expose the new president, his fellow officers and cronies on the board in as penetrating a fashion as modern electronics and a limited budget would allow."

Four decades later, both the Rash record and the mock *National Geographic* show up regularly for sale on eBay.

In late summer of 1963, Rash formed a Foreign Affairs Committee of international correspondents and cultural affairs attaches from the embassies. During a meeting of

This faux National Geographic *cover was produced for the inauguration of NPC President Windsor Booth in 1966.*

this committee on Nov. 22, Rash recounted, "the waiter came to me with the whispered information that President Kennedy had been shot during his trip to Dallas. I passed that information along to the members of the luncheon meeting, and a short time later I left the President's Room to seek additional information."

Rash returned to the luncheon to tell the 14 or 15 representatives of foreign nations what had occurred. The meeting immediately ended, and Rash stood in the door of the room to say good-bye to the guests as they hurried to their offices.

"To my astonishment, as each left, he grasped my hand and offered his personal and his country's condolences," Rash said. "For that brief period, I represented this country to those representatives of another. It was a moment of high emotion."

Rash and Club manager Jim Monfort set up a small memorial for the dead president. A prize-winning photograph of Kennedy taken by George Tames of the *New York Times*, showing the back of the president in silhouette in the Oval Office during the Cuban Missile Crisis, was placed at the Club's entrance over a small table with a white cloth and a vase of white mums. It remained there for the 30 days of mourning.

The new president, Lyndon Johnson, made a personal effort to befriend the Club. In 1965, with less than an hour's notice, he made a surprise visit to trade quips with some of the country's top cartoonists, who had just visited him at the White House. One of the cartoonists, Milton Caniff, apparently invited Johnson to the luncheon in their honor at the Club.

National Press Club memorial to John F. Kennedy, including a photograph by George Tames of the New York Times.

President Lyndon Johnson meets Press Club members in luncheon honoring the nation's cartoonists in 1969. Club President "Pat" Heffernan of Reuters presided.

When he arrived at the Club, Caniff casually said to Club President Bill Blair of the *New York Times*, "I just invited the president to come over for lunch, and he said he might," the Press Club *Record* reported. Within minutes, telephones started to ring and a Secret Service agent appeared in the lobby. A place was quickly arranged at the head table.

When Johnson arrived in the East Lounge, Blair escorted him to the speaker's table. The cartoonists – Caniff, Roy Crane, Mort Walker, Don Sherwood, George Wunder and Bill Mauldin – drew a joint caricature of Johnson, jaunty in an officer's cap as commander in chief. Asked for a few remarks, Johnson said he did not feel about cartoonists like the man who said, "We couldn't find the artist, so we hung the picture instead."

Throughout 1966 and 1967, domestic and international speakers flocked to the Club to talk about the escalating war in Vietnam and East-West tensions. Vice President Hubert Humphrey defended the administration's actions in Southeast Asia, and Australian Prime Minister Harold Edward Holt lent his country's support. California Gov. Ronald Reagan made an appearance as did Madame Chiang Kai-shek, the fiery wife of the longtime Chinese leader. President Ferdinand Marcos of the Philippines told a capacity crowd that a communist takeover in Indonesia during an abortive 1965 coup was averted by the presence of U.S. military personnel, including the 7th Fleet.

On March 29, 1966, Indian Prime Minister Indira Gandhi spoke about the increasing tensions between the two largest communist powers, the Soviet Union and China. "Should we further doubt that it was and still is the design of the Chinese communists to embroil Russia in a general war so that the Red Chinese communists come out the real victor?" she said.

Conflicting advice for the United States on Vietnam abounded in 1967. Afghan Prime Minister Mohammed Hasham Maiwandal told a luncheon that there was no hope for peace talks unless the United States halted bombing of North Vietnam. But South Korea Prime Minister Il Kwon Chung warned that any bombing letup would not produce peace talks.

※◎◎※

April 4, 1968, was a day that not only changed America, but also transformed Washington and the National Press Club. In Memphis, Tenn., assassin James Earl Ray cut down Martin Luther King Jr. As word spread throughout the nation, enraged African Americans rioted, looting and burning central cities. Downtown Washington was not spared.

King first spoke at the Club in 1962, and he was scheduled to appear again at the Club's new Town Meetings on April 9. Instead, he was buried that day.

The Thursday night buffet was in full swing when the news tickers in the Main Lounge clattered with the shattering report.

"When the news of the King assassination hit Washington, the city erupted into violence," remembered Allan Cromley of the *Daily Oklahoman* and *Oklahoma City Times*, who was Club president. "You could look down on F Street and see them breaking windows down there and carrying things away. It was not safe to go onto the streets. I don't remember how I got home."

On Friday night, the Club was jammed with journalists covering the outbreak of violence in sections of Washington. Serving alcoholic beverages was prohibited during the rioting.

Suddenly downtown Washington was not a place where anyone wanted to venture at night, Cromley said. Evening events disappeared, despite attempts by the Club to lure people back with dance bands in the ballroom. "The downtown was not a happy place," he said. Nighttime business at the Club declined, and it took decades for downtown Washington to revive.

To pay tribute to her husband, Coretta Scott King spoke at a luncheon a few years later after writing her book, "My Life with Martin Luther King, Jr.," and she returned many times after that to speak.

In the months following the King assassination, Club members restarted the Town Meetings with debates on such questions as free press, fair trials and the student rebellions, and "the pill." However, tragedy again intervened to cancel a debate in June 1968 on the John F. Kennedy assassination when it coincided with the murder of his brother, Robert.

In the tumultuous year of 1968, all of the presidential and vice presidential candidates spoke at the Club except Richard Nixon and Curtis LeMay. But for Cromley, one of the most heart-stopping events was more personal – when he nearly lost the Club's liquor license.

"I got a call from the District's Alcohol Beverage Board, and the chairman, Joy Symington, wanted to take a look at the men's bar," Cromley said. "I stood in the door to the bar like George Wallace in the school house door and said, 'I'm sorry you can't come in here.' She tried to get our liquor license lifted, but she was outvoted by the two male members of the board."

President Johnson chose the Club's annual meeting in January 1969 to give a farewell press conference just days before leaving office. Johnson signed the guest register even though he was a member of the Club. But by the time Club President John W. "Pat" Heffernan of Reuters had escorted Johnson out, someone had ripped out the page bearing the president's signature. Heffernan put a note in the next issue of the *Record* asking for its return, but to no avail. Johnson,

April 1968 Town Meeting.

J.W. "Pat" Heffernan of Reuters was the first foreign-born president of the National Press Club. Heffernan, who was a British citizen, required a special congressional waiver to become president due to a local District of Columbia liquor license ownership requirement.

by that time back at his ranch in Texas, saw the notice and sent a replacement signature. The original page was never found.

Vietnam and the Middle East continued to be the overriding global issues in 1969. The Club's luncheons were aimed at the international turmoil. W. Averell Harriman, who had been Johnson's chief negotiator at the Paris peace talks on Vietnam, talked about how they had become unproductive. President Nixon's defense secretary, Melvin Laird, told the Club he opposed setting a deadline for U.S. troop withdrawal.

Sen. Edmund Muskie of Maine, who would run for president in 1972, called for changes in the United States' Far East policy. He asked the news media to do more to explain what was happening in Vietnam.

"Over the past eight years," he said, "the news media have proven to be the most consistently reliable guide to facts and to understanding the war. But today we are getting much less than we require for informed public opinion on Vietnam. The result has been less news coverage and less coverage in depth."

Texas billionaire H. Ross Perot, who was working independently to free U.S. prisoners in Vietnam, told the Club he would "support the devil himself" for the release of American POWs. "The treatment of our men in North Vietnam reads like something out of medieval history," he lamented.

But all was not tied to Vietnam in 1969. Americans reached the moon on July 20.

When the Club showed a 27-minute film of the Apollo 11 moon landing, NASA Administrator Thomas O. Paine told the audience that he believed life could and would be extended to other areas of space. "If man can go to the moon," he said, "he can do anything, maybe improve the peas at Press Club luncheons!"

President Lyndon Johnson signs the Club's guestbook after his 1969 farewell press conference given at the Club. First Lady Lady Bird and members look on. Johnson sent the Club another signature after learning that someone stole the page he had signed. (Photo by John Metelsky)

Actress Carol Channing appeared at the Club for a production of "Lorelie" on May 24, 1973. Here Club President Don Larrabee, right, talks with Channing. 1970 Club president, Michael Hudoba of Sports Afield, stands to the left of Channing. (Photo by John Metelsky)

Keeping with the Club's newfound image as the center of news, clocks above the press release shelf reflect the time in nine time zones. 1960 Club President Ed Edstrom of Hearst Newspapers *approves.*

The National Press Club election on Dec. 14, 1956, brought out three generations of Press Club members to vote. Standing left to right and marking their ballots are Dr. Gilbert H. Grosvenor, chairman of the Board of the National Geographic Society and a member of the Club for nearly 50 years; his son Dr. Melville Bell Grosvenor, president and editor of the National Geographic Magazine *and a member of the Club for a quarter of a century; and his son Gilbert M. Grosvenor, on the magazine's illustration staff at the time and later to take on the same role as his father. Standing by is Club President Frank Holeman. Seated are members of the Elections Committee, headed by the veteran chairman Paul J. McCulun of the* Philadelphia Inquirer.

President Hudoba of Sports Afield gets lots of help lighting his cigar from members and friends keen to be on his good side. Hudoba was always lightning quick in his own hospitality, the first to offer a light when someone was searching for a match. Clockwise from bottom left, Neil Regeimbal, Felix Belair, Bob Alden, Ed Prina, Bill Hickman, Vernon Louviere, Don Larrabee, Hudoba, Ken Scheibel, and Stan Jennings.

William Broom of Ridder Newspapers takes the NPC oath of office from President Gerald Ford on Jan. 26, 1975. (Photo by Stan Jennings)

Actor Jimmy Stewart stopped by the Club for a casual dinner with members and President John Cosgrove on Feb. 16, 1961. (Photo by Benjamin E. Forte)

Coretta Scott King and NPC President Lee Roderick of Scripps League meet before her speech on April 8, 1993. (Photo by Marshall Cohen)

Adlai Stevenson, U.S. ambassador to the United Nations, enjoyed his June 26, 1961, appearance, one of many. (Photo by Gene Forte)

India's Prime Minister Jawaharlal Nehru talks with Club President John Cosgrove prior to his Nov. 9, 1961 talk.

NPC President Jack Horner of the Washington Star shakes hands with the Lone Ranger, aka Clayton Moore, at a Family Frolic in the late 1950s.

At a Club "Family Frolic" on June 17, 1956, Club President Frank Holeman is in the passenger seat. Future president John Cosgrove is at the far right.

Drinking and driving was no problem at this Family Frolic picnic in the early 1950s.

Right: Sartorially up to any challenge, members celebrate National Press Club Spring outing in West Virginia. (Photo by Dan Frankforter)

*Below right: "The News Cauldron of the World" is the title of an article in Nation's Business, March 1946, by Carlisle Bargeron, in which this caricature appeared. **First panel,** from left: Junius Wood, W.M. Kiplinger, President Truman, Sir Wilmott Lewis, Paul Wooton, Lord Halifax, The Duke of Windsor, Cardinal Pacelli, Robert Wooley, Homer Dodge, Lawrence Sullivan. **Second panel:** Paul McGahan, Charles Gridley. **Third panel:** Frank Albus, Frank Warfield, Emil Hurja, Joyce O'Hara, Howard Suttle, John O. Williams, Constantine Chekrezi, William Hammers, Bill Doherty, Richard Seelley Jones, Harry Lourie, Ben Stern, Norman Baxter, Bob Watson, Charles Wood, Leo Sack, Jack Edwards, Jim Hood.*

Left: Singer Nat King Cole entertains Club members.

Below: Celebrating the Old West in the early 1950s. Yes, that's a real horse, ridden by entertainer Gordon McRae. The service elevator was repaired afterwards. (Photo by Robert Phillips)

Above: One of the many highlights of the Family Frolics, started by Club President Lucian Warren in 1955, was the annual baseball game between The Press and The Government. Here, Vice President Richard Nixon is at bat in a sandlot in Rock Creek Park. (Photo by Dr. Diesdado M. Yap)

Left: A evening affair at the Club in 1958. (Photo by Benjamin E. Forte)

Margaret Chase Smith announced her bid for the U.S. presidency at a WNPC event in 1964.

CHAPTER FOUR

DOWN FROM THE BALCONY
THE WOMEN'S NATIONAL PRESS CLUB 1919-85

"I would think when there is an official visitor here as the guest of the people of the U.S. and there is a meeting, that all reporters should be welcome on the basis of equality."
— President John F. Kennedy at a news conference, Nov. 29, 1961

Recognizing women as professional journalists did not come easily to the National Press Club, which had begun near the turn of the 20th century in the tradition of all-male social clubs of the time — a retreat to drink, smoke cigars, play cards and exchange information.

But the NPC soon became more than a social club. It quickly gained recognition as a bastion of important press events because it held newsmaker luncheons and heard from presidents, Cabinet members, visiting heads of state and other national and international public officials. From the beginning, women reporters were not allowed to cover these events.

In this atmosphere, in the late fall of 1919, a letter went out to women reporters, society editors, and magazine and government writers in Washington. The language of the letter promoting the idea of a women's press club was deceptively casual.

"The other day when a few of us happened to be together, it occurred to us that it might be both pleasant and profitable for the newspaper and magazine women of Washington to have some means of getting together in informal and irregular fashion," the letter read.

Pleasure and professional advantage would have been reason enough to move ahead. But there was a deeper reason, one not alluded to in the letter, possibly because it was so obvious: Women were barred from membership and participation in the National Press Club and the Gridiron Club, the major journalism institutions in the public life of the nation's capital city.

Washington was ready for a women's professional club. World War I had opened new job opportunities for women as they filled in for men at war. And in the postwar period, Washington had become an important news center. Out-of-town newspapers and press associations were opening bureaus. Washington had a lively political and social scene to be covered.

Also in 1919, only a few months before the letter was circulated, Congress, responding to the pressure of the suffragists, had approved the 19th Amendment to the Constitution giving women the right to vote. But there was another defining event: The National Press Club had just announced it would entertain the Prince of Wales on a highly publicized visit to the nation's capital, and it was made clear that women reporters would be excluded from all activities and interviews.

Cora Rigby, who had recently joined the Washington bureau of the *Christian Science Monitor*, declared a women's club was necessary to combat "the conspiracy of men to keep women off the newspapers or at least to reduce their number, wages and importance."

Cora Rigby, Christian Science Monitor, *founder and second president 1920-28 of the Women's National Press Club.*

Twenty-eight female writers responded to the call and became the first members of the Women's National Press Club.

Of the six original founders, three were reporters: Cora Rigby, Elizabeth King of the *New York Post* and Carolyn Vance Bell, columnist for the Newspaper Enterprise Association. The three others, Florence Brewer Boeckel, Eleanor Taylor Nelson and Alice Gram Robinson, were publicists who had worked in the press room of the Women's National Party in the campaign for suffrage. Robinson spent nine days in jail when she was swept up in a mass arrest of suffragists marching on the White House.

Lily Lykes Shepard of the *New York Tribune* was named the first president in 1919 and was followed by Cora Rigby, 1920-28. They were to lead a progression of prominent, often legendary, Washington reporters in that post.

Although public relations professionals had helped with the formation of the club, its membership was

Lily Lykes Shepard, New York Tribune, *was the first president of the Women's National Press Club in 1919.*

limited to women journalists and government writers. The women's club would emulate the NPC and hold news-making luncheons. Meetings and events would be held in rented space — tea rooms, restaurants and, later, hotels. No plans were made for permanent club quarters. The women lacked the money, and they took a strong professional stand against admitting to membership associate members to help finance club quarters, as the National Press Club had done.

To emphasize that this would not be just a social club, the new organization chose as its first speaker Margaret Bondfield, technical adviser to the British delegation to the International Labor Congress then meeting in Washington. The following luncheon was for Lowell Thomas, just returned from a fact-finding mission for President Wilson. He spoke for the first time in Washington of his meeting with the engaging Lawrence of Arabia. British historian H.G. Wells also was an early speaker.

Over the years, the fledgling women's press club grew and prospered, taking modest steps at first and then growing bolder to compete with the National Press Club for speakers.

In 1927, the club held its first Stunt Party, a cabaret grill, and invited prominent women to attend. That same year, it held its first luncheon for a first lady, Grace Coolidge.

The Roosevelt administration brought the club to prominence. Franklin D. Roosevelt was the first president to speak before the club at one of its luncheons. And Eleanor Roosevelt, noticing the struggle of women reporters for jobs, started holding news-making press conferences for female reporters only, prompting heretofore all-male news bureaus to hire women. Mrs. Roosevelt, by virtue of her syndicated news column, "My Day," became a member of the WNPC.

Helen Essary of the Washington Times-Herald, *1940 WNPC president, with President and Mrs. Roosevelt.*

Mrs. Roosevelt, standing, and WNPC members at an Eleanor Roosevelt press conference.

The Roosevelt White House became the setting of a "Grid Widows" annual dinner, held on the same night as the all-male Gridiron dinner. Press women, wives of Gridiron members and prominent women social and political figures were invited. Press women put on their own satirical costumed show. By the late 1930s, the WNPC had grown so much that the NPC, in its in-house publication *The Goldfish Bowl*, referred to the club as a "rival press club."

While Mrs. Roosevelt helped the status of women journalists, it was World War II that really opened scores of newspaper jobs for women. More women were covering Congress and the White House. There were such well-known figures as May Craig of the

Portland (Maine) Press Herald, Doris Fleeson, of the *New York Daily News*, Josephine Ripley of the *Christian Science Monitor*, Bess Furman of the *New York Times* and Esther Van Wagoner Tufty of the Michigan News Bureau.

After the war, the emphasis at the National Press Club was on getting life back to normal. The Club renovated its bar and showed it off at an evening social event. The year was 1949, and the news story of the moment was that a woman named Florence Chapman had just succeeded in swimming the English Channel in both directions.

At the bar stood Homer Dodge, a courtly gentleman who favored pearly grey spats. As the women filed by, recalled attendee Ada Mae Ade years later, Dodge was moodily staring into his

Esther Van Wagoner Tufty of the Michigan News Bureau (standing) with the Duchess of Windsor. Tufty, known as "The Duchess" was WNPC president in 1941.

partly consumed drink. Addressing no one in particular, he announced in stentorian tones: "Women's place is in the English Channel."

It was to be the last visit for a long time for women to what the *Washington Post* called the "bacchanalian precincts," of the members' bar. "They will not be admitted again," noted the Post.

While battling the National Press Club for fair and equal treatment, the women's club made a life of its own, inviting national and world figures in politics, diplomacy and the arts to luncheon forums and dinners.

In 1951 the WNPC took over Constitution Hall for a USO fundraiser featuring Ted Mack's popular radio "Amateur Hour" with a cast of amateurs drawn from Congress, the diplomatic corps and the military. Annual dinners were given for the diplomatic corps, members of Congress, and the American Society of Newspaper Editors. Every president from Roosevelt to Reagan was an honored guest at either a luncheon or a dinner.

In March 1964, four months after taking office upon the death of President Kennedy, President Johnson unexpectedly announced at a Women's National Press Club dinner the appointment of 10 women to major positions in his new administration. Reporters in evening clothes scrambled for telephones.

President and Mrs. Truman and daughter Margaret present awards to WNPC's 1950 Women of the Year. Left to right, Martha Graham, dance; Dorothy Fosdick, government; Pearl Wanamaker, education; Margaret Truman; President Truman; Mrs. Truman; Olivia de Haviland, theater; Mildred Rebstock, science; Claire McCardell, fashion.

Sen. Margaret Chase Smith also made national news when at a club luncheon in January 1964 she announced that she would be a candidate for the Republican nomination for president.

In the 1940s, 1950s and 1960s, the WNPC hosted dinners honoring women of achievement. Honorees included scientists, physicians, authors and actors. As their numbers and prestige grew, the women began to resent more strongly the National Press Club policy that kept them from attending luncheons featuring top government officials and foreign heads of state.

To these women, their jobs were on the line. They told stories of being assigned to cover a head of state through visits to Congress, White House and embassy receptions, only to be barred when it came to an appearance at the National Press Club. To make matters worse for the women, the State Department often recommended the NPC as the place to make speeches for visiting foreign dignitaries. In some cases, women reporters were removed from the story by their male bosses and a male reporter substituted to cover the Press Club appearance.

Just as the founding members were encouraged by the suffrage campaign, members in the 1950s and 1960s were bolstered by the consciousness-raising of the burgeoning women's movement. They began a lengthy battle that ultimately resulted in the NPC admitting women to membership in 1971.

As early as 1953, the WNPC formed a Professional Committee inspired by Texas newswoman Sarah McClendon. Noting that May Craig and Doris Fleeson had worked on such questions for years, McClendon suggested at a business meeting that the cause might be better served if the club took a strong position, rather than leaving it to individuals.

The following year, the WNPC unanimously adopted a resolution urging the NPC to permit accredited newspaperwomen to cover its news events and simultaneously voted to send letters to Cabinet members and other high officials advising them that women reporters were not allowed in the NPC.

First Lady Jackie Kennedy and May Craig at the WNPC.

From that point on, members of Congress, the Cabinet, world leaders and presidents were petitioned and cajoled in the years-long campaign to open up the NPC's events to all accredited correspondents.

Just as the Eisenhower administration took office, newly named Secretary of Defense Charles Wilson announced his very first news conference would be held at the National Press Club, which barred female reporters from covering the event. Later, Japan's Prime Minister Yoshida expressed his "amazement and shock" to a WNPC member that women were not allowed to cover his luncheon at the NPC.

WNPC member Liz Carpenter of Southwestern Newspapers appealed to the NPC to end its policy, pointing out that: "It is the usual practice of organizations to permit accredited women as well as men to cover their functions, and the WNPC extends this privilege to all male reporters. It is particularly onerous to women reporters to be barred from covering newsworthy functions of another press organization, and we are compelled to protest this discrimination.

"If this policy of discrimination is continued, the WNPC will be forced to make a protest to future speakers before your organization. Toward that end, the board has instructed me to make representation to the Department of State and the Embassies of governments represented in Washington. This is a step I hope can be avoided through prompt action by your board in granting to all accredited reporters, regardless of sex, equal access to the news."

A response was slow in coming.

A tiny item in the Washington Post on Feb. 23, 1955, headlined "Newsmen Admit Girls — To Balcony" alluded to a small step forward in the battle.

The story read: "The all-male National Press Club has lowered its guard against invasion by women of the working press — but only part way. It has decided to admit newspaper women to its balcony if not to its membership rolls."

NPC President Lucian Warren set the rules: Press women would be met at the front desk at 1 p.m. and escorted up the steps to the balcony. As soon as the speakers had finished, the women would be escorted back to the front desk and out the door.

The balcony became a metaphor for discrimination against women reporters, evidenced in the title "Girls in the Balcony," a book by Nan Robertson about the discrimination against women at the *New York Times*.

Bonnie Angelo, 1961 WNPC President and *Newsday* reporter, covered many stories from the NPC balcony. "It was so hot, it was so hot in that balcony," she told Robertson, "All those bodies up there, jammed under the eaves. There were camera crews up there. Television equipment was much bulkier then, and the TV lights were hotter than they are now. It was hard to hear. It was hard to see. People would come early to try to get to the front of the balcony. All this standing — it was like a cattle car. And all the time you were really boiling inside."

At the same time, the NPC appointed a subcommittee to study the admission of women as bona fide members. In 1955, McClendon, who worked in the National Press Building, submitted an application for membership in the NPC, which had just admitted its first black member. The application was duly signed by male sponsors, as required. When weeks went by and she had heard nothing of her application, she contacted the NPC. It had not been received, she was told. McClendon said she then obtained records showing the application had been delivered from Western Union, but it was to no avail.

"I worked in the Press Building until midnight often," said McClendon. "When it was raining or cold and no restaurant nearby, I often wished I could go upstairs to the Club and get coffee or a sandwich." Although there were wire service tickers in the Club, she had to make other arrangements to get the latest stories.

From the time of McClendon's application, 16 more years elapsed before women were admitted. (Years later, the NPC named a room in McClendon's honor. The meeting room off of the Reliable Source Bar and Grill includes a large photo collage of McClendon's professional life.)

All the while, the struggle for access to newsmakers raged on with letters, petitions and telegrams sent worldwide to the likes of British Prime Minister Winston Churchill, German statesman Konrad Adenauer and Jawaharlal Nehru, India's first prime minister. The messages urged the foreign dignitaries not to accept the National Press Club's invitation but to choose another forum. "We know that you and your countrymen would not want to be a party to the fostering of professional discrimination — or discrimination of any kind — and hope that you will take a stand in our behalf," read the messages.

Following Liz Carpenter, through the 1950s and 1960s, Alice Frein Johnson of the *Seattle Times*, Gladys Montgomery of McGraw-Hill, Lee Walsh of the *Washington Evening Star*, Helen Thomas, Frances Lewine of the Associated Press, Bonnie Angelo, Patty Cavin of NBC and Elsie Carper of *The Washington Post* continued to press the issue with the NPC and with the State Department, foreign embassies, members of Congress and the newly formed Commission on the Status of Women.

Secretary of State Dean Rusk, appealed to in person by a WNPC president, suggested WNPC members needed to picket or in some manner embarrass the visiting dignitary or its embassy. From the WNPC's viewpoint, U.S. officialdom seemed to feel it had no role in the matter.

Though the WNPC offered to host a press luncheon or press conference open to all accredited correspondents, both men and women, at a neutral location, there were few takers. When a candidate for the U.S. Senate from Texas, Thad Hutcheson, decided to hold a press conference for Texas reporters at the NPC bar, Sarah McClendon couldn't stand it any longer. She wasn't about to get scooped by competing men reporters from Texas. McClendon banged on the front counter of the NPC reception desk and yelled and screamed about the injustice of it all. Hutcheson, when told of the situation, finished the press conference in the lobby with McClendon included.

Visiting heads of state were another matter entirely. An "old-boy network" existed among NPC members, male press attaches at the embassies – who were often NPC members – and male protocol officials at the State Department. In addition, State Department officials feared that any other forum but the National Press Club would not draw a substantial audience.

At the height of the Cold War, the women found an unexpected ally – Soviet Premier Nikita Khrushchev. Two previous Soviet officials appearing at the NPC made fun of the women's exile to the balcony. But Khrushchev created a diplomatic crisis over the women.

The NPC, the WNPC and the Overseas Writers Club all invited Khrushchev to speak during his historic first visit to the United States in September, 1959. Khrushchev sent word he would not appear at the National Press Club unless women correspondents were admitted. The NPC capitulated, and the three press clubs cooperated in giving the luncheon. But it was held at the National Press Club.

Doris Fleeson wrote Vice President Richard Nixon that "the State Department decided to give the NPC preference as host to Mr. Khrushchev and has placed the WNPC at the mercy of the NPC in the matter of attendance and participation. I regret to say that the NPC has a long record of lack of generosity toward newspaperwomen of Washington, which amounts at times to open hostility."

She asked Nixon to intercede so that women would not have to go "hat in hand" and ask favors of the men of the NPC. She said she hoped he would discuss the situation with State Department officials who had "so cavalierly handed us over to the mercy of the NPC with the patronizing remark that we could expect them to be chivalrous."

Only a few women correspondents were actually admitted. NPC President William Lawrence of *The New York Times* said that after the head table guests and Soviet Union representatives, there would be a maximum of 220 seats available. The "chivalrous" arrangement he worked out was a ration of 1.4 women permitted to attend for every 10 men. The NPC based its numbers on its own estimates of the number of "qualified and accredited" women journalists. WNPC got 33 seats, and its active, professional newswomen had to fill out forms to make sure they had a need to cover the speech. However, as president of the Women's National Press Club, Helen Thomas of United Press International got a spot at the head table.

After the lunch, Mollie Thayer of *The Washington Post* invaded the men's bar, quite by accident, she maintained.

"I'm terribly sorry to have penetrated the Press Club men's bar and caused you such distress," Thayer later wrote President Lawrence. "I just heard fun noises and wandered in. I never heard of the Press Club men's bar and its feminine taboo ... If it's any consolation to you, I didn't see a thing in the men's bar except a score or so of well-tailored backs. So its secrets are still inviolate."

Khrushchev's visit was a watershed event, but far from a decisive one.

Two months later, tempers were still high. When presidential Press Secretary James Hagerty stood up at Mamie Eisenhower's birthday party luncheon given by the WNPC and made favorable remarks about the possibility of women in the National Press Club, the furor in the NPC grew.

President Lawrence complained that there were only a few refuges left, "to which men may retire from the shrill, argumentative voices of the lady reporters."

After the Khrushchev luncheon, French President Charles de Gaulle followed the Soviet premier's lead in making his appearance contingent on women attending, but there the arrangement ended.

Nevertheless, the small success gave the women confidence to take on the State Department, which WNPC members viewed as in collusion with the NPC to keep them out. Early in 1960, Liz Carpenter began a long campaign to have the joint Senate-House Standing Committee of Correspondents begin sponsoring press conferences for foreign heads of state. She appealed to Sen. J.W. Fulbright, chairman of the Senate Foreign Relations Committee, to contact the State Department.

"Almost everything that has been accomplished since then has come about because Liz Carpenter went to Senator Fulbright," said the 1960 WNPC Professional Committee's yearly report. "Things changed right away. Ever since August 1959, the [Women's National Press] Club had been asking the State Department for an appointment to discuss its proposal ... After Senator Fulbright wrote the Department ... [they] suddenly found time for a meeting."

"Accompanied Male Guests Only" read the sign on the door of the members bar.

NATIONAL PRESS CLUB
SPECIAL RULES FOR LADIES

From House Rules as Approved July 30, 1962

11. Ladies shall be admitted to the Club quarters in accordance with the following rules:

a. Ladies, unescorted by a member of the National Press Club, shall be admitted to the Club quarters only when in possession of a guest card issued as hereinafter provided, or when accompanied by one holding a guest card. Such cards shall be issued wholly within the discretion of the Board of Governors and shall be valid only so long as the member making the request for such card remains in good standing as a member or until such card is revoked by the Board of Governors.

b. Ladies' guest cards of admission shall be issued only upon written request of a member of the Club to women members of his immediate family who are more than 18 years of age and who are members of his household. Such request shall be filed in the Secretary's office.

c. Ladies holding cards of admission shall be privileged to bring not more than three guests, except as provided in Rule 11d.

d. Arrangements for group luncheons, teas, dinners and other functions must be made with the Manager of the Club in advance, subject to the approval of the Board of Governors. Arrangements must be made in the name of a member of the Club, on his written authorization, and he will be held responsible.

e. Ladies shall not be admitted to the Main Dining Room, the Main Lounge, or the West Lounge except on Saturdays and Sundays after 12 o'clock noon; on other days of the week after 5:00 p.m., and on special occasions as may be designated by the Board of Governors. Ladies shall not be admitted to the Mezzanine floor of the Club except as approved by the Board of Governors. No ladies shall be admitted to the Card Room or the Taproom at any time.

8-62—1 M

Special rules for ladies.

The State Department reluctantly agreed to consider the issue. Meanwhile, WNPC President Thomas wrote letters to members of the Standing Committee of Correspondents to get their opinions. The responses were mixed. In the end, the Standing Committee's plan for sponsoring press conferences for heads of state failed in part because of resistance by members of the NPC, who were also members of the Standing Committee, and in part because of misgivings within the Standing Committee about the lack of resources and facilities for such events.

Still frustrated, the WNPC Professional Committee continued its efforts into the Kennedy Administration. Kennedy Press Secretary Pierre Salinger wrote at one point that this subject "is a painful one for me."

"I can say without fear of contradiction," Salinger wrote, "that more man-hours have been spent attempting to work out an equitable solution for lady correspondents than almost any other project that we have had since Jan. 20, 1961," the date of Kennedy's inauguration. Have a little more patience, he urged the WNPC, as he sought unsuccessfully to get another organization, the White House Correspondents Association, to sponsor open-to-all press events for visiting heads of state.

But the New Frontier of JFK failed to dent the old frontier of the National Press Club. When Kennedy was asked about the situation at a press conference, he said, "In my judgment, that when an official visitor comes to speak to the Press Club that all working reporters should be permitted on a basis of equality. That is not a social occasion but a working occasion.

"I would think when there is an official visitor here as the guest of the people of the U.S. and there is a meeting, that all reporters should be welcome on the basis of equality."

Chief White House Correspondent Merriman Smith of UPI was annoyed at what he regarded as the frivolous question of equal access to the news. "Sandwiched between Berlin and the bomb," he wrote, "is a crisis of proportions to disrupt normally friendly diplomatic relations; of a divisive nature to set American against American; of sufficient magnitude to require the President himself to deal with it on nationwide television....

"Ladies of the press are granted somewhat grudging access to a balcony where they may sit unfed, unrecognized and whispering little digs about segregation. With distressingly few exceptions, these ladies are deadly earnest journalists and/or feminists. The Press Club balcony has become to them what the wall is to West Berliners.

"Still, it would seem to be a problem that most any Rotary Club could handle back home," Smith wrote.

In the summer of 1963, Elsie Carper was elected president of the WNPC. Carper was encouraged when she received a congratulatory note from Kennedy saying, in part: "You arrive in office at a time of utmost crisis for the lady journalists in their continuing struggle for equal rights ... I know that with your leadership, this fight will continue...."

To members of the WNPC, one of the most bitter and ironic incidents occurred in August 1963 when civil rights leader A. Phillip Randolph and other leaders of the famous Washington Jobs and Freedom March accepted an invitation to appear at NPC after they were urged by the WNPC to appear at a press conference or luncheon open to all men and women correspondents.

When Randolph turned aside all appeals and made his appearance at the NPC anyway, WNPC President Carper, a longtime civil rights reporter, and Frances Lewine, chairwoman of the WNPC Professional Committee, issued a scathing press release in which they called it "ludicrous and at the same time distressing that a group fighting for civil rights has chosen a private and segregated club for its first press appearance in Washington to discuss the March for Jobs and Freedom.

"We find it hard to imagine that this group would not recognize and fight discrimination wherever it exists. The balcony as well as the back of the bus should have special meaning to civil rights leaders," it concluded.

As *Washington Star* columnist Betty Beale wrote, it was a "'low point' of the march effort to see Randolph espousing the cause of anti-discrimination for Negroes in a professional club that so discriminates against women reporters...."

And she noted, "Perhaps the most ironic note of all was that a Negro member of the WNPC, Alice Dunnigan, also was relegated to the balcony."

By then the WNPC was actively competing with the NPC for appearances by speakers. The Professional Committee launched a massive letter-writing campaign to heads of foreign governments and top U.S. officials.

The WNPC Professional Affairs Committee, headed by Frances Lewine, scored a triumph in getting South Vietnam's dragonlady, Madame Ngo Dinh Nhu, who was in the United States to head a delegation to the United Nations, to make her first Washington press appearance at the WNPC. Six hundred people attended the open-to-all event held at the Statler-Hilton ballroom. She went to the NPC several days later. While that event was considered a great success, most of the major speeches were still held at the National Press Club.

In the end, it took the combined efforts of NPC President Joseph Dear of Dear Publications and President Johnson to start to resolve the dispute.

Although no one can prove LBJ was carrying out a promise he made to Liz Carpenter of the WNPC, for several months of his new administration no visiting bigwigs used the NPC as a forum.

British Prime Minister Alex Douglas-Home held a press conference in the rotunda of the British Embassy open to all. The prime minister of Israel accepted an invitation of the Overseas Writers, which was also open to all correspondents. The Embassy of Malaysia announced its prime minister would hold a press conference open to all. Greek Premier George Papandreou held an open press conference at Blair House, following the example of the King of Jordan, who also spoke there.

Finally, on May 11, 1964, under continuing pressure, the governing board of NPC voted 6 to 3, with two abstentions, to let women on the ballroom floor during luncheon speeches. Only they forgot to notify the women. For that reason, only three women reporters attended the May 21, 1964, luncheon for Prime Minister Y.B. Chavan of India. They were Caryll Rivers, who described the event in *Editor and Publisher*, Sarah McClendon and

UPI story on President John Kennedy's message to Elsie Carper on the occasion of her inaugural as WNPC president in 1963.

Press release from the WNPC in August 1963 denouncing A. Phillip Randolph for appearing at a segregated club.

Elizabeth Drew, then of *Congressional Quarterly*. Drew was quoted as whispering: "I'm embarrassed. I didn't come here to fight for women's rights. I just wanted to hear the speech." McClendon said as she slid into her chair: "It sure feels good to be here."

The feeling was not to last. Eleven days later, the governing board reversed itself, 6 to 5, with NPC Vice President Clark Mollenhoff of the *Des Moines Register & Tribune* switching positions. He had been "reluctant" and "wrong" the first time around, he said. He then made references to "governmental figures ... tampering around in the Press Club."

There was plenty of reaction to the reversal. WNPC President Carper called it "regrettable." And, in an editorial, *The Washington Post* joined in:

"What political aspirant will have the hardihood, what foreign potentate will feel potent enough, to choose the National Press Club for public utterances henceforth in the face of the fury of women scorned?"

At long last, the issue was getting serious attention. The battle was joined, and pressure on the NPC increased. On June 29, 1964, at a special meeting of all members, the NPC voted 128 to 50 to permit women reporters to sit with men while covering luncheons.

Mary Gallagher of the *Cincinnati Enquirer* became the first and only woman that day to do so, at a luncheon for Malaysian Prime Minister Tunku Abdul Rahman. She was asked how it felt. "Awful. I'm very nervous. I've never been a pioneer before." The following year she was elected president of the WNPC.

A breakthrough had been made. However, women reporters were still required to enter the NPC through specified entrances and had to clear the Club within 30 minutes after a luncheon ended. While many women journalists were satisfied with this accomplishment, which finally gave them the ability to cover the news on an equal basis with the men, it was not enough for others. To them, equality would only be achieved when women were able to be full-fledged members of the NPC.

In the late 1960s, the final siege over membership in the NPC began. The male diehards saw change coming and didn't like it. Women would alter the flavor of the Press Club, they said. Some resented the thought of having to watch their language in men-only areas, such as the members' bar.

"You let them in this (bleep) place," one holdout was quoted in *The Washington Post*, "and soon they'll be complaining about the (bleep) language."

"You let them in the game room," said another, "and they'll be complaining about the goddam language while they sit there playing bridge or something."

Later, 1973 NPC President Donald Larrabee described the situation at the time: "There was 'closet sympathy'

Liz Carpenter, a WNPC president, worked with President Lyndon B. Johnson to open access for women reporters in the Press Club.

Mary Gallagher, WNPC president, with NPC President William Blair in 1965.

among some male members to admit women but no crusader," he said. "And no one certainly was going to run on the platform favoring women members."

But the change finally happened because people like Larrabee kept up the fight.

Leader of the opponents, Ralph De Toledano, a syndicated writer, drew a grim picture when he said, "First, it's the tap room. Then the billiard room. Then the card room. And eventually, it'll be the men's room."

One hundred members debated the issue in the fall of 1970. Secretary Bob Alden said the time had come for a change: "The Club is the most important non-government news forum in Washington. Women are now an important segment of the national press. A court challenge under the 14th Amendment would be disastrous."

From Bill Coblenz of the Library of Congress came the comment: "The Club should get itself into the 20th century ... What are we afraid of? I wouldn't do anything in this company of men that I wouldn't do in the ladies'."

From Hugo Perez, a Guatemalan correspondent: "I'm a Latin, and you know how we love the ladies. But this club has problems, and it doesn't need another headache."

The soon-to-be president, Vernon Louviere of *Nation's Business* said, "It would severely alter, if not destroy, the character of this 62-year-old institution." As for the notion that the new members would improve the economic base of the NPC, Louviere was dismissive. "The spending habits of women argue against that," he wrote.

Soon after the divisive debate, a mail referendum was scheduled for Oct. 28, 1970, on an amendment to the National Press Club's constitution to admit women as active Club members. The number of responses was huge. In a letter in favor, Alden observed: "If we do not wish to be truly the National Press Club and continue to bar women from membership, we should consider changing our name to the Men's Press Club of Washington, D.C., or the 14th and F Men's Club." While the mail vote was 522 in favor of admitting women and 243 opposed — nearly a 2-to-1 margin — the number was just short of the two-thirds required to change the NPC's constitution.

Immediately after the vote, NPC member Bill Hickman of McGraw-Hill began circulating a petition to bring the issue to the floor of the next membership meeting.

The WNPC knew the time had come to end sex discrimination as well. Within weeks of the NPC's referendum, on Dec. 8, 1970, the Women's National Press Club voted 113 to 6 to admit men and changed its name to the Washington Press Club. A procedural vote completed the process on Jan. 12, 1971. The action had the effect of a pre-emptive strike.

Three days later, at its annual meeting on Jan. 15, the NPC followed suit, admitting women to membership by a vote of 227 to 56. It was a historic moment.

The "Accompanied Male Guests Only" signs came down from the door of the men's bar on Feb. 1. One of the first women to cross the threshold that night was actress Julie Harris, appearing at the National Theater in a play called, ironically enough, "And Miss Reardon Drinks a Little."

In March, the first 24 women members were sworn in. The one-time opponent, now president, Louviere, was on hand to greet them:

"It is with a great deal of honor that I have the privilege of being the president on this auspicious and historic occasion. In a sense, you ladies have carved out a piece of history for yourselves. Look what women have accomplished over the years. Perhaps your names will be added to the list ... Joan of Arc, Amelia Earhart, Carrie Nation, Pocahontas and Lizzie Borden."

Lizzie Borden? His list went on, through Jeanette Rankin and Mata Hari, and Daisy Mae Yokum. At the end the 24 women raised their hands and took the pledge of membership. They were members of the class of 1971. Some were new, but for some it had

The historic vote to admit women, at the annual meeting, Jan. 15, 1971. 227-yes, 56-no.

Sarah McClendon, new member in 1971, planning a Club skit with Bob Loftus and Frank Holeman, in which they would take on the identities of Henry Kissinger, Martha Mitchell, and John Connally.

been quite a wait. Among them was Sarah McClendon, who had been an active newswoman in Washington for 27 years.

"For years I saw Press Club members on the elevator taking their children to Christmas parties and longed to take mine. By the time I could, I brought along my grandchild," McClendon said. "The night I was initiated into the Press Club, I cried before cameras."

While many women were eager to become members of the National Press Club, others who had led the battle for equal access to the news did not join. The battle for them was not for access to the National Press Club bar or card rooms — the inner sanctums of the Club — but to news-making events. With that goal achieved, they decided to remain in the much-loved and venerable club that had begun as the Women's National Press Club.

By this time, their club had received such prominence that *The New York Times* was to write in 1974: "Most journalists now believe that the smaller Washington Press Club is the most prestigious in town."

By the mid-1980s, however, with both clubs admitting women and men and having essentially the same purpose, a merger seemed in the best interest of both. Financially, it made sense, although there was some reluctance on both sides when it came to changing the character of each.

Serious talks of reconciliation and merger began in 1982 after the election of Vivian Vahlberg as the first woman to head the National Press Club. Yet it took three more years before the union was finally consummated.

1984 NPC President John Fogarty recollects that the "breakthrough came in January of his year when the entire NPC board was invited to the WPC inauguration of Susan Garland as president. The event was held at the Phillips Gallery, and it reflected the gallery's warmth. That night you could feel that a threshold had been crossed and the [two clubs] were ready to move forward and, if not forget the past, at least not allow it to impede progress to a merger.

"A dinner was arranged at the NPC shortly after Susan's inauguration," Fogarty said. "Ironically, it was held in the room under the old balcony that many of the WPC/WNPC members hated. While it took another 15 months to get all the details worked out, it was clear that night that we were on the way to a merger and there would be no turning back."

Spearheading the WPC's drive for the merger were Cheryl Arvidson, of Cox Newspapers, 1985 WPC President Susan Garland of Newhouse Newspapers, and Elsie Carper of *The Washington Post.* Representing the National Press Club were President David Hess, Board Chairman Andrew Mollison of Cox Newspapers and NPC Vice President Mary Kay Quinlan of the Gannett News Service. After several weeks of talks and follow-up salesmanship by both sets of leaders to their respective constituencies, the merger was sealed in the spring. The decades of divisiveness ended.

Arvidson remembers the negotiations this way: "When we finally reached the negotiating sessions, we had a long check list of various issues that needed to be addressed, including some changes in NPC policies that were an absolute must if we were to sell the deal to our members.

"We wanted a stronger membership standard. NPC dues were much higher than the WPC dues, so we needed a sliding scale of payments to ease the burden on our members. We wanted to ensure the WPC's highly regarded executive director, Julie Schoo, had a job at the newly merged club, and we needed a place for our archives to be stored and cared for. We also wanted some seats on

President Vivian Vahlberg of the Daily Oklahoman *is proudly sworn in by President Ronald Reagan in 1982 to become the Club's first woman president. (Photo by Stan Jennings)*

WPC President Susan Garland and NPC president David Hess raise a toast to the club's merger in 1985.

the [NPC] Board of Governors to make sure the terms of the merger agreement were honored.

"Although the negotiations were tough," Arvidson said, "my recollection is that the NPC team was very cooperative and willing to go more than halfway to meet us on most issues. Both clubs then had to sell the deal to our respective memberships, which was certainly not a slam-dunk. But in the end, logic prevailed on both sides, and the merger was completed."

On April 29, 1985, the Washington Press Club and the National Press Club united under the NPC's banner.

By 2008, six other women had followed Vivian Vahlberg to the president's office – Mary Kay Quinlan of the Gannett News Service in 1986, Judy Grande of the *Cleveland Plain Dealer* in 1990, Kathryn S. Kahler of Newhouse News Service in 1991, Sonja Hillgren of the Farm Journal in 1996, Tammy Lytle of the *Orlando Sentinel* in 2003 and Sheila Cherry of BNA in 2004.

In the modern NPC, women hold leadership posts in all aspects of the Club, from committee chairs to chairwoman of the Board of Governors. Gone are the days of two separate clubs each competing with the other to host the newsmakers of the day. In their place, the National Press Club remains, stronger and more vibrant, the beneficiary of the combined efforts of more than a half century of Washington journalists, dedicated to the public's right to know. And leading the Club in its centennial year is Sylvia Smith of the Fort Wayne (Ind.) *Journal Gazette*.

Margaret Mead spoke at the Press Club Oct. 9, 1973. Asked if she thought women were really able to take on positions of leadership held by men, she said, "Well, we certainly couldn't do any worse." (Photo by Stan Jennings)

1987 President Andrew Mollison and 1986 President Mary Kay Quinlan, who had worked on merging the National Press Club with the Washington Press Club in 1985. (Photo by Stan Jennings)

The 20th anniversary of women being admitted to the National Press Club was celebrated with original members, left to right, including Helen Thomas, Judith Ellen Randal, Mary Lou Forbes and President Kay Kahler.

Helen Thomas of UPI at podium became the first woman elected to the Club board in 1972 when she became Financial Secretary.

Left: President Lyndon B. Johnson greets reporter May Craig, of the Portland Press-Herald, at her retirement party in 1965. Demure in appearance, Craig was well known for her tough questions at White House press conferences. Right: Esther Van Wagoner Tufty, left, as FDR, and Mary Hornaday as Wendell Wilkie in a 1940 WNPC skit.

WNPC members mocked political issues in their annual satirical skits. This one takes on the 1952 Presidential election.

First Lady Eleanor Roosevelt, center, at a WNPC luncheon, March, 1946, at the Mayflower Hotel.

A stunt party at the Roosevelt White House, put on by the "Gridiron Widows" the same night as the all-male Gridiron dinner.

Club President Judy Grande negotiated a $1 million bequest from Eric Friedheim in 1990 to underwrite the Club's library and archives. (Drawing by Dirk Dugan)

NATIONAL PRESS CLUB

CHAPTER FIVE

PROVIDING INFORMATION
TO THE INFORMATION PROVIDERS

"All I need to become the second-best authority on any subject is access to a first-class library."

– H.L. Mencken, American journalist and social critic

On a Saturday morning in 2007 at the National Press Club, some 20 reporters and their mentors assembled, under the auspices of the Investigative Reporters and Editors organization, for an investigation of their own. Their "target" was themselves. They were learning what it takes to use computers to ferret out abuses of the public trust.

That the venue for this exercise was the Club's Eric Friedheim National Journalism Library was no accident. For the past several years, the Club had worked to improve the ability of journalists to employ the Internet to find patterns of misbehavior or incompetence by public officials and the agencies they run.

One of the reporters in this class was 27-year-old Ben Lando, a Club member who covered energy for UPI. "We were learning how to find documents for our investigatory reports, such as government contracts with corporations, and how to phrase our requests to the relevant [federal] agencies to get the documents," he said.

The Club's library entered the 21st century with the same conundrum as the journalism industry: How to keep the valuable parts of its traditions but also stay relevant to its patrons and adapt to rapidly changing technology that radically changed how journalists do their jobs.

Journalists who once picked up the phone to ask a research librarian to find a senator's middle initial, the name of a campaign contributor or the headquarters of a business now Googled their query, and had the information in seconds. The research component of the library was altered for good.

Club members who once made their way to the reading room of the library to comb through out-of-town newspapers now used a few clicks on the computer to see that day's edition. No wait for the mail.

Now, library visitors were more likely to be in search of a computer than a researcher or an out-of-town newspaper.

The library board encouraged a shift from research to training; by the end of 2007, the director of the library was no longer a librarian but a Club employee who had distinguished herself in planning training programs and forums. The NPC board transferred its $25,000 training budget to the library staff, and the library's new professional fundraiser was tasked with raising thousands more.

The board of the Eric Friedheim National Journalism Library entered 2008 pondering questions about the future: If Club members use the library for two main purposes – training and access for computers – is the library set up to best fulfill those needs? Should computers for Club members' use be available only when the library is open? Is it a better use of the research librarian's time to teach journalists how to do their own research more efficiently?

The Club's library of the early 21st century, with its up-to-date technology and gadgets, is a far cry from its humble beginnings. On May 4, 1908, two months after the formation of the Club, the Board of Governors authorized a Library Committee to purchase a "newspaper file" of leading papers for members to read. Formally dubbed the Library and Charities Committee and put under the chairmanship of Club Vice President Jackson Tinker, the

In the early 1920s, the library in the Albee-Riggs Building was cozy but dark and cramped.

In 1928 a new library opened in spacious quarters on the 14th floor, where the Reliable Source is today.

committee set aside a space in what the House Rules referred to as "the Library floor."

By the following year, the Charities [later designated as the Fellowship] Committee took on its separate role of aiding fellow members in distress, and the Library Committee was re-named the Library and Arts Committee. It solicited donations of books and publications, bought reference materials and acquired art, photographs, cartoons and newspaper matrices for the Club walls. Those matrices, or mats, were lacquered fiber molds used in the hot-lead printing process to cast solid curved plates for high-speed rotary presses. The Club displayed these mats with their banner headlines as part of the paneling in the meeting and dining rooms. To this day, they adorn the Club's premises as reminders of human suffering and folly and the press's duty to report it.

When the Club moved in 1910 to the Rhodes Tavern Building at 15th and F streets NW, a new library was installed, again in a cozy nook. The space featured padded leather winged chairs, Arts and Crafts-style wallpaper, prints donated by members and brimming bookshelves. Frederick J. Haskin, who was beginning his ascent to the Club's presidency, insisted that members request mats and cartoons from their hometown newspapers to complete the interior design of the new digs.

By 1912, the Club's yearbook noted: "A collection of cartoons, showing the history of the times in pictures, and illustrating the growth of the art in America, is also in process of formation." The same yearbook devoted a special section to the library and spelled out its mission. "The library of the National Press Club is planned to aid the working newspaper man in Washington. For this purpose, it includes a representative collection of reference works and government publications…. The general field of literature has not been neglected."

When the Club moved again in 1914 to grander quarters in the Albee-Riggs Building at 15 and G streets NW, the library may have suffered a bit. Photographs from that period show a smaller, dimmer space. Former President Homer Dodge of the *Kansas City Journal* and James Preston, superintendent of the Senate Press Gallery, acted as Club historians in the early years. Preston methodically maintained a scrapbook of the Club's earliest documents. He studied conservation techniques at the British Museum and later served on a National Archives planning committee. He was appointed Club historian in 1916 served unofficially for more than 30 years.

Members frequently contributed their own works or newspaper subscriptions to the growing Club library. In 1913, Lord Northcliffe, publisher of *The London Times*, broke his own rule and granted a free subscription to the Club. Over the years, contributions to the library included the 55-volume collection of the Harvard classics, a complete set of Shakespeare, dictionaries, Bibles, encyclopedias, volumes of poetry, quotation books, government publications and current fiction.

With the move in 1928 to permanent quarters in the new National Press Building, the library expanded to include hundreds of newspapers and magazines, a large reference collection, popular novels and autographed books by Club authors. Pictures taken shortly

Homer Dodge, who served as the Club's unofficial historian from the 1920s through the 1950s, looks over the famed guest book.

after the Club opened show cushy lounge chairs, long library tables, newspapers racked on rods, and an ornate fireplace. The 1928 Club "Yearbook" described the setting as a place where members could find "absolute quiet and comfort. In designing this feature of the Club, the architect selected for its location space that is somewhat detached, and far enough removed to be free from needless sound disturbance." In short, it was far from the bar.

Unfortunately, its remoteness also led to constant theft of books and papers, and few of the reference collections remained intact. Repeated complaints to the Board of Governors and sharp warnings in the house rules did little to deter the losses. "Some character who reckons not the wages of sin walked off with the Club's old Bible," cracked the *Record* in 1962. Some members tried to put the library to use as a workplace for reporters. Instead, it became a drowsy place to sleep off a heavy or bibulous lunch. Books were kept in locked cases, but the greatest concern of some members was the position of the comfy couches to ensure a refreshing nap away from an editor's eye.

Mae Howland Smith preserved many of the valuable archive records from the Club's earliest years.

Progress was made in preserving the Club's archives. Materials collected by Preston and Dodge were turned over to the woman-in-charge-of-everything, Mae Smith, a staff member who brooked little nonsense from wayward co-workers or, for that matter, members. Along with collecting the Club's accounts, overseeing membership rosters and changes and riding herd on Club presidents, Smith safeguarded the official documents, including Board of Governors minutes. During the 1960 presidency of Ed Edstrom of Hearst Newspapers, a subcommittee that included Cabell Phillips, Bruce Catton and Lacey Reynolds was charged with looking into the organization of Club memorabilia, an eclectic and somewhat ragtag collection of gifts and awards from members and foreign dignitaries. It also included, according to one account, "cartoons, letters from world leaders, old newspapers, special editions published for the inauguration of Club presidents, yellowed photographs, receipts, autographed books, first editions, sheets for Club outings, texts of speeches that produced worldwide headlines and shaped the course of history [and] a pile of tape recordings."

At first, Club members volunteered to put the mounting rubble of records in order, but the task was overwhelming. Deciding what should be kept and what discarded was beyond the ken of news people. Photos and cartoons had been damaged by sunlight, and other materials that had been incorrectly filed were unidentifiable.

The library in the 1970s was a comfortable place to read, but service was interrupted by receptions and luncheons. Assistant manager Ernie Ball sorts a daily mail sack of newspapers representing four points of the compass, N E W S.

In 1967, the Club arranged with the Library of Congress to deposit the audio tapes of luncheon speeches dating to 1951. Other records remained in unused shower stalls in the employee locker room and in the writing room off a balcony. Artifacts and paintings deteriorated in the late 1960s and '70s as the Club quarters aged and the Club's strained budget was too tight to preserve them. Member Paul Means, the Archives chairman, saved the valuable John Hays Hammond autographed portrait collection.

In 1976, prodded by growing interest in the nation's bicentennial celebration, Club President Robert Alden of the *Washington Post* appointed a new Archives Committee to try to bring some order to the collection. Records that had been kept in the homes and offices of various members were retrieved. Committee members began to inventory the collection.

Still, the Club was in a quandary of what the library should do. "Whether it is to be a comprehensive source of reference material on American government and history or just a place to take naps, we need a basis for deciding which way to go," said Carl De Bloom of the *Columbus Dispatch*, chairman of the Library Committee in the mid-1970s. In 1974, the Library Committee suggested forming a "Friends of the Library" group and hiring a full-time librarian, but it would be years before those ideas bore fruit.

That year the Club created the National Press Foundation to raise money to purchase reference books. But the books continued to disappear and had to be locked away. Club President Mike Hudoba of *Sports Afield* arranged the donation of a *New York Times* microfilm collection and a film reader. But no one trained users in how to work the reader, nor was the microfilm updated, and eventually the equipment was discarded. Even the 1902 Clifford Berryman cartoon of Theodore Roosevelt, similar to the one that launched the teddy bear craze, disappeared.

Even so, the library continued to hobble along. The first Book Fair and Authors Night was held in 1974 as part of a plan to solicit from NPC member-authors copies of their latest books. The event was chaired by Carl West of Scripps-Howard Newspapers. The event itself was a success, and member Paul D'Armiento of McGraw-Hill nurtured it into an annual event and fund-raiser for the library.

Creating a committee of Club and National Press Foundation members, D'Armiento met with Joseph Duffy, chairman of the National Endowment for the Humanities, and secured a grant of $17,500 to be used to hire an archivist to process the Club's historic materials. In January 1981, archivist Barbara Vandegrift was hired for one year to sort, arrange and catalogue the records. A doctoral candidate in American studies with a graduate degree in library science, Vandegrift had served as director of the library at the George C. Marshall Foundation in Lexington, Va. She brought solid experience in the collection and care of 20th century records.

During the first months of the project, Club treasures were re-discovered. Building attorney Harvey Jacob's files on the demolition of the old Ebbitt Hotel and the construction of the National Press Building on its site, James Preston's amusing recollections on the early days of the Club, and the metal trunk that contained Philadelphia reporter Watson Ambruster's post-civil war morgue were all uncovered. Vandegrift also unearthed autographed photos, programs from spelling bees and mock debates, and turn-of-the-century menus – all fascinating documents of the Club's early days.

As more material was discovered and reported, members responded with enthusiasm, and more records poured into the workspace carved out in the balcony spaces overlooking the Club's main lounge. With half her term behind her, Vandegrift wrote a memo, in June 1981, questioning what would happen to the archives after she left. She asked whether a permanent library-archives could be housed in the Club and funded by the press foundation, and whether a library-archives could administer both the daily research needs of the library and the special needs of a manuscript and archival scholar.

Her questions stoked a serious discussion among Club members that encouraged her to speak out more boldly for the necessity of an expanded staff and resources. "The Club library, in its present condition, interrupted by receptions, plagued by theft, understaffed and under-funded, is not a satisfactory place for serious research or the administration of irreplaceable records," she wrote.

Other press associations in the Washington area such as the Society of Professional Journalists, the American News Women's Club, and the Washington Press Club were willing to unite to create a joint research center, she wrote.

The Club's board began talking about creating a true reference library for journalists. With money donated by the National Press Foundation, a committee headed by former President Arthur Wiese of the *Houston Post* worked with planners and architects to design a press club that emphasized the professionalism of modern journalists. By August 1981, architects requested specifications for a library-archives, launching a joint venture between the Club and the foundation. A prime location on the 13th floor just past the Club's entrance was set aside for the library. In fitting symbolism of how the Club was trying to change its image, the bar and grill were moved up to the 14th floor to make way for the library.

The press foundation secured grants from the Gannett and Benton foundations for designing the library. The Benton Foundation, known for its support of experimental programs in communications, was attracted by the idea of a groundbreaking reference library for journalists that also provided training in the use of the emerging computerized databases. More than 600 Washington journalists were surveyed to determine what services should be offered in the new Club library. When few reporters could answer questions about databases, a computer demonstration was organized at the Club and the survey was

The effort to rename the library had its share of critics. A Washington Times *cartoon, June 29, 1990.*

sent out again. This time, the reporters responded, indicating clearly that print reference materials were important but that they were also eager to see and use the new computerized databases. Follow-up interviews with reporters from small bureaus confirmed that the Club library would be particularly useful for operations that did not have a big reference budget and could not afford an in-house system.

After two years of planning, while shielding the growing archives collection from the construction crews rehabbing the building, the new library and archives opened in October 1984, several months before the grand opening of the new Club. The New Club Committee pondered several options for a name for the library, and settled on the H.L. Mencken Library, honoring the iconoclastic *Baltimore Sun* reporter, critic and raconteur who rose to prominence between the world wars for his critiques of American culture and language.

Some members bridled at naming the library for anyone but a generous donor, following a time-tested policy. Others complained that Mencken had never joined the Club and did not warrant the recognition. But advocates argued in behalf of Mencken's distinguished career and reputation, including his love of libraries.

Despite some predictions that the library would become a white elephant and despite subsequent attempts by the Club management to claim the space for an elegant dining room, the library flourished. At first, two professionals, Vandegrift and Robert Garber, provided full reference assistance from 9 a.m. until 8 p.m. Because of mounting demands from reporters for help in computer searches, the hours were adjusted with more emphasis on midday research to correspond to most news cycles. A third librarian, Barbara van Woerkom, was added in 1988, when regular database demonstrations and searches developed a larger following.

With continued support from the National Press Foundation, current reference titles were placed on standing order and new titles were added annually. Library staff solicited contributions from members and publishers. In 1993, for instance, the in-kind contributions of 350 newspapers, magazines and newsletters were worth over $23,000. Another funding source was added in 1984 with the installation of audiotape recording and duplication equipment. The library provided copies of luncheon tapes for a small fee. Over time, the income from the sale of tapes averaged about $10,000 a year. In one instance, a tape of Independent presidential candidate Ross Perot of Texas generated more than $30,000.

In 1989, Eric Friedheim, editor-in-chief of *Travel Agent* magazine and a 55-year member of the Club, signaled his intention to endow the library. "A library is one of the greatest things you can endow," Friedheim said after contributing to the library at Johns Hopkins University. As for endowing the Club's library, Friedheim recalled his early days as a reporter for International News Service and spoke nostalgically about the old Club library where he had spent many hours.

Eric Friedheim, editor-in-chief of Travel Agent magazine, gave the Club library a major boost with a $1 million endowment in 1990. (Photo by Bachrach)

Working with 1990 Club President Judy Grande of the *Cleveland Plain Dealer*, Friedheim set up a $1 million living trust in which he would take the interest during his lifetime and guarantee the endowed trust for the Library after his death. He asked that the library be named for him.

Some H.L. Mencken fans objected. Editorials and letters to the editor in Washington newspapers raged for weeks. Fueling the debate was the discovery and publication of Mencken's private diaries, written between 1930 and 1948 and sealed for 25 years after his death in 1956. Published in 1989, the diaries revealed that Mencken had held anti-Semitic and racist views. While the diaries had little or nothing to do with the decision to re-name the library, some newspaper editors and others assumed that it had.

The *Washington Times* editorialized that Friedheim "offered $1 million to the Club to drop the Mencken name in favor of his own. The deal was done faster than you can forget that Mr. Mencken was the 'Sage of Baltimore.'"

Grande responded that the attack on the Club was "vicious and wrong.... Mr. Friedheim's endowment is very exciting for the National Press Club. It is the first step in the expansion of the library – technologically and perhaps physically. We are going to begin fund-raising, with Mr. Friedheim's help, to create a business-reference center for financial reporters and to expand our research [service] to small newspapers and broadcast outlets around the country. This – the intent of Mr. Friedheim's endowment – was never mentioned [in the editorial]."

Finally, a compromise was reached when the Board of Governors agreed that the library's reading room would retain Mencken's name, and the main space would bear Friedheim's name.

In 1991, Club President Kathryn Kahler of Newhouse Newspapers moved to incorporate the library as a separate non-profit entity, mainly to provide tax-exempt status for donors. In September, the Friends of the National Journalism Library was established in the District of Columbia, and the following August the new organization received notice of its tax-exempt status from the Internal Revenue Service. This enabled the library to raise substantial sums to help underwrite the library and archives, finance scholarships and pay for journalism prizes.

A Library Expansion Committee was convened under the chairmanship of Paul Merrion of Crain Communications and set to work on planning for a more sophisticated facility with the latest in research technology.

Fund-raising events for the venture continued with gala movie nights held at the Club by the National Press Foundation. Members and donors, in one instance, viewed the film *Mr. Smith Goes to Washington* and welcomed actor Jimmy Stewart, who reminisced about working with the press in 1939. Helen Hayes came at another time to recall the making of *The Front Page*, a movie written by her husband, Charles McArthur. During the 1992 presidential campaign, author Gore Vidal and actor Cliff Robertson regaled members with stories of the movie, *The Best Man*.

Under the guidance of member Andy Alexander of Cox Newspapers, president of the Friends of the National Journalism Library, the Club rebuilt

Jimmy Stewart and Club librarian Barbara Vandegrift in 1991. (Photo by Marshall Cohen)

the library to create a state-of-the-art training center. Major donors then were Michael Bloomberg, the founder of *Bloomberg Business News* and future mayor of New York City, the McGraw-Hill Companies, Compaq Computer Corp., and the Freedom Forum.

"Reporters have moved into computer-assisted journalism quickly and are demanding even more advanced technology from an information center at the press club," Vandegrift noted. "No longer a sleepy place to catch a nap, it's my hope that the library will lead the Press Club in serving the journalism community of the future – one without walls."

But while the Library had a beautiful, up-to-date facility, the Club's archives were relegated to a room in the National Press Building basement. Finding it meant walking down flights of stairs from the building lobby and trekking through hallways to an unmarked door. No one wanted to spend time there. If someone wanted to do research, the archivist had to retrieve the material and bring it up to the Library. With no climate control and water pipes on the ceiling, the Club's historical collection was in danger. But there was no room in the Club itself to house an archives. At the same time, other news organizations were looking for places to house their records, including Society of American Travel Writers, the D.C. Chapter of the American Women in Radio and Television, the D.C. Chapter of the Society of Professional Journalists, and the Overseas Writers.

In 2005, Club Manager John Bloom approached the Friends of the National Journalism Library board with a proposition. The Board of Governors was planning to take over part of the fourth floor to build a National Press Club Broadcast Operations Center. If the Friends group would donate $350,000 from the Eric Friedheim endowment, a climate-controlled archives large enough to house the collection would be constructed adjacent to the broadcast center. The Friends board jumped at the opportunity.

When the new archives opened in January 2006, members could browse through documents in a comfortable reading room, find audio and video tapes and films in a chilled closet, comb through rack after rack of records and mementos, and listen to or watch oral histories provided by women pioneers in journalism and past Club presidents.

Michael Bloomberg, right, donated $100,000 to the library – the seed money that helped establish a computer-assisted reporting training facility. In the center is former President Monroe W. Karmin of Bloomberg Business News, 1996 President Sonja Hillgren and Andy Alexander on far left. (Photo by John Metelsky)

CBS anchorman, Dan Rather talks about his book, Deadlines and Datelines, at a June 25, 1999 book rap. (Photo by John Metelsky)

Rhonda Gray-Young, an archivist intern, sorts through documents in the Club's archives, which opened in 2006. (Photo by Jen Yost)

PROVIDING INFORMATION TO THE IMFORMATION PROVIDERS

Richard G. Thomas, editor of Roll Call Report Syndicate, reviews a web site in the library's new computer training center in 1997. Club Vice President Douglas Harbrecht of Business Week *is standing. Harry Stoffer of Thomson Newspapers is seated. (Photo by Art Garrison)*

1972 Club President Warren Rogers of The Chicago Tribune-New York News Syndicate, pushed to enhance the professional reputation of the Club. (Photo by Marshall Cohen)

CHAPTER SIX

BUILDING A PROFESSIONAL ORGANIZATION

"Our purpose is to foster the ethics of our profession and...to protect the ramparts of the First Amendment whenever they are assailed."

— Warren Rogers, 1972 NPC President

Acrimony between the Nixon Administration and the news media set the stage for the National Press Club to shift the spotlight to the press itself in the early 1970s. This was a sharp departure from its long tradition of highlighting public officials and society. For more than three decades, the Club has aired professional issues and controversies, rewarded journalistic excellence, assisted and trained journalists, and defended press freedom in the United States and abroad.

The Vietnam War soured relations between the government and the press as reporting had become more analytical and interpretive. But it was a speech by Vice President Spiro Agnew at a Midwest Republican conference in Des Moines, Iowa, on Nov. 13, 1969, that dramatically altered the Club's view of its own role.

Television networks carried the speech live as Agnew lambasted an "unelected elite" of network newsmen who determined what Americans learned about national and world news. Agnew decried news commentators' "instant analysis and querulous criticism" of a Nov. 3, 1969, speech by President Nixon. Network executives replied that Agnew's speech was an unprecedented attempt at intimidation. Undeterred, Agnew broadened his attack to include the *Washington Post* and the *New York Times*.

The Nixon administration's relations with the press came to a boil two years later when the *New York Times* published the Pentagon Papers, a massive classified study of U.S. involvement in Vietnam, on June 13, 1971. The Justice Department moved two days later to enjoin the *Times* from further publication of the report. Meantime, the *Washington*

Club President Allan W. Cromley of the Daily Oklahoman *has a few questions for U.S. Vice President Spiro Agnew in 1968. (Photo by John Metelsky)*

Post, Boston Globe and *St. Louis Post-Dispatch* began printing the study as well. On June 30, the U.S. Supreme Court ruled 6 to 3 against the government's attempt to halt the reporting.

Then came Watergate. *Washington Post* reporters Bob Woodward and Carl Bernstein doggedly unraveled the 1972 bugging of the Democratic National Committee headquarters at the Watergate Hotel and the Nixon administration's attempts to cover up the crime. Nixon resigned on Aug. 8, 1974.

At the Club, 1972 President Warren Rogers, a columnist for the *Chicago Tribune-New York News Syndicate,* urged the Club to get directly involved in journalism issues of the day. Aside from the NPC's role as a news forum, the Club primarily had long been a place for socializing. Rogers and others on the recently formed Concerned Members slate, elected that year, decided to shift that emphasis.

Rogers created the Professional Relations Committee "to [keep] an eye on our own observance of journalistic ethics and [stand] watch over the freedom-of-information rights guaranteed in the First Amendment." The committee commissioned a study, conducted by the American University School of Communications, to examine press-government relations in the first four years of the Nixon administration.

"The Watergate scandals grew and flourished in an unhealthy atmosphere of secrecy, official lies, and attempted manipulation of newspapers, radio and television," stated the Professional Relations Committee in the hard-hitting conclusions of its report to the Club's Board of Governors, on July 1, 1973. "Moreover, only an administration so insulated from the press and so contemptuous of its reporting function could have ignored the press's disclosures of scandal over the last year and attempted the complex cover-up which is now breaking down."

Watergate legends Bob Woodward, left, and Carl Bernstein appeared at a Club luncheon on June 5, 1974. (Photo by Stan Jennings)

The report accused the administration of an "unprecedented, government-wide effort to control, restrict and conceal information to which the public is entitled."

Chaired by James McCartney of Knight Newspapers, the committee also chided Nixon for holding fewer news conferences than any president in the previous 36 years, further depriving the public of "vital access to presidential thinking on public issues." It charged Ronald Ziegler, the White House

President Nixon leaves the White House for the last time. Stan Jennings took the picture from the tenth floor of the National Press Building, Aug. 9, 1974.

press secretary, with shutting down communication between reporters and public officials, and it likened the White House's communications office to a "propaganda ministry."

The committee also blamed the White House for fostering legal threats to press freedom, in which four reporters had been jailed for refusing to identify sources.

Finally, the committee took a swipe at newspaper publishers and network officials for protesting too weakly against the Nixon administration's "incursions into press rights, the concealment of information, and the narrowing of news channels."

"When we finished the report, the conservative Board [of Governors] tried to kill it," McCartney recalled. But the report leaked out and was prominently reported in the *Washington Post* and *Washington Star*. Controversy over the leak appeared to reduce its influence at the time, McCartney said, but its impact on the Club became clear as the years passed and as the Club strengthened its professional presence and programs. No longer was it seen mainly as a watering hole for reporters.

The Professional Relations Committee maintained its new watch dog role with a nine-month study of the Ford White House's press relations in April 1975. The committee concluded later that year that the new president had improved the atmosphere with more news conferences and interviews but still tended to stonewall on pertinent questions. The committee found, like previous administrations, the Ford regime hobbled press secretaries by withholding significant information from them.

The shift toward professional ethics caught 1974 Club President Clyde LaMotte of the LaMotte News Service, who specialized in reporting on energy topics. An affable, popular man around the Club, LaMotte accepted a junket to Saudi Arabia sponsored by the oil companies during the height of the Arab oil embargo. When he returned, LaMotte called a Club luncheon with himself as the speaker to report on his findings. Reaction was swift.

"Press junkets were nothing new, but many news organizations were beginning to see them as conflicts of interest," said past President Allan Cromley. "Taking a junket paid for by the industry he covered and then reporting about it at a Club luncheon was just too much for many members. He was forced to resign."

The battles between government and the press engendered a stronger sense of professional pride among many Club members. They called for Club-sponsored awards to journalists for distinguished reporting on a wide range of public issues. Club President Don Larrabee of the Griffin-Larrabee News Bureau, said the Club had long provided a platform for national and world leaders but had done little to acknowledge its own bright stars.

As far back as 1929, the Club had sought to reward some of the best work in Washington correspondence. With money provided by a banker and philanthropist from Peekskill, N.Y., Chester D. Pugsley, the Club awarded the first $1,000 Pugsley Award that year. The winner was John A. Kennedy of Universal Service, who exposed that a staff member for a key senator in tariff negotiations was a paid employee of the Connecticut Manufacturers Association.

The Club hoped the Pugsley would be the beginning of a prize that would rival the Pulitzers in prestige. But it did not last many years.

In 1973, at Larrabee's urging, the Board created the Fourth Estate Award – which has become the Club's most prestigious honor for lifetime achievement – and selected CBS anchor Walter Cronkite as its first winner. He had been a Club member since 1948.

On the evening of the award ceremony, as Larrabee prepared to make the presentation, he was told of a late-breaking news event in the Watergate investigation. He decided to share the news with the gala's audience.

"President Nixon," Larrabee reported, "refused tonight to turn over Watergate-related tapes to Special Prosecutor Archibald Cox but said with greatest reluctance he would prepare a summary of their contents to be verified by Sen. John Stennis of Mississippi." The infamous "Saturday Night Massacre," in which Cox and his chief deputy resigned in protest, followed.

Fourth Estate Award winners Flora Lewis of The New York Times *and Helen Thomas of UPI, on right, photographed on Dec. 9, 1985. (Photo by Marshall Cohen)*

Cronkite spoke of the importance of stripping away veils of secrecy in government, business, labor, lobbies, trade associations and the press itself. He said the big guns trained against the press appeared to have abated for the moment, but the press still faced efforts to undermine its protection of news sources. Journalists, he said, shoulder heavy responsibilities. "Perhaps the greatest of these responsibilities is that of a sort of leadership by default in restoring to this nation a respect for honesty, integrity, candor – belief in those things – and credibility for our institutions," he said.

As Cronkite later told the tale, he noticed people darting in and out of the room while he was talking. Word spread through the audience that Nixon had ordered Attorney General Elliot Richardson to fire Cox. When Richardson resigned in protest, Nixon ordered Deputy Attorney General William Ruckelshaus to fire Cox. He refused and Nixon fired him. Nixon then turned to Solicitor General Robert Bork, who fired Cox.

While the news sparked great interest in the crowd, the show went on, and Cronkite got his award. Larrabee later noted that history had been made many times in the Club's ballroom, so that it was appropriate that night to interrupt the proceedings with another newsworthy announcement – particularly on the occasion of celebrating the Club's first Fourth Estate honoree.

In 1984, Helen Thomas, the doyenne of Washington journalism, was the first woman to be given the Fourth Estate Award. She, too, lamented the growing threat of secrecy in government. "From my view from the bridge," the long-time UPI White House correspondent told the audience, "secrecy is more harmful to a free society than almost any so-called leak. All the presidents have fallen victim to the same syndrome of secrecy, and they all become apoplectic over disclosures that often legitimately belong in the public domain."

Four years later, Fourth Estate honoree David Broder of the *Washington Post* spoke of the blurring of lines between the government and the press through the rise of what he termed the "Washington insiders" – journalists who go into government and return to journalism or managers of political campaigns who then turn up as TV "news" analysts.

"There's a real danger in blurring the line between politicians and journalists, in letting ourselves become androgynous Washington insiders, all of us seeking and wielding influence in our own ways," Broder said. "The people know what to do with politicians who displease them … vote them out of office. But they have no recourse against us in the press. And if they see us as part of a power-wielding clique of insiders, they are going to be resentful as hell that they have no way to call us to account."

Over the years, the Fourth Estate Award has been presented to columnists, correspondents, editors, TV News correspondents and anchors, an author, a photographer and a sports writer. A complete list can be found at the end of the book. All of them had one thing in common: They had devoted their lives to bringing what they saw as truth to the American public. And they had made the profession proud.

In addition to the Fourth Estate Award, the Club presents a series of journalism awards to recognize great work in many different categories of journalism:

- Washington Correspondence Award to recognize the work of reporters who cover Washington for the benefit of the hometown audience.
- Arthur Rowse Award for Press Criticism.
- Robin Goldstein Award for Washington Regional Reporting.
- Edwin M. Hood Award for Diplomatic Correspondence.
- Newsletter Journalism Award.
- Robert L. Kozik Award for Environmental Reporting.

NPC Library Hispanic Committee presentation accepted by 1990 President Judy Grande.

- National Press Club Online Journalism Award.
- John Aubuchon Freedom of the Press Award.
- Sandy Hume Award for Excellence in Political Journalism.
- Joseph D. Ryle Award for Excellence in Writing On the Problems of Geriatrics.
- Angele Gingras Humor Award.
- Ann Cottrell Free Animal Reporting Award.

But the Club wanted to do more for the profession than hand out awards. In 1990, Club President Judy Grande of the *Cleveland Plain Dealer* proposed that the Club underwrite a scholarship to a black, Hispanic or Asian graduating high school student who planned to major in journalism. The news business had been trying for years to attract more minorities, and this would be a way for the Club to promote diversity.

But how to pay for it?

When Ellen Mason Persina of the Canadian Broadcasting Corp. succumbed to cancer at the age of 41 in 1991, her husband, Bill Persina, endowed a scholarship fund in her name.

In 1997, the Club launched an annual 5K run/walk as a regular scholarship fundraiser that has become the Club's largest public event. On a Saturday morning each autumn, hundreds of runners congregate on F Street for the race that takes them toward the Capitol and back. Determined runners lead the pack to finish in minutes. An hour later, the rear is brought up by walkers who just want to be part of the festivities.

Celebrity runners have included Washington Mayor Anthony Williams and Health and Human Services Secretary Donna Shalala. After the race, everyone converges in the Club for a pancake breakfast where awards and prizes are handed out liberally. In recent years, the fundraising has been augmented by a silent auction with items often donated

Nearly 550 runners and walkers competed in the Club's eighth annual 5K Race on Sept. 10, 2005, to raise funds for the Persina Scholarship. (Photo by Marshall Cohen)

Fourth Estate Award winner Tom Brokaw of NBC accepts his plaque from President Tammy Lytle and program chairman Frank Aukofer at a Nov. 19, 2003, dinner. (Photo by John Metelsky)

by Club speakers during the previous year, including actress Angelina Jolie, actor George Clooney, Sen. Barack Obama, televangelist Pat Robertson, actress Jane Fonda and actor LeVar Burton. More money is raised through a simultaneous online auction. The fund-raising allows the Club to award at least one four-year $20,000 scholarship each year. In 2007, the Board specified that the scholarship would be awarded to recipients who contributed to diversity in U.S. newsrooms.

"Some have gone to college who otherwise would not have," said Club President Rick Dunham of *Business Week,* long-time race chairman. "And others have been able to afford their dream school they might not otherwise have been able to pay for."

When Dennis Feldman, who had edited the Club's *Record* for years, died in 1999, his family bequeathed $30,000 for the Club's Feldman scholarship for graduate students. Since then, the $5,000 annual scholarship has helped veteran journalists advance their careers through additional education.

One winner was Terri Williams, who had been a reporter for the *Houston Post* before turning her skills to teaching journalism at an inner-city high school in Houston. The 2003 winner, Paul Burkhardt of Chicago, used his scholarship to attend the Columbia University journalism graduate program so that he could return to Chicago to write about architecture. Said Kathy Kiely, long-time chairwoman of the Scholarship Committee, "By providing some assistance to talent like this, we're making an investment in the future of good journalism."

Professional development became the focus of Club presidents in the early 2000s. Club President Tammy Lytle of the *Orlando Sentinel* re-energized the professional development program with panels and seminars on aspects of the trade from note-taking to story crafting and war coverage. In 2005, President Rick Dunham of *Business Week* launched a mentorship program. It paired seasoned journalists with younger Club members.

Launched with an event that brought *Washington Post* legend Bob Woodward to talk to younger journalists about the art of interviewing, the mentoring program paired 13 veteran and novice journalists the first year. Five or six of the young people got new jobs. "It was a serious benefit of membership," Dunham said.

Beginning in 1972, the Club accelerated its role in defending freedom of the press. "We plan to deal ourselves in on every situation involving infringement of freedom of the press," Club President Warren Rogers said that year. One of his first steps was to telegraph the United Nations to denounce the expulsion of two accredited Taiwanese journalists.

The Club has sent hundreds of letters to leaders around the globe over the years, protesting abuse of press freedom. It protested to Philippine President Ferdinand Marcos about the deaths of 22 news reporters who had been killed in the Philippines between 1979 and 1985. The Club also complained to Soviet authorities in 1986 when Nicholas Daniloff, Moscow correspondent for *U.S. News and World Report*, was arrested and charged with spying. Though Daniloff was eventually released and returned to the U.S., the Club canceled a members' trip to the USSR, slated for November of that year.

The Club posted a plaque in 1985 memorializing 265 journalists who had been killed in the line of duty since the late 1970s. With so many attacks on a free press at home and around the world, the Board formed the Freedom of the Press Committee in 1987 to monitor incidents of press suppression worldwide and to recognize journalists who have had to work under difficult and dangerous circumstances.

The committee organized annual Freedom of the Press days in collaboration with the Committee to Protect Journalists, which presented its report on journalists killed

Terry Anderson of the Associated Press, who was held captive in Lebanon.

Author Salman Rushdie describes how to survive and thrive under a daily death threat when he spoke to the Club in 1993. (Photo by Christy Bowe)

Marking a day of relief and pride for the press.

in the line of duty. The Club established annual Freedom of the Press awards for both domestic and international journalists.

In 1987, the Club protested to Iran's Ayatollah Khomeini about the detention in Lebanon of Terry Anderson of the Associated Press, Charles Glass of ABC-TV, as well as French and British journalists held by local terrorists thought to be sponsored by Iran. The following year the Club established a national headquarters of the Reporters Committee to Free Terry Anderson, who was held captive for seven years, longer than any other American hostage. For a long time, a banner proclaiming "Free Terry Anderson" hung from the press building's front entrance, and Anderson spoke at the Club following his release.

A letter to P.W. Botha, then president of South Africa, deplored press suppression and the arrest of journalists there. In 1993, the Club complained to United Nations Secretary Boutros Boutros-Ghali about death threats leveled by certain U.N.-member countries against author Salman Rushdie for his books lamenting Islamic extremists' treatment of fellow citizens.

In one unusual case, the Club became the ward of a Zairian journalist and his family. In 1994, Kalala Mbenga Kalao, who had been jailed and beaten after writing a series of articles critical of Zaire's President Mobutu, won the International Freedom of the Press Award. Kalao accepted the award at a Club luncheon and denounced the Mobutu regime. Word soon reached him that he would be killed if he returned to Zaire. The Club arranged political asylum for him and helped spirit his pregnant wife, Sylvie, out of Zaire. NPC President Gil Klein of the Media General News Service worked with Trinity

Presbyterian Church in Arlington, Va., to get the Kalaos settled with housing and a job and to arrange for Kalao to study English at Georgetown University.

In 2002, Club President John Aubuchon of Maryland Public Television repeatedly voiced the Club's alarm at threats to press freedom and the public's right to know. When Congress, in the wake of the terrorist attack on the World Trade Centers in 2001, began writing a law to define the powers of the new Homeland Security Department, Aubuchon detected danger. When he spotted a provision that exempted from the Freedom of Information Act certain items that had long been publicly accessible, he dashed off this protest: "In its rush to protect the country from terrorists, Congress should not lose sight of the public's right to know what its government is doing."

When reporter Joel Mowbray of *National Review* magazine was detained by the Diplomatic Security Service, Aubuchon wrote to the State Department: "The National Press Club was astounded by the detention of a reporter.... The apparent intention was an attempt to ascertain the source of classified cables relating to embarrassing problems with U.S. visas in Saudi Arabia.... Such tactics, if employed regularly, quickly would make a mockery of our constitutional guarantees of press freedom."

Shortly after Aubuchon died in 2003, the Board named the Club's Freedom of the Press Award after him to honor his activism and commitment on behalf of free-press issues.

In 2007, NPC President Jerry Zremski of the *Buffalo News* wrote to Russian President Vladimir Putin, expressing the Club's alarm at mounting evidence of the Kremlin's crackdown on press freedom. "What worries us most," Zremski wrote, "is ... that 13 working journalists have been slain in Russia since March 2000. Most notable among these cases is that of Anna Politkovskaya, whose brave reports on Russia's leadership and the war against Chechnya were models for the kind of service journalists must provide to hold their governments accountable. We, as colleagues of Anna's, want you to know that the world community of journalists is watching events in Russia with grave concern." Zremski called on Putin to undertake "an aggressive investigation and prosecution of these cases [to] keep Russian journalists safer and Russia freer."

The Club did not limit its protests to foreign governments. It took strong stands against attempts to interfere with the press in the United States. It submitted amicus briefs in U.S. Supreme Court cases involving public and press access to trials and to grand jury witnesses. It protested a subpoena by the House Committee on Standards of Official Conduct of Thomas Brandt of the *Washington Times* when he refused to reveal sources for his story about the committee's investigation of Rep. Geraldine Ferraro, the 1984 Democratic vice presidential candidate.

In early 1992, a Senate-appointed special counsel subpoenaed three journalists, including Nina Totenberg of National Public Radio, about leaks in the confirmation hearings of Clarence Thomas' nomination to the Supreme Court. In response, Club President Gregory Spears of Knight-Ridder Newspapers wrote: "Compelling reporters to disclose their sources may seem like an appealing shortcut to identify the leakers, compared to questioning all the [Judiciary Committee] senators, aides and staff members.... But bear in mind the precedent that would be set, and consider where it could lead the Senate.... The Congress vigorously defends it powers against unconstitutional encroachment by the Executive Branch. We ask you to consider in the same light the separation between the Senate and the press as spelled out in the First Amendment."

To educate reporters in the difficulties of freely exercising their craft, the Club has not been above play-acting. In 2005, under the aegis of President Rick Dunham, the Club sponsored a mock court proceeding on the risk of divulging classified information. In this case, the story-line involved publication of classified data about flaws in nuclear submarines. A panel of lawyers, a law professor and former judge, a *Los Angeles Times* reporter and a *Baltimore Sun* editor played out a scenario that ended with a decision to publish the story. Given a choice of whether to jail the reporter for refusing to reveal a source, the panelists concluded that, in today's climate of prosecutorial overreaching and judicial impatience with the press, the reporter most likely would be hauled before a grand jury and imprisoned.

The Club's Professional Development Committee conducts seminars for younger reporters and newcomers to Washington on how to cover various federal departments and agencies. Veteran reporters, who have covered the beats, give hints on how to cover Congress, the White House, executive departments and agencies and federal courts.

The Club also encouraged the creation of the Regional Reporters Association, giving journalists reporting for mid-sized city papers a forum to help them compete with major newspapers, wire services and television networks. The association enabled regional reporters to get high-ranking officials to address their group who might otherwise have never agreed to appear – including Presidents George H.W. Bush and Bill Clinton.

"The Club only works these days if it serves as an umbrella for many journalism groups," Dunham said. "To remain vital, it has to offer members opportunities to develop their craft, to advance their careers and to defend press freedom."

Photographer Max Desfor, center, presents an autographed copy of his 1951 Pulitzer Prize-winning Korean War photo to Photography Committee Chairman Marshall Cohen, left, and member Jim Wallace.

Among the Club leaders devoted to professional growth were presidents Frank Aukofer, Art Wiese and David Hess, photographed here in 1997. (Photo by John Metelsky)

David Brinkley of ABC News, second from left, and his wife, Susan, are flanked by Democratic strategist Bob Strauss, left, and Conservative columnist George Will when Brinkley received the Fourth Estate Award in 1987. (Photo by Stan Jennings)

Left: James Baldwin, American author (1924-87) has the rapt attention of Washington Post *writer William Raspberry as he makes a point at an NPC reception prior to his speaking. CNN News Anchor Bernard Shaw is in the background. (Photo by Stan Jennings)*

Below left: Cartoonist Herb Block of The Washington Post *with his Fourth Estate Award in 1977.*

Below: Former Miss America and consumer activist Bess Myerson with Club President Drew Von Bergen of UPI at Consumer Awards luncheon Oct. 20, 1980. (Photo by David Nour)

Bottom: John S. Knight of Knight-Ridder Newspapers, 1976 winner of the Fourth Estate Award, poses with fellow publisher Katharine Graham. (Photo by Stan Jennings)

Left: Rev. Billy Graham makes a point at a 1971 news conference held at the Club. (Photo by Stan Jennings) Right: NPC President John Fogarty of the San Francisco Chronicle presents the Fourth Estate Award to UPI correspondent Helen Thomas in 1984. (Photo by Marshall H. Cohen)

Left: Cokie Roberts of National Public Radio and ABC News warmed the audience as she handed out NPC journalism awards on July 17, 1996. (Photo by Art Garrison) Right: New York Times photographer George Tames won the 1992 Fourth Estate Award.

Left: Keynote speaker Daniel Schorr of National Public Radio at NPC journalism awards luncheon, 1997. (Photo by John Metelsky) Right: Dr. Jack Kevorkian gave a fiery speech on Jul. 29, 1996 in defense of doctor-assisted suicide. He chatted beforehand with member Gordon Smith. (Photo by Art Garrison)

New York Times foreign correspondent Flora Lewis enjoys a caricature presented during her Sept. 9, 1985, Fourth Estate Award dinner. Looking on is Zbigniew Brzezinski, President Carter's National Security Advisor. (Photo by Marshall Cohen)

Jimmy Stewart receives a Certificate of Appreciation from former NPC President Don Larrabee and Chairman of the National Press Foundation Robert Farrell for Stewart's "significant and valuable service" to the National Press Foundation. (Photo by John Metelsky)

Helen Thomas, UPI, greets former White House press secretary Jim Brady and his wife, Sarah, at a Fourth Estate Award dinner on Dec. 5, 1984. Past President Don Larrabee on right. (Photo by Marshall H. Cohen)

Club President Henry L. Sweinhart signs the contract for construction of the NPC Building on Aug. 24, 1925. Also on hand were left to right, James William Bryan, general manager of the new National Press Building Corp.; Lewis Wood, chairman of The Board of Governors; and William A. Crawford, a charter member of the Club.

CHAPTER SEVEN

14TH AND F NW
WASHINGTON, D.C. 20045

"There is only one capital of the United States, there is only one 14th and F streets, and there is only one National Press Club."
– James William Bryan, promoter of the National Press Building

A block from Metro Center, the busiest stop on the subway line, the National Press Building welcomes as many as 7,000 people in a single day to its offices and shops. By noon, the place is bustling with journalists, tourists, shoppers and various professionals speaking a Babel of languages. With a lifespan covering some 80 years, the building has become an integral part of the city and an institution in its own right.

The press building is a tribute to the dreams and business acumen of National Press Club member James William Bryan. He and those who adopted his vision pledged their own money as co-signers of a loan to get it started, and overcame daunting financial obstacles to see it come to life. They tackled financial frights and construction headaches that might have caused the more faint-hearted to duck for cover.

The venture began in 1925, when Club members started looking for a permanent home. Members already had moved three times in 18 years and were hopeful of getting permanent quarters for their clubhouse. But they lacked the wherewithal to purchase permanent space. Bryan came forward with the audacious proposal for a $10 million office building to serve not only the needs of a burgeoning capital press corps and international news center but also of Club members for a roosting place and refuge.

A publisher who had been a Club member since arriving in Washington in 1912, Bryan was also a promoter, ever questing for a new project. He hatched an idea for what would become the largest privately owned office building in the nation's capital – the National Press Building.

Later to become one of the busiest intersections in the country, Pennsylvania Avenue and 14th Street. The old Washington Post is on far right.

NPC members begin tearing down the Ebbitt Hotel on Jan. 6, 1926 (Photo by Harris & Ewing)

Crowds line the street in front of the Fox Theatre shortly after it opened in 1927.

From the start, Bryan set his sights on the site at 14th and F streets NW about two blocks from the White House. Known for more than 50 years as Newspaper Row, the two streets contained a jumble of shops and townhouses near the Western Union telegraph service. Bryan envisioned razing the old structures and erecting a new building. The Ebbitt House, an antebellum hotel whose halls and lobbies were swathed in red plush carpets and decorated with black walnut furniture, boasted one of the most popular watering holes in town. It also occupied a big chunk of the site. Adjacent to the hotel was a two-and-a-half story edifice, once the quarters and law office of the notorious Aaron Burr, vice president of the United States who killed Alexander Hamilton in a duel in 1804. Next to that was the Hooe Iron Building, a cast-iron curiosity that housed the U.S. Geological Survey offices.

In all, the three parcels of land that caught Bryan's eye were controlled by Stormfelz-Loveley, of Detroit, which acted as trustee for the owners. Bryan met with the trustees in New York City to negotiate an option to purchase the site. Neither Stormfeltz nor Loveley took the Club's proposition seriously, but they granted an option holding the property off-market for 30 days. Bryan later recalled: "The option to the property had been obtained through the judicious use in the darkest days of Prohibition of a bottle of genuine Scotch and the payment of one dollar cash in hand."

The Ebbitt Hotel as it looked in 1926, shortly before it was demolished to make room for the National Press Building.

There was one rather significant catch. The owners demanded that the single dollar had to be followed with a payment of $2.85 million at the end of the 30-day option.

Bryan went to work, calling on his wide circle of acquaintances to seek bankers willing to underwrite $6.25 million worth of bonds as well as builders ready to put up an additional $450,000 on a subordinate mortgage. He also opened negotiations to lease theater space in the yet-to-be-constructed building. He called a general meeting of active Club members to ratify the proposal, only to see many influential members rally to defeat it.

Faced with this lack of enthusiasm, Bryan nevertheless persisted. He formed a committee comprised of Henry Sweinhart, the 1925 Club president, and two other influential Washingtonians – John Henry Hammonds, a mining engineer, and John Joy Edson, chairman of the board of the Washington Loan and Trust Co. Neither was a Club member but they agreed to advise Sweinhart on the venture. Their first step was to renew the option, which Bryan learned would cost $12,500.

"The Club did not have that kind of money," wrote Hugh Morrow in *Dateline: Washington*. "Bryan executed a demand note in that amount at the District National Bank where he was told the money could be borrowed if a dozen press club members co-signed it. Those co-signers, along with Bryan, were dubbed The Signers, honored reverentially by subsequent generations of members almost equally with the signers of the Declaration of Independence. Each signer obligated himself personally for a $1,050 share of the note.

"Some may have had that much in the bank, some might have been able to raise that much if sued, some, it can be safely presumed, were not within hailing distance of that much money," Morrow wryly observed.

In any case, the 30 days quickly slipped by, and John Hays Hammond put up another $12,500 option renewal, giving the entrepreneurs another month to scramble for financing.

A special meeting held in the fall of 1925 to approve plans for construction of a new club building. John Joy Edson, leading Washington banker and Treasurer of the National Press Building Corp., shown at the speakers table with Henry L. Sweinhart, president of the Club in 1925.

As that month passed, both the Famous Players-Lasky (later to become Paramount Pictures) and the Fox Theater Corp. showed an eagerness for obtaining a move theater in the nation's capital. Negotiations ensued, and William Fox agreed to advance $500,000 in cash, to be applied to future rent. When the papers for this theater portion of the transaction were drawn, actor Charlie Chaplin, then a guest in Fox's house, was invited to witness the signings. With dramatic flourish, he penned his name in green ink – the color of money.

With the theater agreement settled, the building promoters pushed forward and secured other funding, totaling $6.6 million. There was also a third mortgage held by the building contractors, who effectively advanced the money to pay themselves. Because the Club, under District of Columbia law, could not engage directly in real estate transactions, it formed the National Press Realty Holding Corp., later to become the National Press Building Corp. The new holding company swiftly undertook the task of issuing preferred stock for sale to the public. Most of the stock "salesmen" were Club members, who persuaded friends, fellow members and anyone else they could inveigle to buy into the venture. A number of the country's publishers bought stock shares, along with some wealthy financiers.

Ulric Bell of the *Louisville Courier-Journal* was elected as 1926 Club president to succeed Sweinhart, who had worked hard to help get the project launched. The new president was consumed with getting the construction started. He made many trips to New York to consult with bankers and contractors, always under Bryan's watchful eye. Bryan had been retained as a representative for the holding company. From rented offices across F Street in the Westory Building, Bryan watched the new building rise.

A Chicago architectural firm, George Rapp and Co., won the contract to design the structure. Fuller Construction Co. began work immediately, first tearing down the old Ebbitt Hotel. Before the razing, many Club members gathered souvenirs, and the famous hotel bar was salvaged and today stands in the Old Ebbitt Grill at 15th and G streets, NW, just a block away.

The project got off to a bumpy start. At the construction site, builders were confronted with rising waters in the construction pit. A tributary of the Tiber Creek, running underground through Washington and emptying into the old canals parallel to the Potomac River, flowed at 40 gallons per minute into the excavation. It had to be pumped out continuously.

Another snag arose when the building corporation determined that more rental space, beyond the planned 11 stories, would be needed to make the venture financially viable. Three additional stories were required. A 1910 District of Columbia law, however, forbade erection of any commercial building higher than the distance across the street plus 20 feet, which yielded a rule-of-thumb height of 130 feet – although case-by-case exceptions could be made along broad avenues for buildings up to 160 feet; so 11 stories was the usual height of buildings erected after that date. But the Club used its influence to persuade key members of Congress to enact special legislation enabling the National Press Building to obtain a waiver from the District regulation and rise to 14 stories, thus making it roughly equal in stature to the then tallest commercial structure in town, the 160-foot Cairo apartment building some 12 blocks away at 16th and Q streets, NW.

The three additional floors, along with the boom in pre-Depression prices, drove up costs of the project and meant that more money had to be borrowed. Before the building plans were completed and ready for the ceremony, a cornerstone-laying event was orchestrated for publicity – a ploy that Bryan and fellow stockholders hoped would lure new investors. Over the protests of the project's lawyers and the rest of the building committee, Bryan hatched a plan to sell $1.3 million worth of stock in the National Press Building Corp.

"Actually, at the time the cornerstone ceremonies were held, we were not ready for the cornerstone," Bryan recalled. "In fact, we would not be ready for several months. But we

President Calvin Coolidge was not silent at building dedication, 1927.

Former Club President David Hess, left, and future President Peter Holmes with the original Coolidge dedication cornerstone lost for many years and later discovered in the bowels of the building by President John Cosgrove. Hess put time capsule items behind the cornerstone when it was relaid.

had to have the money then and there or the whole thing would have gone up in smoke."

The cornerstone ceremony began at 2:00 p.m. on April 8, 1926, when Club President Bell, clad in a borrowed cutaway coat, pin-striped trousers and an opera hat, made brief remarks in advance of the keynote speaker, President Calvin Coolidge. Silent Cal arrived at the crowded event as newsreel cameras whirred along 14th Street from Pennsylvania Avenue to F Street. Nearly every Washington correspondent for the nation's newspapers covered the ceremony.

Clad in his own cutaway coat and striped pants, Coolidge scooped up mortar with a gold trowel and officially laid the cornerstone, which was later stored away until the right time arrived to seal it into the building. The press, the U.S. president declaimed in his celebratory speech, is one of the "cornerstones of liberty," and the crowd cheered.

As for Bryan's sham ceremony, he later ruefully admitted: "My face is red and I shamefacedly confess that His Excellency, the President of the United States, who so vigorously wielded the golden trowel … splashed a lot of mortar in vain. For the cornerstone he 'laid' was in the middle of the sidewalk and the memento box of heavy copper, lined with aluminum and jacketed with zinc, containing things of interest to be preserved for the day (mementos of the Club, including copies of the Washington newspapers), rested only a few hours in its temporary place. That night it went into my safe to be held until the Building Committee placed it in the real cornerstone months later."

Ironically, few members at the time realized the ceremony was premature. Coolidge's presence and the glamour of the dedication managed to lend the cash-strapped project a much-needed morale and financial boost. The building corporation sold all of the stock needed to rescue the project, except for some shares set aside for Club members, the architects, builders, suppliers and a few others. Some key investors bought tens of thousands of dollars worth of the shares, including *National Geographic Magazine* ($25,000), McGraw-Hill ($15,000) and Andrew Mellon, then-Secretary of the Treasury ($50,000).

Though symbolic, the laying of the cornerstone signaled the eventual success of Bryan's $10 million dream. The ringmaster himself noted the significance when he boasted, with his characteristic flair for exaggeration, that the "property it occupied is perhaps as valuable a piece of real estate as any in the United States and it greatly will enhance in value as time goes on."

Finally, on Aug. 25, 1927, exactly two years after the building was proposed by Bryan and his mendicant colleagues, the first tenants began moving into their new quarters. The project still was a diamond in the rough as final touches were completed around them. Many of the do-it-yourself tenants painted walls and installed their own fixtures. The *Baltimore Sun* staff, along with Club members, had to walk up 12 flights of stairs for several weeks until the building elevators were installed. Hilliard Harper, a former night copy boy of the *Sun* during Prohibition, said the climb was "no big deal for a 16-year-old, and I didn't complain. Those who did were the bootleggers. They didn't care for the…walk [up] with their pockets full of pint bottles." Six more years would pass until the anti-booze amendment to the Constitution was repealed and the Club could sell liquor legally.

The Fox Theater, later to become Loew's Capitol Theater, opened its doors on F Street soon after the tenants moved in. On Sept. 19, 1927, the opulent entertainment center held its own lavish opening with President Coolidge, his Cabinet and many members of Congress attending.

The National Press Club occupied its new quarters over two days on Dec. 13 and 14, 1927, after spending about $90,000 to furnish the place, and after negotiating a 99-year lease at $1 per year with the building corporation for the space. Though the Club's rent to this day remains $1 a year, it also must pay, among other things, for its share of real estate taxes and utilities. By early 1928, as J. Fred Essary of the *Baltimore Sun* was inaugurated as NPC president, the Club's active membership exceeded 1,800 journalists. By all accounts, the Club was flourishing in its spanking new building.

All was ready, too, for the building's official dedication, and on Feb. 4, 1928, President Coolidge returned to speak at that event in remarks that were broadcast to the nation. As the U.S. Marine Band played, Essary announced that the Club would be open during the fete for "ladies of the members' households" – a lame concession to women, even practicing journalists, who were then barred from membership in the all-male Club.

The building began to fill with tenants, mostly from out-of-town newspapers with Washington bureaus. For the first seven years, it operated in the red, even though the Internal Revenue Service, from 1928 to 1930, leased offices there until its own building was ready. Then came the stock market crash in October 1929 and the onset of the Great Depression. A gleaming edifice of the booming '20s, the building (and Club) were enveloped in the gloom of the early '30s and nearly collapsed with the economy of that decade.

In 1932, newly elected NPC President Bascom Timmons of the

The National Press Building was administered by a separate corporation named by the Club. These impeccably dressed first officers of the building in 1926 are John Hays Hammond, president; H.L. Sweinhart, vice president; John Joy Edson, treasurer; Harvey D. Jacob, general counsel; and James William Bryan, secretary and general manager.

Cheers and good luck all around. Gala celebration the evening of the opening of the National Press Building in 1927.

Houston Chronicle met with former Club President Essary and Jesse H. Jones, who served with the new Reconstruction Finance Corp. As president of the National Press Building Corp., Essary gave Jones, a banker, the grim details of the Club's faltering finances. On Oct.17, the 5-year-old press building went into receivership. Lawrence B. Campbell, then the building's general manager, was appointed a receiver. This gave the Club some breathing space, but foreclosure loomed.

President Herbert Hoover, upon learning of the Club's financial struggle, was angered and urged the Club not to buckle under the pressure from mortgage bondholders. "Don't let them do that [force disclosure]," the president told Timmons. "First mortgage bondholders have been pretty ruthless. They have been foreclosing buildings right and left, getting property in many cases worth far more than the mortgage liability. This practice has spread misery all over the country."

Under mounting default demands, Timmons arched his back and refused to give in. "The good faith of the press club is at stake," he told the bondholders. "If under the circumstances you bondholders foreclose your mortgage, I shall do my best to see that every newspaper tenant moves out of the building, and furthermore, I shall personally chisel off the name 'National Press Building.'"

Some relief arrived when Timmons, Peter Brandt of the *St. Louis Post Dispatch*, and Eugene Leggett of the *Detroit Free Press* were among the reporters traveling in November 1932 on the campaign train of Democratic presidential candidate Franklin Delano Roosevelt. They explained the Club's dismal financial straits and won a promise from Roosevelt that if he won the election he would support an amendment to the bankruptcy laws for aid to debt-burdened associations such as the National Press Club.

Roosevelt kept his promise. Soon after his election, one of two emergency enactments to improve equity reorganization was passed by Congress. Fifteen minutes after Roosevelt signed the conference report making the new language law, Timmons was in U.S. District Court filing the first petition recorded under Section 77-B of the new statute. Later evolving into Chapter 11 of the federal bankruptcy code, the law helped save the National Press Building as well as thousands of other Depression-scourged corporations and other organizations. Along with 77-B and the waning of the Depression's worst effects, prudent management of Bryan's dreamwork put the National Press Building on the road to financial recovery.

The 1940s and early '50s saw ever-expanding use of the building and Club. By 1949, the Club was flush enough to renovate its aging quarters, including refitting its storied Tap Room, the members' bar.

After the war, the Club benefited from the nation's unprecedented era of expansion. Washington became the news capital of the globe. Just as in the beginning in the early years of the century, when the Club occupied two overcrowded rooms above a jewelry store, it was faced with overcrowding in the '50s. As early as 1958, even with the renovation a few years before, space problems persisted, prompting some Club leaders to wonder if it had become too popular.

"The present overcrowding is caused not so much by the growth in membership as by the growth in interest, use and facilities of the Club," said 1957 President Ben Grant of *U.S. News and World Report*. "Thus, there is a lot of satisfaction in the very problems that beset us."

As for the press building's finances, there was encouraging news. Fully occupied, the building raked in rental income in 1949 that exceeded $1.1 million. The biggest tenant was Loew's Capitol Theatre, occupying one-third of the building's rental space and paying $170,000 a year in rent. The second largest renter was the Federal Deposit Insurance Corp.

At the beginning of the '60s, the building was as busy as ever, but hard times loomed. Richard L. Wilson was chosen in 1961 to head the building corporation and immediately wrestled with a loss of tenants and launched discussions about renovating the entire building. Although the corporation had its best year in 1960 and the forecast for '61 was even cheerier, by 1963 the building's largest two tenants moved out. One of them, the FDIC, a 30-year tenant that occupied more than a fifth of the building, shifted to a permanent home about six blocks away.

The year 1961 had marked the end of the long-term lease with Loew's theater, the largest lessee. It was not unexpected, since the theater was losing money and on the brink of closing. Negotiations for a lease renewal had been going on aimlessly for months. So in preparation for what seemed to be an inevitable departure, the Club appointed a planning committee to ponder the future of the building and began consulting contractors, architects, engineers and downtown planners. As that proceeded, the lease with Loew's was extended on a month-to-month basis, until the theater darkened its lights in the fall of 1963.

In June 1963, after months of study, the building corporation invited bids for its most ambitious project to date to modernize the structure and refashion the 3,500-seat theater into ground-floor stores and upper offices. Included in those plans were the eventual automation of the elevators, rewiring of the overburdened electrical system and the installation of new central air conditioning and upgraded plumbing.

In September, the gold curtain descended for the last time in the theatre after the movie, *The Ticklish Affair.* A sparse crowd, typical of the movie house's long struggle to survive in its downtown location, was on hand. Demolition of the historic landmark began soon after, although part of the ornate exterior façade, including the arches, was preserved.

It took three years to complete the six floors and two basements that the theatre had occupied – a year longer than to erect the entire building in 1926-28. But when the project was finished, black granite columns and terrazzo floors, custom-designed offices and one of the most sophisticated elevator banks in the city filled the historic space. As the $6 mil-

Before you build a new press building, you have to break up the old one. On March 18, 1977, the Knight-Ridder staff held a cocktail party to start the process. Here, Bill Eaton, Los Angeles Times, *swings the sledge hammer. Splotches all over are dust in the air. (Photo by Stan Jennings)*

Overdressed but ready to lend his labor, NPC President Ken Scheibel, 1975. (Photo credit: N.E.W.S. photo)

lion facelift continued in 1965, the first tenants began moving into the new space. Fairchild Publications' Washington bureau was the first tenant. The Security Bank soon opened its fourth Washington branch at the corner of 14th and F streets with a novel feature – a sidewalk teller window. Joseph R. Harris & Co., a women's apparel store, opened in March along F Street, followed by Super Music City and Press Liquors.

Addressing the Club membership in April 1966 after the remodeling was complete, corporation president Wilson said, "We have put the National Press Building back in business for another 20 years." His optimism, alas, was short-lived.

By 1974, evidence began to mount that the building as a whole needed more than cosmetic treatment. At 3 a.m. on Nov. 21, the telephone rang at the home of Club President Kenneth Scheibel of *Washington Bureau News*. Charles Sherren of the F.W. Berens Co., on-site manager of the press building, told Scheibel that pieces of brick, mortar and terra cotta had fallen from the F Street façade onto the sidewalk below. Largely because of the hour, no one was injured.

Scheibel directed Sherren to start erecting a scaffold around the F Street and 14th Street perimeter so that pedestrians would not be in danger of falling debris. The cost of the scaffold was $10,000 plus $100 per day rent until the building's walls could be repaired.

Soon after that, during a heavy rainstorm, the building's roof sprang a leak, and water seeped through the 13th floor ceiling into the Club president's office. That same rain had delayed Scheibel's arrival at the office, and likely spared him from injury. When he finally got there, he discovered 60 pounds of plaster, mortar and concrete in the middle of his desk.

Club leaders quickly went to work on a plan to hold the building together. The F Street and 14th Street facades were loosening and the building's south wall, overlooking Pennsylvania Avenue, was bowing out. Scheibel's and subsequent Club administrations provided patchwork fixes to keep the building safe and operable, but a succession of Club leaders through the rest of the decade realized that the 50-year-old structure was in dire need of renovation. In fact, the entire neighborhood around the press building had deteriorated markedly. From the flights to suburbia in the '50s to the urban riots of the '60s, not to mention the influx of prostitutes to the vicinity, all had lent a forlorn and seedy look to the neighborhood. Though known for having the cheapest office space in town, the building began bleeding financially as media tenants, including the *Wall Street Journal*, fled to fancier digs.

The Club and building corporation were faced with two options, either a massive renovation or a new building. In the late '70s attention focused on the idea of stem-to-stern renovation. Frank Aukofer of *The Milwaukee Journal*, the 1978 Club president, relates the story of the Club's exciting but elusive dream of taking over and developing the entire block – bordered by F Street on the north, 14th Street on the west, E Street on the south and 13th Street on the east. The grand scheme called not only for a thorough renovation and expansion of the press building but also rehabilitation of the whole block, including a convention-ready hotel crowned by a vast new Club.

Aukofer credits Australian Henry Keys, a former journalist who then headed the National Press Building Corp., with the big dream of sweeping redevelopment. "We hooked up with John Portman, the Atlanta architect and developer, to build a giant, twin-atrium, 1,300-room convention hotel topped by a new National Press Building of 650,000 square feet, including, of course, a new press club," Aukofer said.

"We were pioneers in [supporting] the redevelopment of Pennsylvania Avenue and, in fact, had lobbied the previous year to save the Pennsylvania Avenue Development Corporation (PADC) from extinction in Congress," Aukofer recalled. "To enhance our position, we bought the land under the Munsey Building (around the corner on E Street), making us the biggest landowners on the block. Ultimately, that purchase made a million dollars for the building corporation and the Club."

The notion of redeveloping run-down Pennsylvania Avenue had been bandied about ever since President Kennedy remarked upon its shabby appearance after his 1961 inaugural limousine ride from Capitol Hill to the White House. Twenty years later, after grandiose plans and several false starts, the PADC Project, created by Congress, got credit for not only the renovation of the National Press Building but also the restoration of the Willard Continental Hotel, the Old Post Office and several other structures along the broad avenue.

"The $160 million Press Club-Portman project, we all figured, would make the Club so rich that we would not only assure its future existence but we would be able to reduce dues besides," Aukofer said. "As with all other Press Club officers and boards before and since, our single-minded interest was the survival of the Club."

To its dismay, the building corporation lost the right to redevelop the block. The defeat of its bid was a bitter disappointment. And the problems with the aging press building itself remained. The Club's Board of Governors pondered other means of dealing with the problem but soon came to believe that renovation was the best choice.

"People began to notice that we had a large and valuable asset here that probably wasn't producing as much as it should," said William D. Hickman, who headed the National Press Building Corp. from 1982 to 1991 and led it through the hectic rehabilitation.

In the years before the project got under way, changes had occurred in the Club's relationship with the building corporation – changes that enabled the Club to seize control of building affairs. As majority stockholder (77.1 percent) of the corporation, the Club had been chastised for not staying abreast of the building's business. In 1972, Club President Warren Rogers of the Chicago Tribune-New York News Syndicate helped change that.

Under his direction, the Club's board took control of the building, made possible by an earlier move in 1970 by President Michael Hudoba of *Sports Afield Magazine* to limit all Club trustee terms to one year, instead of staggered five-year terms. This gave future Club boards the ability to elect slates of their own trustees. By Rogers' administration, the trustees voted all 12 Club officers and board members, plus nine immediate past presidents, to the building's board of directors, thereby gaining majority control. This thrust the Club's board directly into the building's operations and led to a unanimous decision on July 28, 1980, to reconstruct the National Press Building on site from top to bottom.

The $60 million renovation project, unveiled in 1980 to Club members by President Drew Von Bergen of United Press International, called for modernizing the entire facility and the preservation of the architecturally important Fox-Capitol Theatre façade on F Street. The theater arch was to become the ceremonial entrance to the renovated building, a tribute to the long relationship between the Club and the movie palace.

"We wanted to look like we've been on the block for 50 years and we were going to be

Final curtains for the grand old Fox Capitol Theatre as the space is absorbed by the Press Building. (Photo by Harris & Ewing)

here for another 50," Hickman said.

To do that and perform other extensive remodeling, the Club had to make some sacrifices from time to time to come up with enough money for the expensive project. In 1983, for example, the corporation entered into an agreement with 250 limited partners, each of whom invested $250,000, to purchase 98 percent of the building. The Club retained ownership of the land under the building (which it leased to the limited partnership for 45 years), as well as 1 percent of the building itself.

Another highlight of the renovation plan was a 14-story covered atrium, constructed in the former interior light-court of the original press building, a design that would yield significant energy savings. The light-court rose from the seventh to the 14th floors. The design also added on to the original façade, a process that the architects described as "re-skinning." The space between the old

Ornate columns of the theater still stand as the walls around them come crumbling down in 1983 demolition.

and new skins accommodated new plumbing, electrical connections, and heating and air conditioning lines. Alterations also were made to adapt new communications technologies for newspaper, wire service and broadcasting tenants.

Additionally, in the floor-to-roof atrium, two glass-enclosed elevators and a freight elevator were added to the building's existing constellation of one freight and six passenger lifts, thus speeding the structure's vertical traffic. When finished, the project provided 350,000 square feet of office space, 31,000 of retail, and 48,000 for a completely new National Press Club on the 13th and 14th floors.

"Even with all these architectural elements...a strong emphasis is being placed on preserving the significant design or historical features of our existing Club," said 1982 President Vivian Vahlberg of the *Daily Oklahoman*. "For instance, all of our famous newspaper mats are being retained, along with the two-story, wood-paneled main lounge, both of the Club's working fireplaces and much of the wood interior of the present library."

Before the spidery web of scaffolds covered the façade and the renovation began in 1982, a "Roaring '20s" bash, called the National Press Club Wrecker's Ball, celebrated the start of the project on June 25. Attendees danced the night away before the disruption of the construction crews shut down most Club frivolities. The ball signaled the official beginning of the Club's metamorphosis and was an effort to impose a sense of normalcy on the long, dusty, grungy years of construction.

Surprisingly, though some anticipated a sharp drop-off in membership, the Club actually experienced a net increase. In 1982, 130 new members were added, bringing total strength to 4,383. Tenancy in the building, however, plunged.

Initially, the building corporation undertook the reconstruction on its own with construction loan financing from the local National Savings & Trust Co. and San Francisco-based Bank of America. Instead of a complete evacuation, the corporation approved plans for renovating one-fourth of the building at a time. The idea was to maintain an adequate stream of cash and also to reduce disruptions to the tenants who stayed. The corporation figured that if it shut down the whole building, luring tenants back would be difficult.

Front page mats always attracted the eye of Club member Lyle Wilson, UPI bureau chief, photographed in 1958. Almost 40 years later, Rick Zimmerman of the Cleveland Plain Dealer *led a project of hanging a series of offset plates of famous front pages, displayed in the Truman Lounge, Reliable Source dining room and second floor lobby.*

The building was reduced to basic steel structure and concrete floors...then entirely re-built.

A view of The Willard Hotel across 14th Street during reconstruction.

"We asked our tenants to put up with an awful lot of grief, noise and dust," Hickman recalled. "Fortunately, most of them did." But some of the larger ones did not.

For those who stayed, it was an ordeal. One notable example that nearly caused a catastrophe occurred one night during the initial phase of demolition when the building's foundations began to sink into a large hole next door that would become the J.W. Marriott Hotel. Luckily, despite the cracking walls and falling debris from the slippage, the foundation settled, and redevelopment of the press building continued without further disruption. Construction engineers said later that another inch or two, and the building would have toppled over.

Meanwhile, several large tenants moved out to avoid the dust and din, including McGraw-Hill, Reuters, United Press International and the *Baltimore Sun*. Knight-Ridder's bureau chief, Robert S. Boyd, moved his offices to temporary quarters across F Street but

Piece by piece and section by section. (Photo by Stan Jennings)

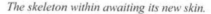

The skeleton within awaiting its new skin.

moved back after the renovation was completed. (About 18 years later, Knight-Ridder, the corporation's largest tenant, left the press building altogether for airier digs astride Metro Center Subway Station.)

As larger bureaus abandoned the place, new offices for small bureaus were configured into the design of the renovated building and provided space for many low-budget news operations. The new building also offered "press room clusters" for those who wanted the independence of their own separate offices in conjunction with like-minded operations.

Just as the project was in its most active stages, in 1981 and '82, economic times changed as interest rates soared to nearly 20 percent – and the anticipated cost of the renovation rose sharply because of the complexity of the work. The Club could no longer afford to complete the project.

Raising the additional money was a long and tortuous process for the Club. In 1983, the building corporation, then wholly owned by the Club (after settling a shareholder lawsuit over the project's rising costs), entered the agreement with the limited partnership. Under that deal, the partnership and corporation agreed on a commitment of $62.5 million in permanent financing when the renovation was completed. The terms were these: That the Club would retain ownership of the land under the building (which it leased to the limited partners for 45 years), and the Club would also retain a 1 percent ownership of the building as well as the right to control the building's operation. Besides the $1-a-year lease that was part of this agreement, the Club retained the right to repurchase the building in the future.

By the end of 1983, the project's first milestone was reached when some tenants began moving into new offices in the initially reconstructed section of the building, just in time for the limited partners to get some tax benefits on their investment. Some 83 news organizations soon were working from the new space that comprised about one-quarter of the entire building, even as the bustle of reconstruction continued apace in the rest of the structure. Among those tenants were the *Chicago Sun-Times*, Crain Communications, *Asahi Shimbun*, Copley Newspapers and the Scandinavian Broadcasting Group.

While progress was made on the office space, the Club's new quarters took shape. The Club's $7 million renovation, under the New Club chairmanship of 1979 President Arthur Wiese of the *Houston Post*, began in 1981. In July, the Board of Governors voted to retain H. Chambers Co. of Baltimore to design a new clubhouse on the 13th and 14th floors. Even as the Club was under construction, both NPC President Vahlberg and her successor, Don Byrne of *Traffic World*, insisted on retaining the Club's main events by continuing newsmaker luncheons and professional activities. During that period, speakers and other guests were ushered into the ballroom through a narrow gauntlet of construction activity where walls and flooring had been stripped to concrete and the exterior wall – 13 stories above the street – removed. Club officers, as they escorted guest speakers, frequently positioned themselves between their guests and the yawning abyss overlooking 14th Street.

Amid the rubble, only a handful of luncheons had to be canceled or shifted to other venues. At times, construction was so chaotic that it engendered a continuous string of jokes from wags in the press corps, who took to de-

Edwin Meese, chief counsel to President Reagan and soon-to-be attorney general, is welcomed by NPC President Don Byrne to a luncheon held at the Capitol Hilton Hotel on Dec. 15, 1983. (Photo by Marshall Cohen).

scribing the project as "downtown Beirut." Cartoonists and Club members Bill Rechin and Don Wilder, creators of "Crock," concocted a series of cartoons printed in the *Record* and posted around the dismembered Club, satirizing life as an NPC member during the renovation. One of their offerings depicted three members playing cards in a makeshift cardroom, door propped open with a piece of plywood and a bare light dangling from the cracked ceiling.

The caption: "I'll see your five pieces of drywall and raise you one 1936 urinal."

Then it finally came to an end. Again, a gala celebration, with the unveiling of the new Club ballroom and a recitation of its 75-year history. On Feb. 11, 1984, Club President John Fogarty of the *San Francisco Chronicle* presided over the black-tie festivities marking the first major event of the elegant ballroom and lounge. Though there were a few remaining finishing touches to be done, the Club in its new and more opulent design was open for business.

The décor blended the open look of the Club's new glass exterior walls and interior atrium glass with a rich and subdued interior reminiscent of the past. Among the many newer features was a redesigned larger ballroom with space for 100 more guests at sit-down events, a casual restaurant dubbed the Reliable Source adjacent to a rectangular, wood-paneled bar on the 14th floor, and an elegant new restaurant called the Fourth Estate overlook-

ing the atrium on the 13th floor. Additionally, the new clubhouse boasted a fully equipped athletic facility and sauna, as well as an expansive library and reading room with computers for reporters' research as well as an archive of the Club's history and memorabilia.

In his remarks to members at the event, Fogarty said, "The Club has come a long way from its beginnings as a place where a group of men could play cards, into an organization whose members are interested in the arts, foreign affairs, economics, business, theater, books, chess, travel and the like. We've evolved into a professional club, and we've done it without losing the Club's character. We are, as former House Speaker Joe Cannon said, 'the largest exclusive club in the world.'"

New plate glass windows show off the Willard Hotel across 14h Street.

Workers lift a marquee place over the building's front entrance in 1985. It welcomed – and sheltered – thousands of members and world leaders until it was dismantled in 2006. (Photo by Stan Jennings)

Amb. W. Averell Harriman enjoyed coming to the Club as a speaker and/or listener, shown here with former arms control negotiator Paul Warnke and 1982 President Vivian Vahlberg. (Photo by Stan Jennings)

Fogarty went on: "We have survived war, prohibition, depression, riots, urban renewal and the deaths of many good newspapers. The Club's obituary has been written many times, but the Club has not died because there have always been enough members who cared about it."

On Oct. 26, 1984, more than 1,000 members and their guests celebrated the final completion of the new Club with a TGIF (Thank Goodness It's Finished) party. Several long-time members attended, including one of the founding members, Jerome Fanciulli, who remembered the brisk day in 1926 when the original National Press Building cornerstone was laid.

Nearly six decades later, on May 21, 1985, after 33 months of reconstruction, a new dedication ceremony for the completed building renovation was celebrated. Accompanied on the dais by Secretary of the Treasury James A. Baker III, Club President David Hess of Knight-Ridder Newspapers presided at the event as a new cornerstone was installed next to the old one. With a grin and gentle tweak of the assembled press, Baker told the crowd: "The right of free speech is a right that's best used briefly." Many reporters smiled as they recalled getting the same advice from their editors.

Reminiscent of the 1926 ceremony, two time capsules were loaded with Club mementoes and placed behind the cornerstones, which were encased in the lobby wall next to the building's main entrance on 14th Street.

The late 1980s were good times for the building corporation, with occupancy rates consistently higher than 95 percent. As the decade progressed, the National Press Building Limited Partnership began paying back the reconstruction loans, which by then had grown to nearly $85 million. In 1989, the partnership considered either selling the building or re-

financing the loan. In the end, the limited partners turned down an offer for more than $100 million, and decided instead to refinance with a $92.5 million loan from Sumitomo Bank, Ltd. The 10-year, interest-only loan carried a 10.915

Treasury Secretary James A. Baker III and President David W. Hess of Knight-Ridder Newspapers at May 25, 1985, ceremony rededicating the building after multimillion-dollar renovation. (Photo by Stan Jennings)

percent interest rate, deemed competitive at the time.

Then the bottom fell out of the downtown real estate market, stripping the building of nearly 30 percent of its market value and forcing management to rent space for much less than planned. Again, the building was in big trouble and it only seemed to get worse.

In April 1991, William O. Vose, a vice president of The Donohoe Companies, the building's property manager, was brought in as president of the press building corporation. His first priority was to assess the financial situation. It soon became clear that because of the unanticipated drop in rental income, the building would be unable to meet its mortgage payments. Vose and other members of the corporation's board initiated discussions with the lender. Sumitomo Bank was willing to forego foreclosure and re-negotiate the loan in part because of its confidence that the building was being operated efficiently under stressful circumstances. But the bank also insisted on receiving all the net cash flow from building operations and some additional payments from the Club.

Recognizing that the fate of the National Press Club was linked to the fate of the building, and aware of Vose's progress in stabilizing the building's finances, the Club in August 1992 merged the positions of Club manager and president of the building corporation. Vose left the Donohoe firm to assume this dual role. He and John Bloom, director of Club operations, put the Club on solid enough footing

National Press Club manager Bill Vose was introduced to the members in 1992. (Photo by Martin Kuhn)

that the Board of Governors in 1995 approved a million-dollar refurbishing of the Club, including an expansion of the library and computer-training center and a remodeling of the 14th floor Reliable Source to embrace the adjacent Truman Lounge.

By 1999, owing to the devaluation of the building as the city's real estate market continued to oscillate, Sumitomo Bank finally threw in the towel. It had been collecting all the cash flow from the building, as excess interest accrued on its loan to the National Press Building Limited Partnership. The building had been struggling over the decade to extend its financing as interest rates declined but faced the certainty of eventual foreclosure with no other remedy in sight.

In a letter in September 2004, John Bloom, the building vice president and manager of the National Press Club, summed up the building's plight. "While investors continued to receive their anticipated, substantial tax benefits," he told the building's limited partners who initially helped finance the reconstruction, "necessary increases, modifications and extensions of the Building's financing in 1989 and 1994, [along with] continuing fallout from the 1986 [federal] tax law changes, and most importantly, fluctuating economic conditions in Washington, D.C., affecting the Building operations decreased the value of the Building, resulting in a multi-million dollar over-financing from which there has been no recovery…. We estimate the difference between the [building's] outstanding loan balance and [its] value exceeded $40 million in July [2004] at the time of the transfer."

That transfer constituted a shift in 1999 of Sumitomo's loan to Resource Properties 54, a real estate investment firm that bought the loan from Sumitomo for a reported $70 million, along with an insistence that the new firm take over management of the building corporation. The principal balance on the note at the time was $92.5 million, not counting millions more in unpaid interest due. In the five years after that sale, Resource Properties received all of the building's net operating revenue in partial payment of interest due on the mortgage, while the balance of unpaid interest continued to accrue. As the numbers grew, it was clear, Bloom later said, "There was no way for the building to keep up with the continuing rise in the unpaid balance due on the loan."

So, in 2004, a new deal was arranged in which Resource Properties sold the note on the building to Quadrangle Management Corp., which owned the adjoining National Place. The building corporation finally gave up its interest in the land underlying the building, which it had mortgaged in 1981 at the start of the renovation. Up to then, the Club had the right of first refusal if the building were ever put up for sale. Resource Properties had paid the Club $500,000 to give up that stipulation; the Club retained only the right to match any future purchase offer "in a short period of time and close the transaction soon thereafter." In this same transaction, Quadrangle made a modest payment to the limited partnership, whose investors received substantially less than they would have received had they approved the $100 million-plus purchase offer in 1989.

Nonetheless, and despite the convoluted financial machinations in the decades after the renovation began, the Press Club retained its highly valuable lease at $1 per year for the 13th and 14th floors of the building plus the cost of its share of the building's taxes and certain other expenses, through 2078.

After nearly four-score years in the real estate business, the National Press Club and its spin-off building corporation were out of the building ownership business in Washington. Quadrangle Management became owner and manager of the press building, and the National Press Club became just another tenant in the building it once controlled. Even so, its long-term lease through the bulk of the 21st century assured it of a spacious home in a prime neighborhood – still just two blocks from the White House and a 10-minute cab ride to Capitol Hill.

Seth Payne led a fundraising mission for the restoration of the historic mats, shown here with Club President Sonja Hillgren in 1996. (Photo by John Metelsky)

Left: Atrium view of the National Press Building in 1985. News shops on top, commercial shops on bottom.

Below: Rick Zimmerman with first batch of selected offset plates.

Left: Paul Means, Club archivist, former entertainment chairman and first non-voting board member, emceeing tribute to Frank Holeman in 1996. Right: The National Press Building faces north, so the Greek Goddess carved above the Fox Arch receives the light of day just once a year during a few days of June. The rest of the year she is in the shade. (Photo by Stan Jennings)

Actor George Clooney and Sen. Barack Obama join forces at a Newsmaker on human rights abuses in Darfur, Sudan, on April 27, 2006. (Photo by Christy Bowe)

Iranian President Mahmoud Ahmadinejad became the first speaker at a Club luncheon to appear by two-way satellite connection. At the head table listening to him are from left, Club President Jerry Zremski; Kaveh Afrashiabi, a Bentley College professor; Clarence Page of the Chicago Tribune*; Donna Leinwand of* USA Today*; Hiroki Sugita of the Kyoda News Agency; Ken Mellgren of the Associated Press and Lucie Morillon of Reporters Without Borders.*

CHAPTER EIGHT

INTO THE 21ST CENTURY

"The Club has a rich tradition because of its physical place, but the Club of the future will have to create a virtual presence."
> – Bill McCarren, who became Club general manager in 2007

It's Monday, Sept. 24, 2007. Outside the front door of the National Press Building, protesters wave signs saying, "Israel is on the Map to Stay," "Iran Funds Islamic Jihad," and "Strong Sanctions Against Iran Now."

Inside the Club, President Jerry Zremski of the *Buffalo News* puts the final touches on the luncheon that is causing the protest. Iran's president, Mahmoud Ahmadinejad, is scheduled to appear in just a few minutes. But unlike the thousands of other speakers who have appeared at Club luncheons for more than 70 years, the Iranian president will not be there in person.

The United States government will not allow Ahmadinejad to visit Washington. His views on eradicating Israel, his support of terrorists throughout the Middle East and his threat to create a nuclear weapon have made him anathema to Americans. Many inside and out of the government warn that war with Iran may be inevitable.

That makes Ahmadinejad news.

For three months, Zremski negotiated with the Iranian government and worked with the Club's new Broadcast Operation Center to arrange for this teleconference. He visited the Iranian ambassador in New York. Ahmadinejad was scheduled to visit the U.N. Would he speak to the Club and take questions by VideoLink?

Everything came together just four days before the event.

"We've never done one like this," Zremski said, "hosting a luncheon with the head of a country that does not have diplomatic relations with the United States."

To explain why the Club has invited someone many people consider a terrorist, Zremski issues a press release saying, "Here at the National Press Club, it's our job to facilitate the news – to help bring newsmakers and journalists together. That's exactly what we're doing here."

In front of two large video screens, a traditional head table made up of noted journalists such as Fox News' Greta Van Susteren, Chicago Tribune columnist Clarence Page and Newsweek's Eleanor Clift waits for the image of the Iranian leader to appear. About 20 TV cameras line the back and sides of the ballroom.

Ten minutes behind schedule, Ahmadinejad pops onto the screen from a U.N. studio. He launches into a rambling speech with long quotations from the Koran. He dodges Zremski's questions about floggings and imprisonment of students, journalists and women. "People in Iran are very joyous, happy people," he exclaims. "They are free in expressing what they think."

If Americans wondered whether the Iranian president was a little weird, the luncheon removes all doubt. It was, as the Washington Post headlines the next day, "Mahmoud Ahmadinejad's Unreality Show."

⚜

Heads of state appearing by satellite? The Club has come a long way since President David Hess of Knight-Ridder Newspapers dedicated the renovated building in 1985. It has evolved into a financially sound, professional center for journalists – just as President

NPC member John Anderson gets a workout in the Club fitness center. (Photo by Christy Bowe)

Warren Rogers envisioned in the 1970s.

Yet, even as members and staff put final touches on plans for a gala centennial celebration on April 5, 2008, the Club still struggled to secure its role as the news business rapidly evolves with new technology.

It wasn't quite the same Club many long-time members remembered. The rowdy behavior and hard drinking of the "Front Page" brand of journalism that had made the Club sometimes a raucous and always amusing place had faded.

"You don't get the ne'er-do-wells in here as we used to get, and it's good for the people, but it's terrible for the Club," 1956 Club President Frank Holeman said in a 1991 oral history. "Here we are sitting in the card room. In the old days, there would be two games going right now, some of them left over from last night."

Instead of drinking heavily at lunch, some members walked through the lobby in their gym clothes on their way to the fitness center where trainer Terry Davis helped them run through exercise routines with treadmills and weights.

CBS News legend Walter Cronkite sniffed at the notion of a Club fitness center when he visited in the late 1990s. "Fitness center?" he exclaimed with a tone of disgust in his voice. "When I was a member here in 1948, we got fitness just one way." He bent his elbow bringing his fist to his mouth as though drinking at the bar. "Up down, up down."

Free tacos were offered in the Reliable Source to attract members on Friday nights, and 2001 Club President Dick Ryan brought in a popcorn machine on other nights to add to the bar's ambiance. The image of chain-smoking reporters disappeared as smoking was banned from the Club, restricted for a while to the bar and Truman Lounge and then banished altogether under a District of Columbia mandate that took effect Jan. 1, 2007.

Perhaps nothing signified the changing of the guard more than the saga of Phryne.

In 1932, the Brazilian embassy donated a 4 x 6 foot painting of a reclining nude by Brazilian artist Antonio Parreiras. It depicted a Greek courtesan known as Phryne, who lay there with a come-hither expression on her face. It was hung in the Main Lounge over the entryway to the bar that connects with the ballroom. "The men loved her," one longtime member said. "If they were having trouble with their wives and girlfriends, they always had Phryne."

By 1982 when demolition began on rebuilding the Club, Phryne was in a sad state. Decades of cigarette and cigar smoke, dust and age faded her vibrant colors. She was stored away with an art conservator. When the renovated club opened, Phryne was not among the new décor. The Club had merged with the Washington Press Club. The women who had battled for so long to gain entry to the Club, wanted nothing to do with Phryne. To many of them, the painting was demeaning and insulting. The Club might as well put up a Confederate flag as hang a depiction of a concubine. The lounge was now used for commercial purposes. Such a painting would not fit well with press conferences and forums.

But Phryne's supporters were not deterred, even by the price tag of restoring the painting. In 1994, a group led by Austin Kiplinger, John Cosgrove and Donald Larrabee formed the Fine Arts Committee of the Silver Owls and asked the Board of Governors if they could take possession of Phryne. Many board members assumed that the committee would not raise the money and that would be the last they would hear about it. But by 1998, the painting was restored in its original vibrant colors. When it was displayed in the Club during the 90th birthday celebration, 90-year-old Sen. Strom Thurmond, who had a reputation as a lady's man, saw her and exclaimed, "Is she still alive?" The committee offered it back to the Club if it would again be hung in the Main Lounge – by then renamed the Holeman Lounge after Frank Holeman. By a decisive nine-to-two vote, the Board voted no.

The Fine Arts Committee lent Phryne to the Metropolitan Club for several years before giving up on returning the painting to the Club. The committee put Phryne up for auction. It was purchased for $80,000 by an anonymous Brazilian. Much of that money went to the library's discretionary fund. No one knows exactly where she is now, but Phryne is not in the Club.

Silver Owls raise a toast to Phryne, the controversial nude removed from the Club lounge in 1982. Owls purchased Phryne, had it restored and lent it to the Metropolitan Club before selling it in 2005 and giving the proceeds to the NPC Archives. From left, Bruce Perkins, John Cosgrove, Austin Kiplinger, Don Larrabee, Jim Corrigan, Warren Rogers, and Todd Kiplinger.

Other art far more valuable than Phryne adorned the renovated clubhouse. An original Norman Rockwell, entitled "Visit to a Country Editor," hangs at the entrance to the Reliable Source Bar and Grill. Rockwell painted it in 1946 for the Saturday Evening Post. It depicts the newsroom of the Monroe County Appeal in Paris, Mo., on a typical Thursday just before it went to press. Shown walking into the newsroom, pipe in mouth and portfolio in hand, is Norman Rockwell himself.

In the Fourth Estate Dining Room hangs an original N.C. Wyeth painting entitled "Buckboard." It shows a bunch of mean-looking hombres riding in a wagon apparently transporting a prisoner whose hands are tied. Wyeth was one of the leading illustrators of his day and father of renowned artist Andrew Wyeth. But how this painting made it to the Club is lost to history.

While not thought of as art when they were produced, front pages of newspapers decorate the Club's lobbies, both on the 13th and 14th floors. On the 13th floor are the fiber matrices, or "mats" used for the rotary presses to print newspapers. From its earliest days, the Club collected them. They were stained, lacquered and imbedded in the walls. They made the transition from one Clubhouse to the next. When the restored Club opened in 1985, the mats were there, but the stain had made even the headlines almost unreadable.

Seth Payne of McGraw-Hill proposed in 1994 that the Club hire an art restorer to painstakingly remove the stain and bring the words of those long-forgotten headlines back to life. Payne and member Stan Jennings organized a fund-raising drive, and by 1996, the work was done.

But these front pages ended in the 1960s. Newspapers were no longer produced on fiber matrices, but on offset plates. At the same time the Club held a reception to thank the donors for the mat restoration, Club member Richard Zimmerman of the *Cleveland Plain Dealer* unveiled a new collection of historic offset plates that now line the 14th floor lobby, the Reliable Source restaurant and the Truman Lounge. The one that draws the most attention is from a small Texas paper, *The McGregor Mirror and Crawford Sun*, that best exemplifies how all news is local. Its headline: "Local Rancher George W. Bush Elected as Nation's 43rd President."

Keeping the Club viable hasn't come easily. Around the world, press clubs closed their doors in the late 20th century when faced with dwindling memberships and rising costs. Downtown clubs in general have suffered from the flight to the suburbs. But the National Press Club has three assets that have kept it alive and vital.

First, because it built the building, the Club pays minimal rent. Even after losing control of the building in 2004, the Club secured a $1-a-year lease until 2078. Second, it can draw its membership from a greater population of journalists and news sources than most any other city in the world. And third, Washington needs a place to serve as a conduit between the news media and those who have something to say.

But the Club had never been a great money maker. Just breaking even was considered a success, even in the economically fat years of the late 1980s. In 1990, President Judy Grande of the *Cleveland Plain Dealer* oversaw the rebuilding of the First Amendment Lounge to enclose the outdoor terrace to enhance the value of that room. She closed a deal with the Harvard Club, begun by President Peter Holmes of the *Washington Times* the year before, to generate more revenue for the Club by subletting a dining room. The deal never produced the promised revenue and proved unpopular with Press Club members before it was terminated.

During the 1991-92 recession, the Club dangled in a precarious financial position as catering revenue dropped and membership was squeezed by downsizing news organizations.

The year 1992 was painful for the board. Through the leadership of Kathryn Kahler of the Newhouse News Service, who had returned to the board after her presidency to serve as chairwoman, Vice President Clayton Boyce of the KRT News Service, Treasurer Monroe "Bud" Karmin of Bloomberg Business News and President Greg Spears of Knight-Ridder Newspapers, the board dismissed manager Harry Bodaan, reorganized the Club's management and made the difficult cost cutting necessary to maintain solvency. The Club's labor union agreed to forego a pay raise for a year, and the board put new emphasis on building membership, reversing a decade-long slide.

The new general manager, Bill Vose, and Director of Operations John Bloom found ways to combine the business of the Club and the National Press Building to realize significant savings and new revenue sources. Their work was so successful that the Club was able to forego an annual dues increase, reduced dues for younger members in 1995 and gave the staff a bonus to make up for some of the foregone wage increase.

New services for members were added to the library, and the Fourth Estate restaurant was reopened for dinner service. A reserve fund was established to weather the next recession. By the late 1990s, the Club was in a predicament not seen in any member's memory – how to avoid paying taxes on the profits. Many members were surprised to learn the Club was a for-profit corporation.

General Manager John Bloom transformed the Club's business model to keep it viable in the 21st century. (Photo by Marshall Cohen)

But the new economic model for the Club required that the Holeman Lounge be used mostly as a revenue-generating room for catering business, not as the relaxing, overstuffed sofa retreat it had been for decades. The Board resisted repeated efforts by long-time members to reserve the lounge for members.

To make the 14th floor feel more like a clubhouse, the Board undertook a major renovation, removing the wall between the Reliable Source Bar and Grill and the Truman Lounge and refurbishing both.

Walk into the president's office in 1996, and one would likely see President Sonja Hillgren of the *Farm Journal* conferring with board members about shades of carpeting or window treatments. Hillgren said the Club had become a hodge-podge of decorating styles, and she insisted that an interior decorator be hired.

Comedian Al Franken humored President Sonja Hillgren and others at an Oct. 11, 1996, address. (Photo by Art Garrison)

With all these changes going on behind the scenes, the Club maintained its high-profile public face.

In 1987, Club President Andrew Mollison of Cox Newspapers was immersed in finding permanent financing for the building. He was also one of the catalysts who helped raise $650,000 for the Washington Press Club Foundation to complete a professional oral history of 59 pioneer women journalists, a project headed by former Washington Press Club President Peggy Simpson of *Ms Magazine*.

Mollison also recalls with pride that he had two Japanese prime ministers speak at the Club during his administration.

"My record was perfect," he quipped. "Both had to resign in disgrace."

Clayton Boyce of KRT News Service devoted his administration in 1993 to rebuilding the Club's management team. But the highlight of his year was the appearance of Palestinian Liberation Organization leader Yasser Arafat, who for decades had been denied permission to travel to Washington. On the day after he signed an historic peace agreement with Israeli Prime Minister Yitzak Rabin on the White House lawn, Arafat addressed the Club.

Boyce asked him what he thought was a serious question.

"Now that you have made peace with the Israelis," Boyce said, "who do you consider your enemy?"

A regular TV show co-produced by the NPC and George Washington University featured television veteran Marvin Kalb (left) shown here with panelist Donna Shalala, Secretary of Health and Human Services, Sen. Alan K. Simpson of Wyoming and White House Budget Director Robert Rubin at the show's 1994 debut.

Arafat thought for just one second, and with his eyes twinkling under his checkered kaffiyeh, he shot back, "You are."

Boyce was speechless for a moment as the audience laughed.

"Well, you're the one asking the questions," Arafat said.

Enduring far longer than the 1993 PLO-Israeli peace agreement has been "The Kalb Report." In 1994, Club President Gil Klein of the Media General News Service wanted the Club to produce a regular broadcast series. At the same time, former CBS News correspondent Marvin Kalb was taking a year's sabbatical from Harvard to teach

Marvin Kalb, host of the monthly Kalb Report at the Club, is a senior fellow at the Joan Shorenstein Center on The Press, Politics, and Public Policy in the Kennedy School of Government at Harvard University. Produced in the Club's ballroom, Kalb hosted 58 of the public affairs programs from 1994 through 2007. (Photo by Christy Bowe)

Defense Secretary Donald Rumsfeld defends strategy in the War in Iraq during a "Kalb Report" show the Club co-sponsored with the American Society of Newspaper Editors in 2002. (Photo by Christy Bowe)

at George Washington University. Michael Freedman, GW's public affairs director at the time, wanted a broadcast outlet to feature Kalb.

Club member Jan DuPlane introduced Klein to Freedman. "The Kalb Report" was born.

As a former CBS correspondent – the last one hired by news legend Edward R. Murrow – and a thoughtful scholar of the news media, Kalb had the stature to draw prominent guests. The premier show on Sept. 29, 1994, was a blockbuster with Kalb juggling 11 panelists ranging from civil rights leader Jesse Jackson to White House Budget Director Robert Rubin, Wyoming Sen. Alan Simpson, Health and Human Services Secretary Donna Shalala and Club members David Broder of the *Washington Post*, Carl Leubsdorf of the *Dallas Morning News* and Susan Page of *USA Today*. In more than 50 shows that followed, Kalb probed presidential campaign reporting, war correspondence, talk show democracy, the transformation of the news business and journalism ethics. He has gone one-on-one with Walter Cronkite, Ted Koppel, Donald Rumsfeld, Hillary Clinton, Roger Ailes and Dan Rather.

After 13 years, shows still pack the ballroom with Club members and GW students, making it the Club's leading professional affairs event. In 2006, the Club honored Kalb with its Fourth Estate Award for lifetime achievement in journalism.

The Club held cigar nights in the mid-1990s to raise money for the scholarship fund. For a while, they were among the Club's most profitable and entertaining events. They raised thousands of dollars by attracting such Washington notables as Supreme Court justices Clarence Thomas and Antonin Scalia, Sen. Conrad Burns, political satirist Mark Russell, and John McLaughlin of the McLaughlin Group. In a dinner and auction organized by Clayton Boyce, one bidding match ran up the price of a box of cigars to $1,700.

"I can remember when every dinner at the National Press Club was a cigar dinner," Russell quipped, referring to the days when it was a men's club.

But it was Justice Thomas, once caught in the news media's crosshairs during his confirmation hearing, to whom the best line is attributed: "Any time I can sit in the press' living room and blow smoke, I'm glad to do it."

※◎◎※

With the emergence of the Internet, the Club again wrestled with defining a journalist. In 1993, Carl Malamud, founder of the Internet Multicasting Service, introduced the Internet to the Club at a forum in the ballroom. Displayed on a big screen, the service was slow and often unresponsive. But journalists got the idea that this was something revolutionary. Somehow – seemingly like magic – one could type something into a computer in Washington and retrieve information from a library in Australia. The potential for journalism research was immediately obvious. Everyone was saying the Club had to become a cyber station, whatever that was. The impact the Internet would have on the news business was far less clear.

Anyone could set himself up as an online journalist, and anyone did. Did that mean online journalists were on an equal footing with professional reporters who worked for a newspaper company, a television network or a radio news service?

In 1998, President Doug Harbrecht of *Business Week* unwittingly set himself up as the lightning rod for this issue. He invited Matt Drudge, founder and chief contributor for the online *Drudge Report,* to be a luncheon speaker.

"It set off a firestorm – first when traditional journalists were outraged that Drudge from the online world was invited to speak," Harbrecht said. "Then from Drudge fans, conservatives and online-denizens who felt Drudge wasn't given the respect and fairness he deserved."

Harbrecht withstood a petition drive among members demanding that the luncheon be canceled. Drudge showed up in his signature fedora and parried tough questions fired at him from the audience and Harbrecht.

This was the first time that online bloggers like Drudge were engaged by traditional print and broadcast journalists in a full and frank discussion of standards, fairness and efficacy, Harbrecht said. "You can say online 'won' and continues to win," Harbrecht said. "But Drudge said things at that lunch that will always be quoted whenever he is in the news, like 'It's okay to be right 60 percent of the time.'"

To keep long-time members engaged, the Club created the Silver Owls in 1985 for people who had been members for at least 25 years. After 50 years, they became Golden Owls.

Owlhood was the brainchild of Bernie Goodrich, a one-time *Washington Star* reporter who later went into public relations. As the building was under construction, he noticed a lot of the older members weren't showing up. President David Hess of Knight-Ridder Newspapers gave his blessing on the new organization that elected Goodrich its first chairman – or Head Hoot – and held its first hoot on May 22, 1986.

"Distancing ourselves from any form of senior citizens, we're really ol' owls, just like that bird in our logo," said former President Frank Holeman, a charter Silver Owl member. More than 20 years later, the Owls still are a mainstay of the Club as they hold their hoots and preserve the Club's heritage.

But in early 2001, a stark reality hit the Board. The Club had more members over 80 than under 30. Certainly the Club had always recruited members when they arrived in Washington usually at the prime of their careers, and they stayed to the end. Club membership was aging. The Board decided it had to do more to draw younger members. For years it had had offered a less expensive under-35 membership category. Now it created a new under-30 category with dues 60 percent lower than full membership. The thinking, Membership Director Julie Schoo told the Board, was that if a member could be recruited and kept for three years, he or she likely would be a member for life.

By 2007, the Club had a thriving Young Members Committee that worked almost as a club within a club. Issuing its own online biweekly newsletter – the Club Buzz – the committee organized events for play and work. "Breakfast with Champions" and "Cocktails with Champions" brought well known senior journalists like CNN's Bill Schneider, Hearst's Helen Tomas and the *Washington Post's* Dana Milbank to talk with younger journalists about their craft. With the International Correspondents Committee, the Young Members arranged gatherings at the Swedish and Finnish embassies and with reporters from the Russian state news agency. Panels on magazine writing and travel writing were juxtaposed with a wine tour of Virginia vineyards.

"We're building camaraderie among a core group of people," said committee chairwoman Kate Hunter of Congressional Quarterly.

NPC Silver Owls May 29, 1992. Frances Hardin purrs WWII favorite "Lilli Marlene" while honky tonk piano player Les Karr tickles the ivories. (NPC photo by John Metelsky)

Younger members had reached a critical mass so that they were a thriving part of the Club, making it a truly multi-generational organization.

⊰≼ ⊘⁄≻

Sept. 11, 2001. A day that will live in infamy, just like Dec. 7, 1941. Club President Dick Ryan of the *Detroit News* was at a press breakfast hosted by the *Christian Science Monitor* at the St. Regis Hotel on 16th Street with about 25 other reporters. Democratic strategists James Carville, Stan Greenberg and Robert Shrum told reporters that President Bush would face a tough re-election campaign because his poll numbers already were so low. Just as the breakfast broke up, Shrum answered a cell phone call and exclaimed, "A plane has just crashed into the World Trade Center." Reporters left quickly.

As Ryan and former President Gil Klein walked through Lafayette Park in front of the White House on their way back to the National Press Building, the skies were crystalline blue. The two reporters speculated on whether the crash could have been an accident, and if it wasn't, what did it mean? If they had walked that way just minutes later, they would have been overrun with people fleeing the White House. As they entered the press building lobby, Ryan looked up at the television monitors and saw the second plane crash into the World Trade Center. It was no accident. Both Ryan and Klein sped to their offices in time to hear about a plane crashing into the Pentagon. Washington was under attack.

In the National Press Club that morning, general manager John Bloom looked forward to a banner day. Every room was booked. That September was anticipated to be the highest grossing month in the Club's history. More than 500 people were attending events when the planes began to hit.

"I had (Club AV director) Howard Rothman put TVs all over the Club so people could see what was going on," Bloom recalled. "We were hearing all kinds of rumors about a bomb at the State Department and attacks on the Metro and that another plane was out there. I looked out the window, and it looked like one of those old monster movies with a crowd of frantic people running down the street.

"I got the staff together and said the best thing we can do is stay cool, keep the business going," Bloom said. "I said it was too dangerous to go outside. A couple of employees freaked out, and I said they could go home. I didn't want them here so upset. During the course of the day, we started closing down events, then the dining rooms. At 5 p.m., we closed the bar. I was the last person out."

2002 President John Aubuchon of Maryland Public Television pushed the Club to do more to promote freedom of the press.

Meanwhile Ryan, like all Washington reporters, worked all day reporting the news. By the time he finished, he said, the Club was closed. He had nothing to do but go home. "The streets were eerily quiet."

Business in the Club plummeted in the weeks after the attack. People were afraid to come to Washington. With all the talk of dirty bombs, people did not want to be so close to the White House. Bloom told the Board that major cutbacks had to be made. The Fourth Estate dining room was closed in the evenings; staff hours cut back. "I told the Board to go into emergency mode," Bloom said. But the Club never closed, not even on the day after the attack.

"It was touch and go for the Club," Ryan said. "But the year ended up okay."

Freelance writer Sheila Cherry was sworn in by Washington Mayor Anthony Williams in 2004 to be the first African-American president of the Club. Master of Ceremonies Aram Bakshian, left, applauds.

Still, a somber mood hung over the Club. Antics such as actress Goldie Hawn giving Ryan a big smooch after he presented her with a Club mug and former professional wrestler and Minnesota Gov. Jesse Ventura mugging for 35 TV cameras gave way to more sober luncheons. When John Aubuchon of Maryland Public Television was inaugurated as the next president in January 2002, he featured New York City firefighters and police officers at an inaugural party that for the only time in anyone's memory did not produce a laugh.

In 2004, the Club passed another milestone by inaugurating freelance writer Sheila Cherry as the first African-American Club president. Contrary to the fracas over admitting Louis Lautier as the first black member 48 years earlier, Cherry's inaugural, with District of Columbia Mayor Anthony Williams swearing her in, was a joyous affair.

"Serving as president of the NPC was an honor and a privilege for me, as it would be for any journalist," Cherry said. "To be perfectly frank, I would greatly welcome the day when the fact that I happened to be African American is merely an interesting footnote."

For Cherry, the biggest event of her administration was hosting 10 heads of state at the same time when an Eastern European delegation of new and anticipated NATO members made the Club their first stop after meeting with President Bush.

For 15 years, Club manager John Bloom's job was to grow the Club's business without undermining its character and traditions. That's no easy task. Getting more revenue out of the same rooms without anyone noticing is a magician's act that Bloom performed with such dexterity that every president and every Board came up with new ideas for spending money. Bloom would find it.

Club president Rick Dunham holds the NHL Stanley Cup Trophy during a luncheon speech by NHL Commissioner Gary Bettman in 2005.

"The Club has to change with the times," Bloom said. "We weren't making it on memberships. The Board realized we needed other revenue streams that were not intrusive to the Club. We went with more press conferences. We charged for the room, the breakfast, the microphones, the Web casting, the satellite feeds."

From 1995 to 2006, he said, revenue from catering grew by 25 percent a year. The Club's revenue went from $4 million in 1992 to $12 million in 2007. But the growth in catering could not be sustained much longer. The Club required some other revenue source.

Bloom eyed an idea proposed by the Club's long-range planning committee chaired by former President Larry Lipman of the *Palm Beach Post*. It called for the Club to create a broadcast studio.

"Howard (Rothman) and I saw that in the press conference business that was the missing piece of the puzzle," Bloom said. "Jerry (Zremski, the treasurer) and Rick (Dunham, the president) greased the skids with the board. We pitched it and gave the

Board three weeks to decide. We built it in less than a year."

That makes the process sound easier than it actually was. Rick Dunham of *Business Week* said Bloom came to him with the idea during Dunham's first week as president. "It became one of the 'musts' of my presidency," he said. "I wanted it done the sooner the better, and we cut the ribbon on the last hour of my presidency." The first job was to secure the lease for the only space in the building that had ceilings high enough for a broadcast studio. Then the Club had to rip out everything that was there and rebuild it with a state-of-the-art broadcasting and editing equipment.

"We understood from the start that it was a gamble, but felt it worth the risk because even if it didn't pan out, we had minimized the Club's financial liability and were strong enough to withstand failure," said former Club President Jonathan Salant of Bloomberg.

"Frankly, in many ways, it was a nerve-wracking accomplishment," said 2007 President Zremski of the *Buffalo News*. "First we had to ask the hard questions: What would be the member benefit? What is the potential financial reward – and what are the risks? What is the competition like? And what if we don't do this?"

Bloom and Rothman provided answers that calmed their worries. Rothman became an evangelist for the project, seeing big profits for the Club. Still, a shiver ran through the Board of Governors when the final cost of building the Broadcast Operation Center was more than $2 million, double the projection.

Club president Rick Dunham cuts the ribbon opening the new Broadcast Operations Center in January 2006 as Secretary Sylvia Smith, Treasurer Jerry Zremski, and Vice President Jonathan Salant watch. (Photo by Marshall Cohen)

Howard Rothman, director of multimedia services, works with Broadcast Operations Center Manager Tiina Kreek to prepare a televised press conference in 2007. (Photo by Christy Bowe)

"You have no idea how much nervousness and lost sleep this cost me," Zremski said. "But, thankfully, the BOC has proved to be worth every penny."

As promised, the Broadcast Center enhanced the Club's press conference business. After making a presentation in the Club, many speakers come down to the studio where they do one-on-one interviews. As the Toyota press conference mentioned in chapter one showed, the Center can coordinate news events across the country and around the world. Also, the Club developed training programs to help print journalists become comfortable with broadcast reporting for what is rapidly becoming a multimedia business.

The Broadcast Center was expected to do $2 million worth of business in 2008 and grow from there, Bloom said, just before retiring in July 2007.

"What was important in John Bloom's era was that he was pro-active to changes in journalism," Dunham said. "He created an economic model where the Club could not just survive but thrive when membership was declining and the journalism business was in turmoil."

It is nothing short of amazing that the National Press Club has lasted so long – long past its original purpose of providing a watering hole for reporters. Consider for a moment that it depends on the volunteer labor of journalists, who are working in a highly competitive, rapidly changing and oftentimes all-consuming profession. These volunteers not only maintain the active professional programs but also become knowledgeable in Club finances, management, labor negotiations, restaurant and bar business and membership recruitment. Even more amazing is that volunteers built the largest private office building in Washington at the time and rebuilt it in the teeth of cutthroat downtown commercial real estate competition. Board members have wrestled with city bureaucrats and international financiers.

Why do they do it?

For many presidents, perhaps it has to do with the thrill of walking into the ballroom with some of the greatest actors on the world stage. For one year, they are movers and shakers in the nation's capital. But it's more than that. Visitors from press clubs in Europe and Asia are amazed at the size of the National Press Club and the scope of its programs. Across the nation and around the world, people have heard of it. Nowhere else in the world is there a club run by journalists – not by governments or companies – that offers as much as the National Press Club. Few people get to be part of something that is not only the best in the world, but – as Eric Sevareid said – "absolutely bursting with irreverence."

National Press Club, June 1, 1982 with legendary TV commentator Eric Sevareid who said the Club was "absolutely bursting with irreverence." (Photo by John Metelsky)

As the Club enters its second 100 years, its leaders planned to emphasize the National in the National Press Club name. Taking advantage of Internet Web streaming technology, events at the Club can be instantly available everywhere. Club services are promoted to journalism schools so that professors can download video from luncheons, newsmakers, press conferences and professional affairs events for use in their classes.

Manager Bill McCarren, who took office in July 2007, comes from an entirely different background from the Club's past professional managers. Harry Bodaan came from restaurant management. Bill Vose from commercial real estate development. John Bloom from hotel and club management. McCarren is a journalism business entrepreneur who founded U.S. Newswire in 1986 and was president of Medialink Public Affairs when he accepted the job as NPC general manager. He is also the first professional manager who was a longtime Club member. In 2005 he received the Club's Berny Krug Award as an outstanding volunteer.

McCarren's mission is to use the brand name and reputation of the Club to expand it worldwide on the Internet.

"The Club has a rich tradition because of its physical place, but the Club of the future will have to create a virtual presence," McCarren said. "We see this as a way to attract members from around the world."

To keep growing, the Club needs a revenue-producing online presence consistent with its mission, he said. A virtual Club with some buzz will attract new members. He sees the Club's mentoring program expanded to young journalists nationwide. The virtual Club can keep journalists up on the changing role of the news business and the

Ways and Means Committee Chairman Rep. Charles Rangel, (D-NY), shares a pre-luncheon moment with President Jerry Zremski and National Urban League president Mark Morial on April 17, 2007. (Photo by Rex Stucky)

job market. What used to happen around the bar and in the library a few years ago will be happening online.

And the Club has a duty to inform a skeptical public about the importance of journalism in defending democracy.

"A recent Pew poll found that 50 percent of high school students think it is wrong for the press to publish stories against the wishes of the president," McCarren said. "So we have a problem with the public right now and we have a bigger problem coming down the road."

Bill McCarren, who took over as general manager in July 2007, plans to expand the Club internationally through the Internet. (Photo by Darlene Shields)

It's Friday, Nov. 9, 2007 on the corner of 14th and F streets, the place where it all began 100 years ago. If Graham Nichol and James Hay suddenly reappeared here today to reenact their chance meeting of February 1908, they would recognize the Willard Hotel across the street, but nothing else. Certainly not the National Press Building that requires one to lean way back to see the top where the Club perches.

If they strolled through the Club with its flat-screen, electronic signs, its library full of computers, people taking blogging classes and TV reporters scurrying through pulling carts full of cameras, they would be astounded and amazed. A "virtual Club" connecting members worldwide? What nonsense.

Pianist Jack Matos plays a modern Jingle Bells for NPC revelers and guests from left to right: Kate Culpepper, Nick Kolakowski, Jack Oldfield, and Tara Butler at the Club's annual holiday party on Dec. 19, 2006. (Photo by Marshall Cohen)

But in one part of the Club, they would be quite comfortable. Hidden away back behind the Reliable Source Bar and Grill, where no one but Club members are allowed to enter, is the card room. On this day, as on most every Friday, about 10 or 11 members gather after lunch to play some poker.

"We're just a bunch of old reporters who like to swap stories about the people we knew and the events we saw," says regular Jerry Rosen. "We all like poker. Poker is an old newspaperman's game. Whoever heard of a press club without a poker game?"

One can almost hear the echo of Graham Nichol out there on the corner with James Hay in the bone-chilling air: "Hells bells, why don't we get up a press club?"

Marine Gen. Peter Pace, chairman of the Joint Chiefs of Staff, shares a light moment with a long-time friend and Club member Ivan Scott, center, and Speakers Committee member Ken Dalecki. Pace gave a luncheon update on the military situation in Iraq on Feb. 17, 2006. (Photo by Christy Bowe)

Sebastian Junger, author of "A Death in Belmont," left, and John Prendergast, author of "Not on Our Watch," right, enjoy an animated discussion with Club member Sandra Mertz during the 2007 Book Fair. (Photo by Marshall Cohen)

A record 10 prime ministers, including seven from former Communist countries, visited the Club on March 29, 2004, for a Newsmaker that drew some 300 attendees. (Photo by John Metelsky)

President Bill Clinton receives his membership card from NPC President Sonja Hillgren in 1996.

Club President Jack Cushman welcomes GOP presidential candidate George W. Bush and key advisors for a well-attended press conference in May 2000. From the left, former Secretary of State Henry Kissinger, Bush, Cushman, former chairman of the Joint Chiefs of Staff Colin Powell, former National Security Advisor Brent Scowcroft and former and future Secretary of Defense Donald Rumsfeld. (Photo by John Metelsky)

Actresses Lynda Carter, left, and Joan Collins meet with Motion Picture Association of America President Jack Valenti on Nov. 28, 2006 prior to their luncheon address on aging in America. (Photo by Marshall Cohen)

NPC President Jerry Zremski presents the "Crawlin' King Snake" trophy to Tony Snow, White House press secretary, who won the battle of the bands against CBS anchorman Bob Schieffer's band Honky Tonk Confidential at an NPC centennial fundraiser in 2007. (Photo by Marshall Cohen)

Elizabeth Dole needs a pen for guest book in 1984. President John Fogarty assists. (Photo by Stan Jennings)

Past President Frank Aukofer, Milwaukee Journal and his wife, Sharlene, were feisty competitors at the 1996 club chili cook-off. (Photo by Art Garrison)

Celebrants toast the new millennium in the Club ballroom. (Photo by Marshall Cohen)

Billionaire Ross Perot shakes hands with member George Embrey as 1991 NPC President Kay Kahler looks on. (NPC photo by John Metelsky)

Baseball legend "Iron Man" Cal Ripken Jr. chats with Chris Campo, left, guest of member John Fales, and Izzy Salant, son of former NPC President Jonathan Salant, April 13, 2007. (Photo by Marshall Cohen)

Club President Jonathan Salant holds the trophy for the divisional championship of the Metropolitan Media Softball League, which the NPC team won in 2006. (Photo by Marshall Cohen)

Former Club presidents, staff and other celebrants light candles on the NPC's 90th birthday cake on April 3, 1998. (Photo by Marshall Cohen)

Club President Monroe Karmin presents actress Sharon Stone with an NPC mug in 1995. (Photo by Marshall Cohen)

Supreme Court Associate Justice Clarence Thomas enjoys a smoke with members on cigar night in 1996. Clayton Boyce, club president in 1993, on left. (Photo by Marshall Cohen)

Sen. Hillary Clinton (D-NY) was a luncheon speaker on May 23, 2006. While seated with NPC President Jonathan Salant, someone shouted, "Will the president please stand up?" Someone whispered, "You, too, Jonathan," and the senator and president burst out laughing. (Photo by John Metelsky)

Club members Jennifer Michaels and Jim Wallace enjoy the Club's pool table. The pool and card room is the one place non-members can never go. (Photo by Marshall Cohen)

Jazz musician Wynton Marsalis autographs a luncheon ticket for Wes Pippert of the University of Missouri's Washington journalism program at his Oct. 20, 2005, appearance. (Photo by Marshall Cohen)

Comedian Whoopi Goldberg charmed members, guests and staff on April 7, 1997. Here she is with staffer Kate Goggin, who assisted the Speakers Committee in organizing many of the Club's trademark luncheons. (Photo by Christy Bowe)

Former CBS Anchor Walter Cronkite at the Club in 1997. (Photo by Marshall Cohen)

NATIONAL PRESS CLUB PRESIDENTS
1908 - 2007

1908	William P. Spurgeon	Washington Post
1910	Arthur J. Dodge	Kansas City Journal
1912	Frederick J. Haskin	Haskin Syndicate
1913	John T. Suter	Chicago Record Herald
1913	Oswald F. Schuette	Chicago Inter Ocean
1914	Frank B. Lord	Philadelphia Evening Bulletin
1916	Theodore Tiller	Washington Times
1917	Grafton S. Wilcox	Associated Press
1918	Gus J. Karger	Cincinnati Times-Star
1919	Earl Godwin	Washington Times
1920	Mark L. Goodwin	Dallas News
1921	Avery C. Marks Jr.	Washington Times
1922	Robert B. Armstrong	Los Angeles Times
1923	Carter Field	New York Tribune
1924	George F. Authier	New York World
1925	Henry L. Sweinhart	Havas News Agency
1926	Ulric Bell	Louisville Courier-Journal
1927	A.H. Kirchofer	Buffalo Evening News
1927	Louis L. Ludlow	Columbus Dispatch
1928	J. Fred Essary	Baltimore Sun
1929	Russell Kent	Birmingham News
1930	Norman W. Baxter	Washington Post
1931	Eugene S. Leggett	Detroit Free Press
1932	Bascom N. Timmons	Houston Chronicle
1933	Raymond P. Brandt	St. Louis Post-Dispatch
1934	William C. Murphy Jr.	Philadelphia Public Ledger
1934	Marke Foote	Booth Newspapers
1935	Marke Foote	Booth Newspapers
1936	George W. Stimpson	Houston Post
1937	Charles O. Gridley	Denver Post
1938	Harold Brayman	Philadelphia Public Ledger
1939	Arthur Hachten	International News Service
1940	Richard L. Wilson	Des Moines Register and Tribune
1941	Melbourne Christerson	Associated Press
1942	Clifford A. Prevost	Detroit Free Press
1943	Felix T. Cotten	International News Service
1944	Sam A. O'Neal	Chicago Sun
1945	Edward Jamieson	Houston Chronicle
1946	Paul Wooton	New Orleans Times Picayune
1947	Warren B. Francis	Los Angeles Times
1948	Joseph H. Short Jr.	Baltimore Sun
1949	John C. O'Brien	Philadelphia Inquirer
1950	Radford E. Mobley	Knight Newspapers
1951	Carson F. Lyman	US News & World Report
1952	Truman T. Felt	Miami Daily News
1953	Theodore F. Koop	CBS Radio
1954	Ernest B. Vaccaro	Associated Press
1955	Lucian C. Warren	Buffalo Courier-Express
1956	Frank Holeman	New York Daily News
1957	Ben J. Grant	US News & World Report
1958	John V. Horner	Washington Star

1959	William H. Lawrence	New York Times
1960	Ed Edstrom	Hearst Newspapers
1961	John P. Cosgrove	Broadcasting Publications
1962	George Cullen	Bureau of National Affairs
1963	Bryson Rash	NBC
1964	Joseph A. Dear	Dear Publications
1965	William M. Blair	New York Times
1966	Windsor P. Booth	National Geographic
1967	L. David LeRoy	US News & World Report
1968	Allan W. Cromley	Daily Oklahoman & Oklahoma City Times
1969	John W. Heffernan	Reuters
1970	Michael Hudoba	Sports Afield
1971	Vernon Louviere	Nation's Business
1972	Warren Rogers	Chicago Tribune-New York News Syndicate
1973	Donald R. Larrabee	Griffin Larrabee News Service
1974	Clyde LaMotte	LaMotte News Service
1974	Kenneth Scheibel	Washington Bureau News
1975	William Broom	Ridder Publications
1976	Robert Ames Alden	Washington Post
1977	Robert E. Farrell	McGraw-Hill
1978	Frank A. Aukofer	Milwaukee Journal
1979	Arthur E. Wiese	Houston Post
1980	Drew Von Bergen	United Press International
1981	Joseph R. Slevin	Washington Bond Report
1982	Vivian Vahlberg	Daily Oklahoman
1983	Don Byrne	Traffic World
1984	John R. Fogarty	San Francisco Chronicle
1985	David W. Hess	Knight-Ridder Newspapers
1986	Mary Kay Quinlan	Gannett News Service
1987	Andrew Mollison	Cox Newspapers
1988	Lee Roderick	Scripps League
1989	Peter A. Holmes	Washington Times
1990	Judy Grande	The Plain Dealer
1991	Kathryn S. Kahler	Newhouse News Service
1992	Gregory Spears	Knight-Ridder Newspapers
1993	Clayton Boyce	Knight-Ridder Tribune News Service
1994	Gilbert F. Klein Jr.	Media General News Service
1995	Monroe W. Karmin	Bloomberg Business News
1996	Sonja Hillgren	Farm Journal
1997	Richard Sammon	Congressional Quarterly
1998	Doug Harbrecht	Business Week
1999	Larry Lipman	Palm Beach Post
2000	John H. Cushman Jr.	New York Times
2001	Richard Ryan	Detroit News
2002	John Aubuchon	News Night Maryland, Maryland Public Television
2003	Tammy Lytle	Orlando Sentinel
2004	Sheila R. Cherry	Bureau of National Affairs
2005	Richard Dunham	Business Week
2006	Jonathan Salant	Bloomberg
2007	Jerry Zremski	Buffalo News

WASHINGTON PRESS CLUB PRESIDENTS
1919 - 1984

1919	Lily Lykes Shepard	New York Tribune
1920	Cora Rigby	Christian Science Monitor
1928	Sallie Pickett	Washington Star
1929	Ruth Jones	Washington Star
1931	Martha Strayer	Washington Daily News
1933	Genevieve Forbes Herrick	Chicago Tribune
1935	Winifred Mallon	New York Times
1936	Mary Hornaday	Christian Science Monitor
1937	Doris Fleeson	New York Daily News
1938	Hope Ridings Miller	Washington Post
1939	Ruby Black	United Press
1940	Helen Essary	Washington Times-Herald
1941	Esther Van Wagoner Tufty	Michigan News Bureau
1942	Christine Sadler	Washington Post
1943	May Craig	Portland (ME) Times Herald
1944	Edith Gaylord	Associated Press
1945	Bess Furman	New York Times
1946	Alice Rogers Hager	Skyways Magazine
1947	Ruth Cowan	Associated Press
1948	Dorothy E. Williams	United Press
1949	Jane Stafford	Science Service
1950	Ruth Montgomery	New York Daily News
1951	Josephine Riley	Christian Science Monitor
1952	Marie Sauer	Washington Post
1953	Hazel Markel	Mutual Broadcasting and Washington Daily News
1954	Liz Carpenter	Southwestern Newspapers
1955	Helen Hill Miller	Special Writer
1956	Alice Frein Johnson	Seattle Times
1957	Gladys T. Montgomery	McGraw-Hill
1958	Lee Walsh	Washington Star
1959	Helen Thomas	United Press International
1960	Frances L. Lewine	Associated Press
1961	Bonnie Angelo	Newsday
1962	Patty Cavin	NBC
1963	Elsie Carper	Washington Post
1964	Miriam Ottenberg	Washington Star
1965	Mary Gallagher	Cincinnati Enquirer
1966	Eve Edstrom	Washington Post
1967	Gerry Van der Heuvel	Newhouse News Service
1968	Margaret Kilgore	United Press International
1969	Marjorie Hunter	New York Times
1970	Louise Hutchinson	Chicago Tribune
1971	Vera Glaser	Knight Newspapers
1972	Mary Lou Beatty	Washington Post
1973	Wauhillau La Hay	Scripps-Howard Newspapers
1974	Ron Sarro	Washington Star
1975	Peggy Simpson	Associated Press
1976	Ellen Wadley	CBS News
1977	William J. Eaton	Los Angeles Times
1978	Marguerite H. Sullivan	Copley News Service
1979	Toni House	Washington Star
1980	Ann McFeatters	Scripps-Howard Newspapers
1981	Carol R. Richards	Gannett News Service
1982	Miles Benson	Newhouse News Service
1983	Betty Anne Williams	Associated Press
1984	Susan Garland	Newhouse News Service

FOURTH ESTATE AWARD WINNERS

Edmund Burke said there were Three Estates in Parliament; but, in the Reporters' Gallery yonder, there sat a Fourth Estate more important far than they all. It is not a figure of speech, or witty saying; it is a literal fact—very momentous to us in these times.

The National Press Club confers the annual Fourth Estate Award on the person, who in the judgment of the NPC Board of Governors, has achieved distinction for a lifetime of contributions ot American journalism.

1973	Walter Cronkite, CBS News
1974	James Reston, *New York Times*
1975	Richard Strout, *Christian Science Monitor & New Republic*
1976	John S. Knight, Knight-Ridder Newspapers
1977	Herb Block, *The Washington Post*
1978	Vermont Royster, *Wall Street Journal*
1979	Clayton Kirkpatrick, *Chicago Tribune*
1980	Theodore H. White, author
1981	Nick B. Williams, Los Angeles Times
1982	Simeon Booker, Johnson Publications
1983	Eric Sevareid, CBS News
1984	Helen Thomas, UPI
1985	Flora Lewis, *New York Times*
1986	Art Buchwald, Los Angeles Times Syndicate
1987	David Brinkley, ABC News
1988	David Broder, *The Washington Post*
1989	Russell Baker, *New York Times*
1990	Mike Royko, *Chicago Tribune*
1991	Peter Arnett, CNN
1992	George Tames, *New York Times*
1993	Eugene Roberts, *Philadelphia Inquirer*
1994	Charles Kuralt, CBS News
1995	Shirley Povich, *The Washington Post*
1996	Charles McDowell, *Richmond Times-Dispatch*
1997	Jim Perry, *Wall Street Journal*
1998	Mary McGrory, *The Washington Post*
1999	Carl T. Rowan, Syndicated Columnist
2000	Jack Germond, *Baltimore Sun*
2001	Robert Novak, Creators Syndicate, Inc.
2002	Brian Lamb, C-SPAN
2003	Tom Brokaw, NBC Nightly News
2004	William J. (Bill) Raspberry, Washington Post Writers Group
2005	Austin H. Kiplinger, Kiplinger Washington Editors
2006	Marvin Kalb, The Joan Shorenstein Center for the Press & Public Policy, Harvard University
2007	Paul Steiger, *Wall Street Journal*

NATIONAL PRESS CLUB MEMBERS AS OF JUNE, 2007

Ailis C. Aaron	Wolf Hastings Group
Stephanie Aaronson	Public Broadcasting Service
Nader Abed	Al Jazeera
Helen Lesser Abrams	
Howard S. Abramson	Transport Topics
Magda Abu-Fadil	Institute Profesional Journalists
Andrew Ackerman	Bond Buyer
Nels J. Ackerson	Ackerson Kauffman Fex, PC
Bill Adair	St. Petersburg Times
Francesca Adams	
Roland Adams	Dartmouth College
Ann-Marie Adams	Howard University
A. John Adams	John Adams Associates
Hazel Ward Adcock	
Monroe Aderhold	U.S. Department of Commerce
Linda J. Adler	Freelance
Alison Adler	Freelance
Alexander Adler	Alexander Adler & Associates
Bruce A. Agnew	Freelance
James Agnew III	Blakey & Agnew
Maureen Lamour Agron	National Physicians Association
Francisco Aguirre	Diario Las Americas
David M. Ahearn	Freelance
F. Gregory Ahern	Investment Co. Institute
Laurie Ahern	Mental Disability Rights International
C. Naseer Ahmad	AZI Consulting Inc.
Timothy Ahmann	Reuters
Steven J. Akey	Bridgestone Americas Holdings, Inc.
Satohiro Akimoto	Mitsubishi International Corp.
David S. Aland	
Frank Albert	Foreign Affairs Consultant
Sheldon Alberts	Canwest News Service
David J. Albritton	Raytheon Co.
Hugo Alconada	Diario La Nacion
Robert A. Alden	Washington Post (Retired)
Charles S. Aldinger	
Lorna Aldrich	
Gladys B. Aleman	
Andrew N. Alexander	Cox Newspapers
Nick Alexander	International Food Information Council
Larisa Alexandrovna	Raw Story Media
Kate Alfriend	
Fatma Al-Khalifa	Embassy of Kuwait
Feroza Allee	The Washington Center
Johnny W. Allem	Johnson Institute
Thomas B. Allen	Freelance
Paul J. Allen	
C. Stanley Allen	
Alexis B. Allen	Aerospace Industries Association
Ross Allen Argus	Media Group
Ira R. Allen	Center for the Advancement of Health
David Randal Allen	Communications Office, Inc.
Jonathan Allen	Congressional Quarterly
Maryon Pittman Allen	Maryon Allen Co.
Anne Allen	Morris & Gwendolyn Cafritz Foundation

William Kent Allen	U.S. News & World Report
Jim Allison	WGMS-FM
Robert N. Alls	WHYY-FM
Robert Alotta	Alotta Ink
Bruce S. Alpert	The Times-Picayune
Ali A. Al-Sabah	Embassy of the State of Kuwait
Naila Al-Sowayel	Saudi Press Agency
Natalie Ambrose	Institute for Alternative Futures
John Samuel Amestoy	Mazda North American Operations
Arthur L. Amolsch	Washington Regulatory Reporting
Adlai Amor	Global Fund for Children
Harry O. Amos	
Kirsten Amundsen	Atlantic Council
Vineeta Anand	AFL-CIO
David A. Andelman	Forbes.com
Ric Andersen	U.S. House of Representatives Press Gallery
Mahlon G. Anderson	AAA Mid-Atlantic
Laird B. Anderson	American University
John T. Anderson	Delphi Corp.
Brian D. Anderson	Oblon Spivak
Howard T. Anderson	Stier Anderson, LLC
David T. Anderson	U.S. Department of Housing & Urban Development
Paul L. Anderson	U.S. Government Accountability Office
Peter C. Andrews	
Clara Padilla	Andrews El Hispanic News
Leonard E. B.	Andrews National Arts Program Foundation
Helena D. Andrews	The Politico
Catherine L. Andriadis	DuPont
John-Manuel Andriote	Health & Science Reporting
Salome Angrand	Medill News Service
Cyrus A. Ansary	Investment Services International
Joseph Charles Anselmo	McGraw-Hill
Kathleen Antrim	The Examiner Newspapers
James G. Apple	International Judicial Academy
Marc L. Apter	St. Mary's College of Maryland
John T. Aquino	Aquino
William G. Arey	
Dean R. Armandroff	American Medical Association
Lew Armistead	LA Communications
Liz Schevtchuk Armstrong	Scriptor Exemplar
Larry Arnold	Bloomberg News
John Arnold	Federal Mediation Conciliation Service
Kenneth P. Arnold	T. Dean Reed Co.
Martha Arnold-Charnay	
Kristen Collie Arostegui	Hearst Newspapers
Rudy Arredondo	Nationall Hispanic Political Reporter
Golam Arshad	Daily Inquilab (Bangladesh)
Cheryl Arvidson	Council of Insurance Agents & Brokers
Wondimu Asamnew	Embassy of Ethiopia
Edith Evans Asbury	New York Times (Retired)
Elaine Asch	Strato Publishing Co., Inc.
Annie Barden Ashby	U.S. Department of Education
Carole Ashkinaze	Freelance
Gihane Askar	Washington Times
James R. Asker	Aviation Week & Space Technology
Karin Assmann	Spiegel TV
Genevieve A. Ast	Canadian Broadcasting Corp.
Laura Head Atkinson	Business Software Alliance

Elaine Mitchell Attias	Freelance
Tracey A. Attlee	Freelance
Kemi Aubuchon	
Stephen M. Aug	
Ann M. Augherton	Arlington Catholic Herald
Melissa August	Freelance
James Augustine	Medical Science Communications, Inc
Ali Suleiman Aujali	Embassy of Libya
Frank A. Aukofer	Artists & Writers Syndicate
Elizabeth Auster	The Plain Dealer
Amy Auth	Office of U.S. Representative Virginia Foxx
David E. Autry	Disabled American Veterans
Patricia Avery	
Zagloul Ayad	Voice of the Arab World TV
Herman Ayayo	Tax Analysts
H. Brandt Ayers	Anniston Star
Tim Ayers	Ayers Associates
Merribel S. Ayres	Lighthouse Consulting Group LLC
Mary Ellen Ayres	U.S. Department of Labor
Yolanda Ayubi	
Maria Luisa Azpiazu	EFE News Service
B.F. Chip Backlund	Better Banks Group
Anne C. Bader	Fund for Peace
John J. Bader	IntelliSpace, Inc.
Theodore Baehr	Movieguide
Robert M. Baer	
Barbara Bahny	Willard InterContinental
Rachael Bail	McLean Drama Co.
William B. Bailey	Al Ahram Newspaper
Sue Bailey	NBC News
Jess L Baily	U.S. Department of State
Jackson Bain	Bain & Associates. Inc.
Dona B. Bainbridge	D.H. Bainbridge Associates
Gary H. Baise	Kilpatrick Stockton LLP
Pam Baker	Freelance
Russell Baker	
Norman L. Baker	Defense Daily
Gerard Thomas	Baker Times of London
Aram Bakshian	American Speaker
Douglas Bakshian	Asian Development Bank
Jill Braden Balderas	kaisernetwork.org
Joseph A. Baldinger	Cohen & Baldinger Law Offices
Lolita Baldor	Associated Press
Douglas Baldwin	Baldwin Comunications Group
Tom Baldwin	Times of London
C. Louise Ball	Ball & Ball, PC
Jeffrey Ballou	Al Jazeera
Michael Balmoris	AT&T Services
Margaret M. Bamber	International Brotherhood of Teamsters
Joanne Cronrath	Bamberger
James Bamford	
Hildegard Banes	German Press Agency
Nina Bang-Jensen	Coalition for International Justice
Alseny Ben	Bangoura Africalog
Justin Bank	Annenberg Political Fact Check
Evon Banks	U.S. Environmental Protection Agency
Anne Banville	Banville & Associates
Walter B. Barbe	Keystone College

Ben Barber — U.S. Agency for International Development
Paul A. Barefield — University of Louisiana Lafayette
Edward J. Barks — Barks Communications
J. Robert Barlow
Jeanne K. Barnett
Laura Barnitz — Global Health Council
Ana Baron — Diario Clarin Newspaper
Jill H. Barr — Development Research Associates
Malcolm G. Barr — Hampshire Alliance Inc.
Laurence Barrett
Mavis Perry Barrett
Barbara Barrett — The News & Observer (McClatchy)
Theresa Barry — Bloomberg News
Jerome Barry — Embassy Series
Bertram F. Bartlett — Bartlett Communications Institute
Oscar Bartoli — Freelance
Paul Barton — Arkansas Democrat-Gazette
John F. Barton — U.S. Information Agency
Paul Basken — Chronicle of Higher Education
David H. Bass — Qorvis Communications
Gerald M. Bastarache — Freelance
Quentin R. Bates
Jacqueline Bates
William M. Bates — Bates Associates
Clayton W. Bates, Jr. — Howard University
Rebecca Batts — U.S. Department of Transportation
Linda Bauer — Freelance
Robert N. Baugniet — Gulfstream Aerospace
Everett A. Bauman — El Universal
Ronald M. Baygents — Kuwait News Agency
Nedra Bayne — GroMedia News Group
Michelle Bazie — Center on Budget & Policy Priorities
Geo Beach — Tempest Media Productions
James M. Beall
William Beaman — Reader's Digest
Mary Ledwin Bean — Federal Deposit Insurance Corp.
Maurine Beasley — University of Maryland
Danielle M. Beauchamp — Freelance
Jody Beck — Scripps Howard Foundation
Tobin C. Beck — United Press International
Sarah R. Becker — Freelance
Mary Louise Becker
Steven Kline Beckner — Market News International
James R. Becraft
Frances Bedford
Cora Prifold Beebe
Jane W. Beeder
James Beizer
Robert Beizer — Gray Television
Myron Belkind — Associated Press
Marion K. Bell
Werten F. W. Bellamy — Center for Technology Transfer
William S. Beller
Dominic Bellone — Voice of America
Laura Haines Belman
Adam A. Belmar — ABC News
Jon Belmont — Associated Press Broadcast
Brandon Belote III — Northrop Grumman Corp.

Don Belt	National Geographic Magazine
Beth Belton	Associated Press
Nicholas R. Beltrante	Beltrante & Associates
Lewis B. Beman	
Naftali Bendavid	Chicago Tribune
Robert Bendiner	
Vicki Bendure	Bendure Communications
Claudio F.	Benedi International Press Bureau
Robert A. Benenson	Congressional Quarterly
Matthew K. Benjamin	Bloomberg News
Carole A. Bennett	
Carol Bennett	
Susan Bennett	Newseum
Michael Benson	
Miles R. Benson	Newhouse News Service
Nicholas Benton	Falls Church News-Press
Phillip J. Berardelli	Freelance
Dorothee Berendes	db Media Productions
B. Richard Berg	
James R. Berg	Matson Multi Media
J. Louis Berger	
James R. Berger	Trade Reports International Group
Laurence Bergreen	Freelance
Pat Bergstresser	
William Berkley	Freelance
Sarah Coffey Berkowitz	Reuters
John L. Berlau	Competitive Enterprise Institute
Max Derley	Bloomberg News
Steven Berman	
Daniel Berman	Environment & Energy Publishing .
Michelle D. Bernard	Independent Women's Forum
George Vincent Bernard	Scott Foresman & Co.
Henry R. Bernstein	
Leo Bernstein	
Roger Bernstein	American Chemistry Council
Norman Bernstein	Norman Bernstein Management. Inc.
Chris Berry	WMAL Radio
Paul Lawrence Berry	Paul L. Berry & Associates LLC
Alison Bethel	Nassau Guardian
Roy Anthony Betts	U.S. Postal Service
Jamila M. Bey F	reelance
Jeffrey C. Beyer	Farmers Group, Inc.
Iryna Bezverkha	Embassy of Ukraine
Dipka Bhambhani	McGraw-Hill
Pradeep Bhavsar	Daman Ganga Times
June M. Bierbower	Omaha World Herald
Lauren A. Bigge	Air Force Magazine
Otis Bilodeau	Bloomberg News
Clara Bingham	Freelance
Molly Bingham	Freelance
Dan C. Biondi	
Barbara A. Bird	IT Business Developers, LLC
Stephen V. Bird	National Journalism Center
Sharon Campbell Biron	
Rosette S. Bishop	
Ian Bishop	Lowell Sun /Media News Group
John Bisney	American Petroleum Institute
Larry Bivins	Gannett News Service

Alan Bjerga	Bloomberg News
Helene La Gaccia Bjornson	
Uyless Black	
Edwin Black	Feature Group News Service
Donald Eric Black	Lama Media
Keith Blackman	Burson-Marsteller
Kenneth D. Blackshaw	
Stephen B. Blakely	Employee Benefit Research Institute
Larry Blanchard	CUNA Mutual Group
Joan Gill Blank	Grapetree Productions
Peter L. Blank	Kiplinger Washington Editors, Inc.
Jim Blasingame	Small Business Network, Inc.
Peter E. Blau	
Marie Taylor Blay	
Kenneth Lee Blaylock	
Samuel Bleicher	U.S. Department of State
Sue Blevins	Institute for Health Freedom
Laura Blinkhorn	Congressional Quarterly
Jeff Bliss	Bloomberg News
Carolyn Bloch	Bloch Consulting Group
Victor Block	Freelance
Mamerta R. Block	
John R. Block	Block Communications, Inc.
William Block	Pittsburgh Post-Gazette (Retired)
Raymond L. Blockus	
David W. Blomquist	NJ.Com
John Bloom	National Press Club
Michael Bloomberg	City of New York
John T. Blozis	National Geographic Society
Jolene M. Blozis	U.S. News & World Report
Jane Blume	International Association of Fire Fighters
Elizabeth I. Board	EPCglobal Inc
L. Peyton Bobo	Gazette Newspapers
Elaine Gansz Bobo	PhRMA Co.
Christopher Boesen	Tiber Creek Consulting, Inc.
Katherine Boettrich	
John Boffa	Boffa & Associates
Claudia L. Bogard	Federal Aviation Administration
Marylin Sue Bogner	Institute for the Study of Human Error, LLC
Jaya Bohlmann	Sodexho Food Service
Jacklyn P. Boice	Advancing Philanthropy
Jean-Francois Boittin	Embassy of France
John L. Boland	Public Broadcasting Service
Elaine Bole	UNHCR
Nona G. Bolling	
Jacques N. Bonjawo	Microsoft
Kathleen Bonk	Communications Consortium Media Center
Jack Bonner	Bonner & Associates
Michel Bonny	Freelance
Eric Bontrager	Environment & Energy Publishing
Simeon Booker	Johnson Publishing Co.
George B. Bookman	
Diane E. Booth	Freelance
Robert L. Booth	National Geographic Magazine
Anne Marie Borbely-Bartis	States' Energy Council
Rick Borchelt	Genetics & Public Policy Center
Ezio Borchini	
Joseph Borda	Editorials

Kristina Borjesson	
Harvey Borkin	
Donald J. Borut	National League of Cities
Edgar D. Boshart	Foster Natural Gas Report
Scott Bosley	American Society of Newspaper Editors
Kerry Bothwell	New Zealand Embassy
Herman B. Bouma	Buchanan Ingersoll PC
Mary Ann Bourbon	
Frank Bourgholtzer	
Tony Bourgholtzer	Clinical Cardiology Publishing Co.
Sally Ruth Bourrie	
Mrs. Maxwell-Peg Boverman	
Christy Bowe	ImageCatcher News
Edwin W. Bowers	Ed Bow Unlimited
Michael A. Bowers	Pearson Government Solutions
Brian E. Bowers	Stars & Stripes
Dennis R. Boxx	Lockheed Martin Corp.
Clayton W. Boyce	American Trucking Association
C.A. Boyd	MCS Inc.
John Boyd	Traffic World
John Alton Boyer	
Robert J. Boyer	Care First Blue Cross Blue Shield
Katherine Boyle	E&E Publishing, LLC
William Brack	Black Star Publishing Co.
Len Bracken	BNA, Inc.
John Bradburne	Bradburne Consulting, LLC
Chris Bradburne	National Center for Biodefense
Richard Bradee	
Eugene M. Braderman	
Lou Ann Bell Bradley	
Gene E. Bradley	
David Bradley	Atlantic Media Co.
Cheryl Bradley	National Association of Social Workers
Jessica Brady	
Mikhail Bragin	International Affairs Journal
Elizabeth Brannan	La Prensa of Panama
William A. Brannigan	
Kathleen Brannigan	Greystone Partners
Kay Bransford	Bransford Marketing Partners
David M. Braun	National Geographic Society
Jill C. Braunstein	National Academy of Social Insurance
Karrye Braxton	Global Business Solutions, Inc.
Jerome F. Brazda	Brazda Healthcare Information
Brent Breedin	Brent Breedin & Associates
Mark E. Brender	Space Imaging
Marion A. Brewer	
Theodore Bridges	Hazardous Cargo Bulletin
Henry Brier	
John D. Briggs	Howrey LLP
Lucy C. Brightman	
Edward Earl Brighton	Urban Maglev Interest Group
Helen J. Brinegar	
Andrew C. Briscoe	Sugar Association
Stephen Brobeck	Consumer Federation of America
Joshua Brockman	
Scott Brodbeck	WTTG-TV
David S. Broder	Washington Post
Patricia M. Broderick	Teaching/K-8 Magazine

Ian Brodie	Times of London
Kenneth Brody	Winslow Partners
Erin Broekhuysen	John Snow, Inc.
Jere Broh-Kahn	
Tom Brokaw	NBC News
Art Brothers	Beehive Communications
Stuart N. Brotman	American Television Experience
Deborah J. Brower	D.J. Brower Fine Arts
Robert S. Brown	
Charles D. Brown	
David H. Brown	
Nona B. Brown	
Betti Brown	BNA, Inc.
Patricia Brown	CMP Media
Tracey L. Brown	Cochran Firm
Lillian Brown	Georgetown University
Kent L. Brown	Highlights for Children
Holmes M. Brown	Institute for Applied Economics
David Brown	Manhattan Project Ltd.
Ira D. Brown	PanAmSat
Jamesetta Foster	Brown Sister 2 Sister
Jefferson T. Brown	U.S. Department of State
Elizabeth S. Brownstein	
Alice Brueck	
Geoffrey Brumfiel	Nature Magazine
Michael P. Bruno	Aerospace Daily & Defense Report
Merry P. Bruns	ScienceSites Communications
J. Charles (Chuck) Bruse	Allstate Insurance Co.
Thomas Eugene Bryan	
Magalen O. Bryant	
Nancy B. Bryant	Bryant Consulting Group
Anne L. Bryant	National School Boards Association
Cheryl Buchta	McGraw-Hill
Anne W. Buckley	AHK Realty
John L. Buckman	Freelance
Phillip J. Budahn	U.S. Department of Veterans Affairs
Meredith S. Buel	Voice of America
J. William Buff	
Shawn S. Bullard	Duetto Group
Marcia L. Bullard	USA Weekend
Dena Bunis	Orange County Register
W. Clark Bunting	Discovery Communications, Inc.
Jean Marie Bunton	Security Industries Financial Association
Michael I. Burch	Nature Works, Inc.
Nathan A. Burchfiel	Cybercast News Service
Stephen Burd	Chronicle of Higher Education
Cherryale C. Burge	Maryland Public Television
Tim Burger	Bloomberg News
James Burke	Donovan/Burke Inc.
Lori Burkhammer	Water Environment Federation
Michael Burnham	Greenwire
Martin Burns	AARP
Sascha Burns	Patton Boggs
Tim Burr	Freelance
Thomas Burr	Salt Lake Tribune
Margaret Burroughs	
Bernard Burt	
Jeffrey Busch	Safe Blood International

George W. Bush	President of the United States
Howard M. Bushman	Howard M. Bushman Ltd.
James G. Busse	Freelance
Ramesh Butani	HB Productions LLC
Jonathan A. Buth	Fairfax County Health Department
Tara Butler	National Governors' Association
Patrick Butler	National Organization for Women
Louis G. Buttell	
Corey Byers	Free Lance-Star
Paul H. Byers	Gateway Video Services, Inc.
N. Alicia Byers	Library of Congress
Gayela Bynum	U.S. Department of Housing & Urban Development
Harry F. Byrd Jr.	Rockingham Publishing Co.
Dennis E. Byrne	U.S. Small Business Administration
Carolyn D. Caddes	Photojournalist
George Cahlink	Roll Call
James A. Calderwood	Zuckert, Scoutt & Rasenberger
Bret Caldwell	International Brotherhood of Teamsters
Robert E. Calem	Freelance
V.F. Callahan	Callahan Publications (Retired)
Lawrence L. Calvert	
Duncan H. Cameron	Cameron Communications
Elaine Camhi	Aerospace America
Greta C. Campbell	
Brian Campbell	ABC News
Richard E. Campbell	Argus Press
Leonie L. Campbell	Asian American Justice Center
Scott L. Campbell	Washington Policy & Analysis
Jim Campi	Civil War Preservation Trust
Owen F. Campion	Our Sunday Visitor Inc.
James W. Canan	Aerospace America
Edward Cannon	Cannon Corporate Consultants
Antonio Cano	El Pais
Joseph A. Cantlupe	Copley News Service
Audra S. Capas	5 Star PR, LLC
Milton F. Capps	Nashville Post Co.
Noel Card	
Robert Carden	Carden Communications
Carl W. Cardin	
Arlene R. Cardozo	University of Minnesota
Jaime M. Carino	Maya Media The Manila-U.S. Mail
Carlton Carl	Association of Trial Lawyers of America
Paul N. Carlin	Carlin Enterprises, LLC
Patricia J. Carmack	Masi Max Resources, Inc.
Gregory Carmichael	
Thomas Riley Carmichael	U.S. Department of State
Ellen Carnevale	Population Reference Bureau
Amanda Carpenter	Eagle Publishing
Rebecca Carr	Cox Newspapers
Allen Carrier	Pfizer Inc.
Susan Carroll	
Howard J. Carroll	
Rory Carroll	American Metal Market
Barry J. Carroll	
Dianne Carson	
Steven L. Carson	Manuscript Society News
Deb Carstoiu	Biotechnology Industry Organization
Leah A. Cartabruno	

Hodding Carter	
Vic Carter	WJZ TV
Cynthia Carter	FDAnews
Don E. Carter	Knight Ridder (Retired)
Jeffrey T. Carter	U.S. Coast Guard
Winthrop P. Carty	Population Reference Bureau
Gary Caruso	
Robert Case II	World Journalism Institute
Joan W. Cassedy	ACIL
David M. Cassidy	Belo Broadcasting
William B. Cassidy	Traffic World
Chris Casteel	Daily Oklahoman
Chris Castelli	Inside Washington Publishers
David A. Castelveter	Air Transport Association of America
Glenna Castillo	
Karen Dia Cathey	Bon Vivant LLC
Mike Causey	WTOP Radio
Patricia A. Cavanaugh	Transport Topics (Retired)
John H. Cawley	U.S. Department of Commerce (NOAA)
John B. Caylor	Emerald Coast Times Publishing Co.
Barbara Cebuhar	U.S. Department of Health & Human Services
Guy Cecala	Inside Mortgage Finance
Margaret Chadbourn	Market News International
Gail Russell Chaddock	Christian Science Monitor
Adrienne Bosworth Chafetz	
Conrad Chaffee	Tokyo-Chunichi Shimbun
Henry S. Champ	CBC
Shobhana Chandra	Bloomberg News
Isolde Chapin	Washington Independent Writers
Edwin T. Chapman	
Irwin M. Chapman	Bloomberg News
R. Stanley Chapman	Kansas City Star/Traffic World
Pamela Chappell	
Kevin Chappell	Johnson Publishing Co.
Antigoni Charalambous	Embassy of Cyprus
Melissa Charbonneau	CBN News
Kathleen A. Charles	
Laura E. Chatfield	United Press International
Sumana Chatterjee	Women for Women International
Taoufik Chebbi	Embassy of Tunisia
Jean Chemnick	Congressional Quarterly
Edwin Chen	Bloomberg News
Anna C. Chennault	TAC International
Doral Chenoweth	Columbus Dispatch
Sheila R. Cherry	BNA, Inc.
Daisy Chew	
Rahul Chhabra	Embassy of India
Wang Chi	Washington Journal of Modern China
Nicholas Chiaia	
Helen H. Chien	Chien-Hsieh Translators
Kimberly Chipman	Bloomberg News
Kenneth Choi Chosun	Daily Newspaper
Hyung-du Choi	Munhwa Daily
R.L. Chomiak	Freelance
Phil Chordas	Chordas Enterprises
Nicholas T. Christakos	Sutherland, Asbill & Brennan LLP
Annmarie Christensen	Global Health Council
Donald Christiansen	Informatica

Katherine M. Christie	
Lawrence C. Christopher	Consultant
Janice King Chutick	
Paul Ciampoli	McGraw-Hill
Mehmet Kasim Cindemir	Hurriyet Daily
Stephen Citarella	
Joseph Clabes	National Thoroughbred Racing Association
Judith G. Clabes	Scripps Howard Foundation
Susan Clampitt	Susan Clampitt & Associates
Russell B. Clanahan	
Michael Clark	
June L. Clark	
Tom Clark	CTV Canadian TV
Timothy Clark	Government Executive Magazine
Paul S. Clark	Hill & Knowlton
Michael Clark	Markcorp Inc.
John Clark	Sonnenschein Mass & Rosenthal LLP
Jennifer A. Clark	
Oliver F. Clarke	Gleaner Co.
Richard C. Clarkson	Rich Clarkson & Associates
Richard Pierre Claude	
Carol Clawson	
A. Ricky Clemons	National Urban League
Eleanor Clift	Newsweek
Eli Clifton	Inter Press Service
Paul Clolery	NonProfit Times
Julie Clow	CBC
Adam Clymer	Annenberg Public Policy Center
Patrick Coburn	State Journal-Register
Roger J. Cochetti	CompTia
J. Thomas Cochran	U.S. Conference of Mayors
Lyman B. Coddington	
Robert C. Cody	
Karen James Cody	BNA, Inc.
Mary Fran Coffey	
Mary B. Coffman	Medill News Service
Philip C. Cohan	
Marshall H. Cohen	Big Marsh News Photos
Robert A. Cohen	Braintreee
Stanley E. Cohen	Crain Communications Inc. (Retired)
Zachary Coile	San Francisco Chronicle
George Abbott Colburn	Starbright Media Corp.
Carol Cole	
George M. Coleman	
Roy M. Coleman	
Michael Thomas Coleman	Albuquerque Journal
Frank Coleman	Distilled Spirits Council
Jeanne Collier	
Terese Colling	
Reid Collins	Freelance
David L. Collogan	McGraw-Hill
Michael Colton	CBC
Jeffrey Coman	
Adrienne M. Combs	Joint Force Headquarters
Caroline Jennifer Comport	Tribune Broadcasting
Neisa Condemaita	Azteca America Television
Thomas J. Condon	
George E. Condon	Copley News Service

Carole K. Cones	Safe Blood International
Carrie Conko	George Mason University
Joseph L. Conn	Church & State Magazine
Tara Connell	Gannett Co., Inc.
William A. Connelly	
James M. Connelly	Moscow News
Adele Conover	Freelance
Mihai Constantin	Romanian Television
Lenora W. Conway	
Roger Conway	U.S. Department of Agriculture
David T. Cook	Christian Science Monitor
Charles E. Cook	Cook Political Report
Anne Cook	FDA News
Rhodes Cook	Rhodes Cook Letter
Joseph F. Coombs	Washington Business Journal
Robert J. Coontz	Science Magazine
Michael J. Cooper	Freelance
B. Jay Cooper	APCO Worldwide
Shawn E. Cooper	PG&E Corp.
Elliot T. Cooper	Richmond Times-Dispatch
Josephine S. Cooper	Toyota Motor North America, Inc.
Esther Coopersmith	Coopersmith Real Estate Co.
Richard P. Coorsh	Federation of American Hospitals
Debra Cope	Promontory Financial Group
Peter Copeland	Scripps Howard News Service
Tara Copp Cox	Newspapers
Douglas Cornell	TEAL Group Corp.
John H. Corr	
Jerome R. Corsi	
Lawrence E. Cosgriff	
John P. Cosgrove	
Sylvia A. Costen	Freelance
Raymond L. Courage	
Nancy Covey	McGraw-Hill
Jeffery A. Cowart	Foundation of American Communication (FACS)
Norman J. Cowen	
Hansel Cox	National Association of Manufacturers
William T. Coyle	U.S. Department of Agriculture
John R. Coyne	
James P. Coyne	
Amanda M. Coyne	Anchorage Press
Martin J. Coyne	McGraw-Hill
Susan Crabtree	The Hill
Dr. Mary Faye Craft	Mary Faye Craft & Associates
Maureen Cragin	Boeing Co.
Jim Craig American	Petroleum Institute
William O. Craig	Hearst Newspapers
John E. Craig	National War College Alumni Association
Brenda Laukaitis	Craine American Medical Association
Arnold Crane	Freelance
Martha Craver	Kiplinger Washington Editors, Inc.
Olita (Claire) Crawford	
Vince Crawley	Army Times Publishing Co.
James W. Crawley	Media General News Service
Albert B. Crenshaw	Washington Post
Hilda Crespo	Aspira Association, Inc.
Paul Crespo	Univision Radio Network
Hope Cristol	

Howard Criswell Jr.	Freelance
Allan W. Cromley	Daily Oklahoman (Retired)
Jeffrey Cronin	Center for Science in the Public Interest
Walter Cronkite	CBS News
Raymond S. Crosby	Crosby Marketing Communications
Ralph W. Crosby	Crosby Marketing Communications
Sean Crowley	M&R Strategic Services
Paula Cruickshank	CCH, Inc.
Janice R. Crump	JRC Communications
Jason Cuevas	Southern Co.
David J. Cullen	David Cullen Public Relations, Inc.
Annette Culler	Penney International Marketing & Communications
Tony Culley	Foster CFCO International
Barbara J. Culliton	Genome News Network
Katharine Culpepper	National Geographic Society
Kenneth V. Cummins	Capitol Inquiry Inc.
Thomas Curley	Associated Press
D. Patrick Curley	St. Lawrence Business Consultants
Nicole Currier	Embassy of Canada
Jennifer I. Curtin	Association of Government Accountants
Frances Jo Curnell	Curtis American Peakes Limited (Radio)
Dale Curtis	Dittus Communications
Brenda Curtis-Heiken	U.S. Department of Agriculture
Richard H. Curtiss	Washington Report on Middle East
John H. Cushman	New York Times
Bernard J. Cutler	
Joseph F.H. Cutrona	
Curtis C. Cutter	Interworld Consultants Inc.
Sandra Cutts	Fannie Mae
Peter Cutts	Peter Cutts Photography
Marian A. Czarnecki	
Robert W. Czeschin	
Gina Daddario	Shenandoah University
Kenneth B. Dalecki	Kiplinger Washington Editors, Inc.
Robert E. Daley	Kettering Foundation
Aaron Dalton	Freelance
Michael R. Dalton	
James J. Dalton	
Tim Daly U.S.	Department of Veterans Affairs
Joseph R. Damato	Seyfarth Shaw
Steven B. Dana	IMAS Publishing Group
James T.L. Dandridge	U.S. Department of State
Joseph F. D'Angelo	Hearst Newspapers
Hope M. Daniels	American Style Magazine
Alex Daniels	Arkansas Democrat Gazette
John Danner	Native American Communication-NACOM
Thomas B. Darr	Administrative Office Pennsylvania
Chaman Lal Datta	Freelance
Vanita Datta	SAIC
Harold L. Davey	
Joseph David	Freelance
Mark G. Davidson	McGraw-Hill
Anne Davies	Sydney Morning Herald
Jennifer Davis	Freelance
Andrew Davis	American Press Institute
Stephen C. Davis	Morningside Partners, LLC
Jeffrey A. Davis	Sawmill Marketing Public Relations
Susan Ann Davis	Susan Davis International

Thomas S. Davis	Tom Davis Associates
Joseph E. Davis	Veterans of Foreign Wars
Virginia Dawson	
Wainwright Dawson	Free Press Reports
Jim Dawson	Physics Today Magazine
Russell A. Dawson	Potomac Communications Group, Inc.
Dennis Scott Day	Boeing Co.
Adrian Day	Global Analyst Newsletter
Charles W. Day	WGMS-FM Radio
Daniel S. Dayton	Office of Naval Research
Santiago Real De Azua	Inter-American Development Bank
Arnaud de Borchgrave	
John de Lorenzi	
Marino de Medici	
James R. De	Santis Florida Council Economic Education
Curtis C. Deane	WoodleyLion Consulting
Rhondalee A. Dean-Royce	National Corn Growers Association
Barbara Ray Deans	Freelance
David R. Dear	
Betty Debnam	Mini Page Publishing Co.
Bernd Debusmann	Reuters
Jill T. Decker	Freelance
Brett M. Decker	Export-Import Bank of the U.S.
Terry James Dee	Freelance
Robert DeFillippo	Prudential Financial, Inc.
Stanley E. Degler	
Mary L. Deibel	
Carolyn S. Dejanikus	
Darrell Delamaide	
Paul Delaney	National Public Radio
George B. Delaplaine	Great Southern Enterprises, Inc.
Chris Delboni	Freelance
Norman G. Delbridge	Freelance
Christine Dell'Amore	National Geographic News
Paula L. Delo	
Campbell DeMallie	FDIC
Edward DeMarco	Bloomberg News
John S. DeMott	Freelance
Diana Denman	Freelance
Kevin B. Dennehy	Recon Magazine
Lee W. Dennison	National Endowment for the Arts
Diana Denny	
Richard Dent	WYRE Radio
James S. Denton	Heldref Publications
Albin J. Derecki	
Evan G. DeRenzo	Washington Hospital Center
Ch. L. Deroche	
Michael DeSenne	Smart Money
Frank deSerio Avio	Galleries, Inc.
Alan L. Dessoff	Alan L. Dessoff Communications
Julie DeVader	FHL Bank Topeka
Paul J. Deveney	
Urmila Devgon	
Daniel C. Devine	
Carrie Devorah	Freelance
Stephanie Woods Dhue	Nightly Business Report
John M. Diamond	Stanford Univeristy Press
Miguel Angel Diaz	Freelance

Thomas DiBacco	Broadhead & Co.
Jason Dick	Atlantic Media/Congress Daily
Linda Ann Dickerhoof	Network Solutions, LLC
Margaret L. Dickey	Margaret L. Tomlinson. ESQ
Paul Dickson	Author
Howard F. Didsbury	World Future Society
Michael E. Diegel	National Federation of Independent Business
Lawrence D. Dietz	Symantec Corp.
Russell Dinnage	Environment & Energy Publishing
Magaye C. Diombokho	Le Diplomat
Daniel DiPierro	CBS News
Lee E. Dirks	Dirks, Van Essen & Murray
Joseph DiSciullo	Tax Analysts
Dee Ann Divis	The Examiner
Lisa Dixon	Kiplinger Washington Editors, Inc.
Wilson P. Dizard	Post Newsweek Tech Media/Government Computer News
Joan Dizikes	U.S. Department of Labor
Jennifer Dlouhy	Hearst Newspapers
Muriel Dobbin	
Timothy H. Dobbyn	Reuters
Matthew DoBias	Crain Communications, Inc.
Frank Dobisky	Dobisky Associates
Julia M. Dobson	Freelance
Walter H. Dodd	
Catherine Dodge	Bloomberg News
Enid Doggett	Ketchum Public Relations
Thomas W. Doggett	Reuters
Robert Doherty	Reuters
Alice A. Doherty-Williams	
Marilou Donahue	
Steven Donahue	Language Magazine
Arnold E. Donahue	Pactrade Inc.
Thomas G. Donlan	Barron's Magazine
Ryan J. Donmoyer	Bloomberg News
Dorothy C. Donnelly	
John M. Donnelly	Congressional Quarterly
James A. Donoghue	Flight Safety Foundation
Cathryn Donohoe	Washington Times
Claire M. Donovan	
Edward Dooley	
Amy Doolittle	Federal Times
Margot Dorfman	U.S. Women's Chamber of Commerce
Dina Dorich	U.S. Department of Labor
Dennis B. Doris	Dennis Doris & Associates
Steven Dorsey	American University
Christine M. Dorsey	National Wildlife Federation
Harold Dorwin	Smithsonian Institution
William Douglas	McClatchy Newspapers
Keri Douglas Nine	Muses International
Frederick Douglass	IV Frederick Douglass Organization
Randolph V. Dove	EDS
M. Bruce Downey	
Laura Downhower	
Darian Downs	
Bruce Downs	
Daniel J. Doyle	
Michael Doyle	McClatchy Newspapers
Jessica Ryen Doyle	Observer-Dispatch

Natalie Doyle-Hennin	Rainbow Sufer Institute for Digital & Media Literacy
Murray Drabkin	
Mark Drajem	Bloomberg News
Roberta Hornig Draper	NBC News
Kevin Drawbaugh	Reuters
Larry Dreiling	High Plains Journal
David C. Dressler	Freelance
Elizabeth Drew	Scribner Publishing
Josh Drobnyk	Morning Call
Allen Drury	
Lisa J. Dry	American Seed Trade Association
Jerry Dryer	Dairy & Food Market Analyst, Inc.
Edwin J. Dryer	Foley & Lardner
Jan Du Plain	Du Plain Enterprises Inc.
Don Dudley	WRNN-TV
Anne Duffy	
Jeff Dufour	The Examiner
David Duitch	Belo Broadcasting
William E. Duke	W.E. Duke & Co.
Betty Cole Dukert	
Shirley M. Duncan	
Robert Steven Duncan	IESE Business School
Lucia Duncan	Jet Setter
Michael John Duncan	Potomac Radio News
Mikel Dunham	
Richard S. Dunham	Business Week
Frederica H. Dunn	U.S. Department of Homeland Security
Linda C. Durkee	
Clive L. DuVal	
Henry Duvall	Council of the Great City Schools
Jeffrey Dvorkin	Committee of Concerned Journalists
Scott A. Dykema	Federal Deposit Insurance Corp.
James Dykstra	Edington Peel & Associates
Eelco H. Dykstra	George Washington University
Eleanor Herman	Dyment Aquitaine, Inc.
Charles E. Dynes	
Bainbridge Eager	Bainbridge Eager & Assoc Inc
Gregg S. Early	KCI Communications
Peggy Eastman	Medical Publishing Enterprises
Anthony T. Easton	Worldbeat Publications
Carole Kennon Eaton	
Sabrina Eaton	The Plain Dealer
James Eberle	America's Community Bankers
Igor J. Eberstein	Eberstein Charra Associates
Hamid Ebrahimi	Project SEED
Timothy Guy Echols	University of Georgia
Laura L. Eckart	U.S. House of Representatives Periodical Press Gallery
Toby Eckert	Copley News Service
Paul Eckert	Reuters
Judith Ecochard	Freelance
Donald Ediger	Freelance
Charles L. Edson	Nixon Peabody LLP
Marvin R. Edwards	Freelance
Thomas J. Edwards	CD Publications
Karen Coble Edwards	KCE Public Affairs Associates
Bob Edwards	XM Public Radio/XM Satellite Radio
Tanise Edwards-Evans	Freelance
Robert Carlton Effros	International Monetary Fund

Marc F. Efron	Crowell & Moring LLP
Katherine Egan	Bennett Astro News
James G. Ehrhorn Jr.	WSBA/WARM-103/WSOX
Curtis Eichelberger	Bloomberg News
Martin Einhorn	System Quality Corp.
Charles N. Eischen	
Albert Eisele	The Hill
Hanan Elbadry	Egyptian TV News Division
Donald Leigh Elder	MediaWise Associates
Earle Eldridge	Traffic World
Camille Elhassani	Al Jazeera
Phoebe Eliopoulos	Freelance
Abby Ellin	Freelance
Geoff Elliott	News Limited
Sue L. Ellis	
Richard Ellis	Getty Images
Susan Ellis	U.S. Department of State
Friedrich M. Elmendorf	Consumer Bankers Association
Wesley Elmore	Tax Analysts
Jessy Elmurr	Al Jazeera
George A. Embrey	Columbus Dispatch
Mieko Endo	Kyodo News
Deniz Enginsoy	Anatolia News Agency
Michael English	Maryland Public Television
Joseph Enoch	ConsumerAffairs.com
Kay Enokido	Hay-Adams Management Co.
Aaron Epstein	Freelance
Keith Epstein	Business Week
Edward Epstein	San Francisco Chronicle
Noel Epstein	Washington Post
Mercedes Erickson	
Stanford A. Erickson	Transport Topics
Carl E. J. Ericson	
Ken Ericson	Westin Rinehart
Eddie Escobedo	El Mundo Newspaper
C. Jeffrey Eshelman	Independent Petroleum Association
Kenneth Eskey	Scripps Howard News Service
Adele C. Espeche-Danes	Tender Loving Petcare
Virginia Espie	
Edward P. Essertier	
Mason L. Essif	Ogilvy Public Relations Worldwide
Martha (Marti) Estell	U.S. Department of State
Bernard Etzinger	Embassy of Canada
Toni Eugene	
Michael D. Evans	MEM International
Emily Evershed	
Ann Ewing	
Ky Ewing	Office of Ky P. Ewing, Jr.
Carl R. Eyler	Hawkins Publishing Co., Inc.
Lee Eyler	Hawkins Publishing Co., Inc.
David Lewis Eynon	
William D.	Falcon Freelance
John Fales	Washington Times
Richard W.C. Falknor	NS Associates
Hallie C. Falquet	University of Maryland
Cornel Faltin	Axel Springer Publishing
Odom Fanning	
Joseph Farah	WorldNetDaily.com

Mary-Frances Faraji — Schering-Plough Corp.
Jennifer S. Farland — Fannie Mae
John W. Farley — Phillips International, Inc.
Rita Katz Farrell — Freelance
John Farrell — Denver Post
Jill S. Farrell — Judicial Watch, Inc
Larry C. Farrell — The Farrell Co.
Suraiya Farukhi — Argonne National Laboratory
Zachary D. Fasman — Paul Hastings Janofsky & Walker
Leila Fatehi — Meridian Institute
Fariborz S. Fatemi — Oxfordshire Associates
Ronald Faucheux — Campaigns & Elections Magazine
Stephanie Faul
Laura Faul Folger — Nolan Fleming Douglas Inc.
Mary Sue Faulkner — National Rifle Association
Helen Bernstein — Fealy Freelance
Lawrence W. Feinberg
Robert M. Feist
Jonathon S. Feit — Feit Family Ventures Corp.
Morgan Felchner — Campaigns & Elections Magazine
Karen I. Feld — Capital Connections
Shirley Feldman
Carole Feldman — Associated Press
Elliot J. Feldman — Baker & Hostetler LLP
Esther Felices — Embassy of Spain
Edward R. Felker — SNG Newspapers Inc.
James A. Fellows
John C. Felmy — American Petroleum Institute
Frances Felt
Mary P. Felter — Capital Newspaper
Peter E. Feltman — CCH, Inc.
Kenneth E. Feltman — Employers Council on Flexible Compensation
Patricia Fenton — Freelance
Teal P. Ferguson — Freelance
Barbara G. B. Ferguson — Arab News
Milton Carr Ferguson — Davis Polk & Wardwell
Donald L. Ferguson — Fleishman-Hillard
Rodney Ferguson — Lipman Hearne, Inc.
Tracy N. Ferguson — Maryland State's Attorney Office
James Fetgatter — AFIRE
James Fetig — Georgia Institute of Technology
Joseph Feuerhard — National Catholic Reporter
Ruth Fichenberg
Amy L. Fickling — McGraw-Hill
David Field — Airline Business Magazine
Rebecca Field — Potomac Television
John Paul Fielder — National Association of Manufacturers
Todd Fielding — Freelance
James E. Fields
Cheryl M. Fields — National Association of State Universities & Land Grant Colleges
Christie Findlay — Campaigns & Elections Magazine
Max Fine
Evelyn Fine
Blythe F. Finke — Freelance
Mark Andrew Finkenstaedt — Mark Finkenstaedt Photography
Mark P. Finks — Long & Foster Real Estate
James J. Finn — Avaya
Joseph Finnerty — Stenger & Finnerty

Paul D. Finney	BNA, Inc.
Kenneth Fireman	Bloomberg News
Julie Fischer	Freelance
Betsy Fischer	NBC News
James Fischl	American Legion
David M. Fish	Verizon
William H. Fishback	University of Virginia
Gershon W. Fishbein	Environews Inc.
Mary Jane Fisher	
James Fisher-Thompson	U.S. Department of State
Michael E. Fishman	
Marta Fita	WPROST (Poland)
Benedict Fitzgerald	Benedict Fitzgerald
Alison Fitzgerald	Bloomberg News
Tonya M. Fitzpatrick	Bronze World Travel Media Group
Richard Flanagan	World - Generation
James C. Flanigan	Flanigan's Communications
John P. Fleming	
Sophie P. Fleming	
Douglas R. Fleming	Stampa Generale, SRL
Richard E. Fletcher	Masonic Service Association
Adrianne Flynn	Capital News Service
Kara Flynn	Pew Initiative Food & Biotechnology
Tegan M. Flynn, Esq.	Vinson & Elkins, LLP
Herbert H. Fockler	
Patrick Fogarty	Associated Press Broadcast
John R. Fogarty	White House Bulletin
Julius Fogel	Fogel Foundation
Jean Folkerts	University of North Carolina
Mary Lou Forbes	Washington Times
John Joseph Ford	
Elizabeth Ford	
Werner H. Fornos	
Heather Forsgren Weaver	
Art Forster	Federal Election Commission
Michael G.	Forsythe Bloomberg News
Lawrence G. Foster	
Lawrence D. Foster	McGraw-Hill
Rich Foster	Newseum
Allan Fotheringham	Financial Post
Christopher Fotos	Aviation Week
Helen Strother Fouche	
Adrienne Fox	
Morley E. Fox	Central Arizona Project Association
Donald R. Foxvog	
Trish Foxwell	Travel Publications
Mary Lou Foy	Washington Post
Emmanuel S. Francois	NOAH
Scott Frank	American Institute of Architects
Richard S. Frank	National Journal
Alan S. Franken	Alan Franken Inc
Mary Beth Franklin	Kiplinger Washington Editors, Inc.
David Freddoso	Evans - Novak Inside Report
Donald J. Frederick	Freelance
David W. Frederickson	David W. Frederickson & Co.
Elissa Blake Free	Georgetown University Law Center
Neal Freed	Freed Photography, Inc.
Michael Freedman	George Washington University

Dan Freedman	Hearst Newspapers
Sharon T. Freeman	All American Small Business Exporters
Allison Anne Freeman	E & E Publishing
Mary B. French	Army Magazine
Priscilla Friedersdorf	Island Sun Newspaper
Mrs. Eric Friedheim	
Jock Friedly	Storming Media
Lisa Friedman	Los Angeles Daily News
John T. Friedman	NCQA
Peter Friedmann	Lindsay, Hart, Neil & Weigler
Jane F. Friedmann	Northern Virginia Community College
Brian Friel	National Journal
Michele Frisby	ICMA
Michael Frome	
Norman C. Fu	China Times
Frank Fuhrig	Deutsche Presse-Agentur
James C. Fuller	
Joan S. Fulton	Freelance
David Fuscus	Xenophon Strategies
Donald J. Gaetz	Bay Beacon
Fernando Galaviz	Centech Group Inc.
Barry G. Gale	Gale International LLC
Gary M. GUS Gallagher	Gallagher International
John Gallagher	Traffic World
Tom Gallagher	Traffic World, Air Cargo World
Mercedes Gallegos	El Correo
Jerry Gallegos	U.S. House of Representatives Press Gallery
Anthony E. Gallo	Seventh Street Playhouse
Joseph J. Gancie	Gancie Associates
Jeff Gannon	Freelance
Campbell Gardett	
Charles S. Gardner	
Jack H. Gardner	
Robert W. Gardner	Association for Manufacturing Technology
John Gareeb	
Robert Garfield	Crain Communications, Inc.
Jay Garfinkel	BIC-TV
William Garland	Freelance
Lee Garling	
Wilson Lynn Garner	BNA, Inc.
Arthur Garrison	Freelance
Milton Garrison	
Anne Garside	
Rita Garson	MEDCO
Linda Gasparello	King Publishing Group
Michael Gawenda	Age Newspaper
Marilyn Geewax	Cox Newspapers
Anne Gehrett	Gehrett & Co.
Robert Gehrke	Salt Lake Tribune
Debbie Geiger	Geiger & Associates
Stephen J. Geimann	Bloomberg News
Jerome M. Geisel	Crain Communications, Inc.
Charles R. Gellner	Global Security Analyses
John B. Gemma	
R. Bruce Gemmill	Campbell Associates
Elizabeth George	Congressional Quarterly
Neil J. George	KCI Communications
Andreas Georgiou	International Monetary Fund

Ash Gerecht	
Mike Gerecht	CD Publications
Jack Germond	
Darren Gersh	Nightly Business Report
Kathryn Waters Gest	Powell Tate/Weber Shandwick
Jean Franklin Getlein	
Victoria Gewirz	Victoria Gewirz Photography
Edmund Ghareeb	Embassy of the United Arab Emirates
Bimal C. Ghosh	VA Medical Center
David M. Giammarco	CTV Television Network
Leslie J. Gianelli	Johns Hopkins University
Thomas W. Gibb	Universal Studios
Gwen Gibson	Freelance
William E. Gibson	South Florida Sun-Sentinel
Viola G. Gienger	Bloomberg News
Jeff Giesea	FierceMarkets, Inc.
Patti Giglio	PSG Communications, LLC
Diego Gilardoni	Swiss Public Television
Sarah Gilbert	BBC
Craig Gilbert	Milwaukee Journal Sentinel
Robert H. Giles	Nieman Foundation Harvard University
Dorothy B. Gilliam	George Washington University
Thomas Gillilland	Art in the Hand Gallery
C.M. Sandy Gilmour	Sandy Gilmour Communications
Samuel M. Gilston	Gilston-Kalin Communications, LLC
John Gilstrap	Freelance
Edward Giltenan	Investment Company Institute
Sylvia Gimenez	NAHRO
Gerry Gingrich	U.S. Department of Defense
Steven Ginsburg	Reuters
Joanne Giordano	U.S. Post Office
Greg Giroux	Congressional Quarterly
Terrence J. Giroux	Horatio Alger Association
Yves Gisse	Consultant / International Economic
Jonah Gitlitz	
Vera Glaser	Freelance
Andrew J. Glass	The Politico
Jane H. Glazer	
Gwen Glazer	Nationaljournal.com
Craig Glazer	PJM Interconnection, LLC
Tim Gleason	University of Oregon
Howard Gleckman	Business Week
Robert W. Glenn	National Education Association
Heidi Glenn	Tax Analysts
Ben Goad	The Press-Enterprise
Harold J. Goald	
Kate Goggin	U.S. Department of State
Chour Thong Goh	Embassy of the Republic of Singapore
George M. Gold	Concept Solutions, Inc.
Peter Gold	Fuji Television
Kevin M. Goldberg	Cohn & Marks LLP
Ted Goldman	American Lawyer Media
Michael Goldman	Bloomberg News
Julianna Goldman	Bloomberg News
Jana Goldman	NOAA
Jacobo Goldstein	
Avram Goldstein	Bloomberg News
Peter Goldstein	Kiplinger Washington Editors, Inc.

Frederick Goldstein — Law Office of Frederick Goldstein
Carter H. Golembe — Golembe Reports
Howard Goller — Reuters
Francis D. Gomez — ETS - Education Testing Services
Norman Gomlak, Jr. — Baltimore Sun
Bruce Goodpasture
Bernard A. Goodrich — Goodrich Associates
Lawrence J. Goodrich — High Stakes Writing, LLC
Martha Goodway — Smithsonian Center for Materials, Research & Education
Irwin Goodwin — Physics Today (Retired)
Lucy L. Gordan — Foreign Press Association of Italy
David F. Gordon — American Trucking Associations
Laura Gore — American College of Emergency Physicians
Thomas K. Gorguissian — Al Wafd Egyptian Daily
Beth Gorham — Canadian Press
Timothy J. Gorman — Gorman Group. Inc,
Carolyn Gorman — Insurance Information Institute
William Gormly — NBC News
Shihoko Goto — United Press International
Mary G. Gotschall — Athena Group
Robert Lee Gould — Constellation Energy
Carol Gould — Current Viewpoints
Douglas Gould — Douglas Gould & Co.
Jessica Gould — Washington City Paper
Raghubir Goyal — Asia Today International
Gene Grabowski — Levick Strategic Communications
Dorothy Graham
John P. Gramlich — Baltimore Sun
Stanley I. Grand
Leonard Grant
Cissy Finley Grant — Almanac Newspapers
Robert C. Grant — Inter-Mark Associates
Pamela Wade Grant — U.S. Environmental Protection Agency
Jacqueline Grapin — European Institute
John Grasser — U.S. Department of Energy
Gilman Drew — Grave National Institutes of Health
Denise Graveline — Don't Get Caught
Sarah Gray — NISH
Julia Betty M. Gray — Washington Daily News
Benson L. Grayson
Ruth G. Graze — Graze Advertising
Richard G. Green — American Dental Association
Mark D. Green — Daily Oklahoman
Arthur E. Green — U.S. Department of State
Joel Greenberg — DCPR
Michael Greene — Council for Responsible Nutrition
James M. Greene — NBC News
Keiron Greenhalgh — McGraw-Hill
James Greenhill — Durango Herald
Karen Greenwald — The Burbank Group, LLC
William W. Greenwood — ABC News
Betsy Samuelson Greer
Franklin Greer — GMMB
Diana Gregg — BNA, Inc.
Kimon Gregory — CBS News
Angela Greiling — Keane Bloomberg News
Eric Greitens
Cynthia Grenier — National Interest

Jeffrey Grieco	U.S. AID
Robert J. Griffin	FDA WebView
Patricia K. Griffith	Toledo Blade/Pittsburgh Post Gazette
William M. Grigg	
Charlotte Grimes	Syracuse University
Walter Grimes	W.B. Grimes & Co.
J. Edward Grimsley	Richmond Times-Dispatch (Retired)
Ferde Grofe	Military Combat Library
Sam L. Grogg	University of Miami
Joseph M. Gromelski	Stars & Stripes
Tracy Taylor Grondine	American Farm Bureau Federation
Maureen Groppe	Gannett News Service
Ethan Grossman	Ethan Grossman Engineering
Linda Grover	Obsidian Arts Inc.
Edward A. Grunberg	RCA Global Communications
Robert W. Grupp	Cephalon, Inc.
Matt Gryta	Buffalo News
Hernan Guaracao	Al Dia Newspapers
Elliott H. Gue	KCI Communications
Markus Guenther,	Ph.D. Westdeutsche Allgemeine
Marie C. Guerrero	National Rural Electric Cooperative
Daniel W. Guido	McGraw-Hill
Denny Gulino	Market News International, Inc.
Deborah Gump	Committee of Concerned Journalists
Kathy Gurchiek	Society for Human Resource Management
Hugo D. Gurdon	The Hill
Lawrence Simpson	Guthrie Covington & Burling
Joanne M. Haas	Freelance
David L. Haase	Mindshare Interactive Campaigns
Alan Habbick	Canadian Broadcasting Corp.
Jennifer Haberkorn	Washington Times
Jessie Hackes	WorldReach Communications
Joe Hackett	Embassy of Ireland
Dar Haddix	
Leila Hadley	Freelance
Norma R. Hagan	Freelance
Rebecca Hagelin	Heritage Foundation
George J. Hagerty	Franklin Pierce College
Karim A. Haggag	Egyptian Press & Information Office
Keith Alan Haglund	Science News
Lorna J.B. Hagstrom	Daytona Beach News Journal
Bradley Hague	
Philip Y. Hahn	Blue Ridge Leader
Susan L. Hahn	Gridiron Club
Gordon Haight	101 Communications
Mary Rose Hall	
Marlene W. Hall	LMT
John Hall	Media General (Retired)
Jean Halliburton	
Liz Halloran	U.S. News & World Report
Millie Hallow N	ational Rifle Association
Douglas Halonen	Crain Communications, Inc.
James S. Halota	Halota Enterprises, Inc.
Dirck Halstead	Digital Journalist
Thomas Hambrick	Yomiuri Shimbun
William Hamby	William Hamby Communications
Fukiko Aoki Hamill	Freelance
Stanley Hamilton	

W. Mark Hamilton	American Mental Health Counselors Association
John Hamilton	Hamilton Productions, Inc.
Tara Hamilton	Metropolitan Washington Airports Authority
Janet C. Hamlin	
William E. Hammersla	Trusted Computer Solutions
Corinne F. Hammett	Freelance
Jeanne E. Hammond	Greenwood Publishing
Timothy Hammonds	Food Marketing Institute
Cheryl Hampton	National Public Radio
Mark A. Hamrick	Associated Press Broadcast
John M. Hanchette	St. Bonaventure University
Paul Handley	Agence France Presse
Donald K. Hanes	
Joanna Hanes-Lahr	Hanes-Lahr Public Relations
Paul W. Hanley	Office of the Chairman of the Joint Chiefs of Staff
Jerry Hannifin	
John R. Hanny	
Laurence A. Hanrahan	
Sara Hansard	Crain Communications, Inc.
J. Woods Hansen	
Geri Hansen	Literacy Worldwide Foundation
Tam Harbert	Freelance
Douglas A. Harbrecht	Kiplinger.com
Frances Anne Hardin	International Monetary Fund
Peter Hardin	Richmond Times-Dispatch
James W. Harff	Global Communicators
Peter A. Harkness	Governing Magazine
John H. Harms	
Toby Harnden	Sunday Telegraph
Kenneth R. Harney	Washington Post Writers Group
Sherry Harowitz	Security Management Magazine
Benjamin Harper	Medill News Service
Tim Harper	Toronto Star
John Harrington	Freelance
Lucille E. Harrington	Harrington Associates
Ty Harrington	Harrington Communications
Donna Harris	Crain Communications, Inc.
Barbara Harris	Envision EMI, LLC
Ralph Harris	Reuters
Charles Harris	Yomiuri Shimbun
E. Bruce Harrison	EnviroComm International
Joan Harrison	Harco Publishing
Katie Harrison	Hearst Newspapers
S.L. Harrison	Menckeniana
Joseph Harrow	News-Feature Press, Inc.
Nancy Ann V. Hart	
William M. Hart	
William Hart	Radia Free Asia
Roderick P. Hart	University of Texas at Austin
Marjorie B. Harter	U.S. Department of Agriculture
Carl Hartman	Associated Press
Robert T. Hartmann	
Robert S. Hartmann	National Rehabilitation Hospital
Anne Hartzenbusch	Spanish Language Intrepreting
Mary E. Harvey	
Jack Harvey	Blackburn & Co., Inc.
William B. Harwood	
Khalid Hasan	Daily Times (Pakistan)/Friday Times

Ahson Saeed Hasan	Morningside Partners LLC
Robert H. Haskell	Martinsville Bulletin
Elizabeth Hassett	
Robert Hastings	BAE Systems
Michele E. Hatty	USA Weekend
Robert Hawk	
David Hawkings	Congressional Quarterly
G. Austin Hay	U.S. Department of Transportation
Phillip Wayne Hayes	North Bridge Communications
C. Evans Hays	American Embassy
Richette L. Haywood	PALS, Inc.
Hasan M. Hazar	Ihlas Holding Media Groups
Charles Hazard	
Ed Hazelwood	Aviation Week & Space Technology
Jubi Headley	The Sports Philanthropy Project
Martha Ann Healy	
Susan E. Heavey	Reuters
Mark E. Heckathorn	American University
Roy Heffley	
John D. Heffner	John D. Heffner, PLLC
Bernard F. Heiler	Gilbert House of Middleway
Grover Heiman	
Alice C. Heires	
Margaret Heldring	America's Health Together
Kristiina Helenius	Embassy of Finland
Janet Heller	Freelance
Michael J. Heller	
Marc R. Heller	Watertown Daily Times
Edward L. Helminski	Exchange/Monitor Publications
Gerhard B. Helskog	TV2 Norway
Barbara K. Hembree	Federal Home Loan Bank
Edwin L. Heminger	Courier
Mark Hemingway	Market News International
Michael Hempen	Associated Press
Gene H. Hemphill	New Holland North America Inc
John Hendel	United Press International
Bruce E. Henderson	
Hazel Henderson	Author
Richard Dean Henderson	Commercial Vehicle Safety Alliance
Karin Henriksson	Svenska Dagbladet
Edgar R. Henry	Kiplinger Washington Editors, Inc.
Hi Soo Shin Hepinstall	Freelance
Kristofer Steven Herlitz	Herlitz Co., Inc.
Ken Herman	Cox Newspapers
Stephen A. Herman	Goldman Sachs & Co.
Thomas Herman	Wall Street Journal
Sylvia Hermann	
Alan Hermesch	Alan Hermesch Public Relations, LLC
Debra Gersh Hernandez	
Maurice G. Herndon	
Gloria E. Herndon	G.B. Herndon & Associates
Patricia Herold	Freelance
Jill Herzog	Social & Health Services, LTD
David A. Hess	
David W. Hess	National Journal
Barbara Hesselgrave	Centre City Studios
Otto J. Hetzel	Otto Hetzel Esq.
Kathleen Eleanor	Hickey Freelance

William D. Hickman	Bill Hickman Associates
Peter J. Hickman	Hickman International Consultancy
Robert H. Hicks	Buffalo Bulletin
Yoskiki Hidaka	Global News & Communications
Masano Hidaka	Global News & Communications
Bill Hieronymus	BrazilPortfolio
Maria C. Higgins	U.S. Department of the Army
Keith M. Hill	BNA, Inc.
Terry Hill	Franchising World
Patrice Hill	Washington Times
William O. Hillburg	Los Angeles Newspaper Group
Thomas H. Hillery	Dorchester News
Meredith Hindley	Nationall Endowment for the Humanities
Mary E. Hinds	Press Telegram Newspaper
Cragg Hines	Houston Chronicle
William Hingst	Mastocytosis Society, Inc.
Katsumi Hino	Tokyo Broadcasting System
Joseph U. Hinshaw	
Alice M. Hirsch, Ph.D.	North Allegheny School District
Olga Hirshhorn	
Elaine Hiruo	McGraw-Hill
Shinichi Hisadome	Tokyo Shimbun
William P. Hoar	United Communications Group
Robert Hochstein	Columbia University
Robert F. Hoel Filene	Research Institute
Audrey Hoffer	Milwaukee Journal Sentinel
Gail Hoffman	GlobalSecurity.org
Mark A. Hofmann	Crain Communications, Inc.
Ed Hogan-Bassey	
James H. Hogue	International Publications
Joe Holbert	State of Alaska
Christina Holder	Prison Fellowship
Holly Holeman	
James R. Holland	AARP (Retired)
Jesse Holland	Associated Press
Judy Holland	Hearst Newspapers
William Holland	McGraw-Hill
Melanie Hollands	Harvard Univeristy
Andrew L. Holloway	
Peter A. Holmes	Semloh Advisors
Samuel C.O. Holt	Consultant
Simma Holt	Freelance
Margaret G. Holwill	U.S. Department of State
Jennifer Homer	ASTD
Joseph J. Honick	GMA International LTD
Jerome Hoobler	
Patricia S. Hook	Freelance
Heather A. Hope	
Melissa B. Hope	Email News
Cheyenne Hopkins	American Banker
Stephen Horn	HBL Media Ltd.
Carol J. Horner	Knight Center for Specialized Journalism
Daniel Horner	McGraw-Hill
Mark Horner	Mullen
Nicholas Horrock	Connection Newspapers
Thomas J. Horton	Orrick Herrington & Sutcliffe LLP
Nancy Horton	
Phillip G. Hough	International Business Development

Delia Linares Housein	Venezuelan News Agency
Carrie Housman	American Red Cross
Brant Houston	University of Missouri
John H.F. Hoving	Hoving Group
Atlanta M. Howard	
William J. Howard	Discovery Tours
Ellen Howe	Transportation Security Administration
Sarah Howell	BP America
Jonathan Hoyle	Embassy of Great Britain
Anne W. Hoyt	Grupo Radio Centro
Wade Hoyt	Toyota Motor Sales USA, Inc.
Francis Hsu	U.S. Department of State
Arkie G. Hudkins	Arkie Hupkins Cartoons & Illustrations
Beverly G. Hudnut	Commission on the National Guard
Betty Hudson	National Geographic Society
Ernest B. Hueter	
John Hughes	Bloomberg News
Debra Hughes	D.A. Hughes & Associates
Ann Hughey	Bloomberg News
Nellie F. Hull	
Susan L. Hullin	Hullin Metz & Compnay LLC
Robert W. Hume	U.S. Coast Guard Auxiliary
William B. Hummer	Bank News & Comment
Linda Hunt	Freelance
Ann A. Hunter	Freelance
Kathleen Hunter	Congressional Quarterly
Stephen R. Hunter	Loft Press, Inc.
Mark L. Hurley	Campaign for Tobacco Free Kids
John Edward Hurley	Confederate Memorial Association
Karina Hurley	Hispanic Communications Network
Lawrence Hurley	Los Angeles Daily Journal
Meredith S. Hurt	
James Hurt	NBC News
John D. Husband	
Samira Hussain	CBC Television
Iftikhar Hussain	Voice of America
Sharafat Hussain	Weekly Thikana
Omer Daffallah A. Hussein	
Sam Husseini	IPA Media
Philip A. Hutchinson	
Gereon H. Huth	EPMS, Inc.
Harrison Hutson	
David F. Hyatt	National Automobile Dealers Association
Barbara P. Hyde	American Society for Microbiology
Justin Hyde	Detroit Free Press
Jay Hyde	National Governors' Association
Anna Iannuzzo	A.N.S.A. Italian News Agency
Jerome Idaszak	Kiplinger Washington Editors, Inc.
John Iglehart	Health Affairs Journal Project HOPE
Tadayoshi Ii	TV-Asahi America Inc.
Laura Iiyama	
Jayne Brumley Ikard	
Tom Inglesby	American Motorist Magazine
George B. Irish	Hearst Newspapers
Osita Iroegbu	American Lawyer Media
Rodney D. Irvin	Eastman Chemical Co.
Ismaila Isa	Democrat Newspaper
Gerald R. Ives	BNA, Inc. (Retired)

William E. Jackman	Freelance
Estelle S. Jackson	Freelance
Herb Jackson	Bergen Record
Caroline Jackson	Jackson Enterprises, Inc.
Valarie N. Jackson	McGraw-Hill
Llenda Jackson-Leslie	American Civil Liberties Union
Madeleine Jacobs	American Chemical Society
Robert Jacobs	NASA
Sharon Jacobs	PR Newswire
Andrew Jacobson	MCG Capital Corp.
Victoria M. Jaggard	National Geographic News
Mary Clare Jalonick	Associated Press
Joseph Jamele	
Betty Miles James	
Carol L. James	Carol James Communications
Kathleen Hall Jamieson	Annenberg Public Policy Center
Donna Jamieson	Maloney
Larry Janezich	U.S. Senate Radio & TV Gallery
Peter Allen Janhunen	Airline Pilots Association
Bart Jansen	Congressional Quarterly
Frances K. Jaques	
Judit Ja'Rai	Hungarian Radio
H. Judith Jarrell	Capitol College
Laurence Jarvik	The Idler
Matthew J. Jeanneret	American Road & Transportation Builders Association
Raymond Jefferson	McKinsey & Co.
Terry L. Jemison	U.S. Department of Veterans Affairs
Wayland L. Jenkins	Historic Hope Foundation, Inc.
Michael V. Jennings	Financial Analytics Corp.
Madelyn P. Jennings	Gannett Co., Inc.
Jeanne S. Jennings	JeanneJennings.com
John H. Jennrich	Federal Energy Regulatory Commission
Kristin Jensen	Bloomberg News
Eino E. Jenstrom Finncorr	Press International
Hye Jeong	Daily Press
Tetsuya Jitsu	Nikkei Newspaper
Mary G. Johancen	U.S. Army
Tracy Johnke	
Maurice Johnson	
Dennis A. Johnson	American Planning Association
Steven A. Johnson	ASI Marketing
Sandra K. Johnson	Associated Press
Cathy Johnson	Control Risks Group
Gordon O. F. Johnson	Johnson Associates
Frank S. Johnson	Johnson Group
Kimberly Johnson	McGraw-Hill
Alex Johnson	MSNBC.com
Ken Johnson	Pharmaceutical Research America
Arthur W. Johnson	Safe Travel America, Inc.
David A. Johnson	Scripps Howard News Service
Stephen C. Johnson	The Lima News
Lynn Marie Johnson	U.S. Department of Transportation
Paul Johnson	WRC-TV
Nicholas Johnston	Bloomberg News
Margret Johnston	Deutsche Presse-Agentur
Jeff Johnston	Greystone Partners
Marie G. Johnston	U.S. Department of the Navy
William Johnstone	

Compton S. Jones	Freelance
Arthur J. Jones	
Claudia Jones	AT&T
Edward W. Jones	Free Lance-Star
Nicholas G. Jonson	McGraw-Hill
Robert E. Jordan	National Association of Tax Practitioners
Rosiland Jordan	NBC News
George Jordan	Star-Ledger
Lisa Jorgenson	J.L. Jorgensen & Association
Julian Josephson	Freelance
Rajesh Joshi	T&F Informa UK Ltd.
Ramona Joyce	American Legion
Stephen Joyce	BNA, Inc.
Horace Freeland	Judson Freelance
Sebastian Junger	Freelance
R.N. Jurgenson	News Photo Worldwide
Debra Kahn	Environment & Energy Publishing
Marvin Kalb	Harvard University
Deborah Kalb	The Hill
Harold B. Kaltenheuser	Freelance
Assem Kamal	Al-Ahram International
Joe Kamalick	ICIS News
Jerry Kammer	Copley News Service
John Francis Kamp	Wiley Rein & Fielding
Tsutomu Kanayama	Sophia University
Frank R. Kane	
Theodore Kanter	Theodore's Furniture, Inc.
Anne Kantor	
Gilbert B. Kaplan	King & Spalding, LLP
Herbert E. Kaplow	
Alex Kaplun	Environment & Energy Publishing
Joyce Karam	Al-Hayat Arabic Daily Newpaper
Mary Lou Karch	Karch Group
John R. Karickhoff	
Lorie Karnath	Freelance
Kensuke Karube	Jiji Press
Klaus Kastan	German Public Radio
Theana Yatron Kastens	Central European News
Jose Katigbak	Philippine Star
Satomi Kato	
Yoichi Kato	Asahi Shimbun
Hidenaka Kato	Nikkei Newspaper
Oscar Katov	OK Communications, Inc.
Michelle Katz	HC Strategies
Frank Kauffman	Fleishman-Hillard
Toshifumi Kawano	Mainuchi Shimbun
Shin Kazama	Fuji Television Network, Inc
Mary Hope Keating	
Victor (Pete) Keay	
Gary Kebbel	John S. & James L. Knight Foundation
Barbara A. Keebler	National Catholic Educational Association
Joe Keenan	U.S. Senate Press Gallery
John C. Keeney	Hogan & Hartson
Kenton Keith	Meridian International Center
William C. Keller	
Ed Kelley	Daily Oklahoman
A. Benjamin Kelley	Public Health Advocacy Institute
Leslie Kelley	Viacom/MTV Networks

Edward V. Kelly	American Maritime Officers
Janis Kelly	Flash Corp.
John Kelly	John Kelly Associates
Charles Brian Kelly	University of Virginia
Thomas Kelsch	Stars & Stripes
Gary Kemper	European Pressphoto Agency
Rudy H. Kempter	
Dr. Charles H Kendall	National News Research Syndicate
Stephanie A. Kennan	Alston & Bird LLP
Marthajane Kennedy	
Dr. Allan Kennedy	Morgan State University
Douglas Kennett	Boeing Co.
B. Allen Kenney	Tax Analysts
Arthur Kent	Fast Forward Films, Ltd.
Philip A. Kent	Phil Kent Consulting Inc.
Jeffrey S. Kent	U. S. Senate Press Gallery
Nancy Kercheval	Bloomberg News
Ellen Renee Kesten	SAGA Agency Inc.
Dr. Joan Keston	Pentagon Force Protection Agency
Perry Ketchum	Ketchum Metz Inc.
Arthur B. Keys	International Relief & Development
William P. Kiehl	PD Worldwide
Kathy Kiely	USA Today
Phillip J. Kiesner	Kiplinger Washington Editors, Inc.
John Cantwell Kiley	
Pamela Reeves Kilian	Scripps Howard News Service
Edward Killham	Killham Associates
Linda Killian	Boston University
Erin Killian	Washington Business Journal
Peter Kim	Korean Information Service
Young-Ho Kim	Washington Christian Broadcasting
Penn T. Kimball	
Darcel G. Kimble	PNC Financial Services Group
Claire Kincannon	Dancing Ink Press
Gary C. King	Freelance
Jeffery S. King	Freelance
Robin King	Aluminum Association
Katherine King	George Washington University
Llewellyn W. King	King Publishing Group
Roland H. King	National Association of Independent Colleges & Universitites
Jeanne Kingman	
Nathan Kingsley	Total Communications International
David Kinsman	American College of Physicians
Bogdan Kipling	Kipling News Service
Austin H. Kiplinger	Kiplinger Washington Editors, Inc.
Knight A. Kiplinger	Kiplinger Washington Editors, Inc.
Todd L. Kiplinger	Kiplinger Washington Editors, Inc.
Robert Kirchner	Shenandoah Group
Donald Kirk	Freelance
Elise K. Kirk	
Ken Kirk	Assciation of Metropolitan Sewer Agencies
Joel Kirkland	McGraw-Hill
Harry Kirsbaum	Freelance
Mitsuru Kitano	Embassy of Japan
Mark Alan Kitchens	AARP
Richard P. Kleeman	
Herbert G. Klein	
Gilbert F. Klein	Media General News Service

Marvin Klemow	
Jeffrey R. Kline	Hispanic Radio Network
Sally Kline	Journal Newspapers, Inc.
Kristyn Kline	Socknat Senate Periodical Gallery
Craig Klugman	Journal Gazette
Michael Knapik	McGraw-Hill
Don Knight	
Merv Knobloch	U.S. Department of Labor
Jonathan Knowles	Autodesk
Robert H. Knox	
George W. Koch	Kirkpatrick & Lockhardt
Robert C. Kochersberger	North Carolina State University
Dexter C. Koehl	Travel Industry Association of America
Don Koehler	Georgia Agricultural Commodity
John Koenig Jr.	Associated Press (Retired)
Stephen Koff	The Plain Dealer
Nicholas Kolakowski	Magazine Group/Hi Magazine
Emi Kolawole	Annenberg Political Fact Check
Ken Kolbe	Grand Valley State University-WGUU
Nick Kominus	Agro Washington
Yoshihisa Komori	Sankei Shimbun
Yoshiyuki Komurata	Asahi Shimbun
Michael A. Konczal	Manning Selvage & Lee
Akio Konoshima	
Adam D. Konowe	Sullivan Higdon & Sink
William K. Konze	
Richard Koonce	Richard Koonce Productions
Julia Koppius	Embassy of the Netherlands
Tuna Koprulu	
Daniel W. Kops	Barry Telecommunications Inc.
Paul Koring	Globe & Mail
Richard J. Kosmicki	Dilenschneider Group
Grace J. Koss	
Ihor O. E. Kotlarchuk	
Nick Kotz	Freelance
Bill Kovach	Committee of Concerned Journalists
Gerald J. Kovach	NeuStar, Inc.
Peter J. Kovach	U.S. Department of State
Alan Kovski	McGraw-Hill
Gary Kozel	GK Consultants
Myriam Kozik	
Donald D. Kozusko	Kozusko Harris Vetter Wareh LLP
Michael B. Kraft	
Frederick V. Krais, Jr.	Communications Publishers Inc
Gene Kramer	Freelance
Lawrence Kramer	CBS News
Linda Kramer	People Magazine
Adam Krantz	National Association of Clean Water Agencies
Thomas Kranz	Inman Law Firm
Ralph M. Krause	
Paul M. Krawzak	Copley News Service
Andrew T. Kreig	Wireless Communications Association
Durrell M. Kreisher	Copley News Service
Adam Krell	Auteur Productions LTD
Gerald Krell	Auteur Productions LTD
W. John E. Kress	National Museum of Natural History
Thaddeus R. Kresse	Washington Post Radio
Harriet M. Kriesberg	

Barbara Kivimae — Krimgold Center for the Advancement of Health
David K. Krohne — Institute of Scrap Recycling Industries
George M. Kroloff — George Kroloff & Associates
Kathryn Kross — Bloomberg News
Joseph C. Krovisky — U.S. Department of Justice
Daniel E. Kubiske — Freelance
Rod William Kuckro — McGraw-Hill
Al Kuettner — UPI
Gene Kuleta — Metro Networks
Raj Kumar — Development Executive Group
Tom Kunkel — University of Maryland
John F. Kurie — Mecklenburg Times
Yulii Kurnosov — Waggener Edstrom
Scott Kuschmider — Office of U.S. Representative Dale E. Kildee
Yeiichi (Kelly) Kuwayama
Jai Hong Kwon — MBC TV & Radio, South Korea
Leonore M. Laan
Gary LaBella — Recreational Vehicle Industry Association
Pauline A. Labrie
A. Joseph LaCovey
Christopher Lagan — Data
Brian K. Lagana — Pedorthic Footwear Association
Janis Lamar — Northrop Grumman Corp.
Brian P. Lamb — C-SPAN
Brandon J. Lambert — Fuji Television
Lisa Lambert — Reuters
Adam J. Landis — Freelance
Ben Lando — United Press International
Catherine J. Landry — McGraw-Hill
Kimberly Lankford — Kiplinger Washington Editors, Inc.
Maura Kelly Lannan — Freelance
Edward A. Lapham — Automotive News
Wayne LaPierre — National Rifle Association
Fermin Lares — Tal Cual, Venezuela Daily News
Catherine Larkin — Bloomberg News
Annette Larkin — Rational Public Relations
Donald R. Larrabee — Griffin-Larrabee News Bureau
Daniel M. Larson — Texas Instruments
Christina Larson — Washington Monthly
Fred C. Lash — VSE Corp.
Jennifer Laszlo — Israel Project
Lynden Theodore Latiak
Val Lauder — University of North Carolina
Matt Lauer — Qorvis Communications
Annie L. Lauler — Annie Lauler Corp.
Nathan Lauterstein — Gannett Co., Inc.
Bianca Lavies — National Geographic Society
Patrick Lavigne — NRECA
Carl Edgar Law — Freelance
E. Janice Law — Galveston Daily News
William M. Lawbaugh — NASA
Jessica Lawrence-Hurt — Heldref Publications
Belford V. Lawson — Federal Communications Commissions
Philip Lax — Chathill Management Inc.
Mell Lazarus — Creators Syndicate. Inc.
Anna L. Lea — Helen-Sperry Lea Foundation
Robert D. Leahy — Leahy & Associates LLC
Craig C. Lebamoff — U.S. Department of State

Sabah Lebbar	Maghreb Arab Press
Renee C. LeBoeuf	SAIC, Science Application International
Michael L. Ledford	Lewis-Burke Associates LLC
Donald E. Ledwig	Consultant
Ha Won Lee	Chosun Daily Newspaper
Harry Sunmyung Lee	Korea Press International
Kwang Chool Lee	Korean Broadcasting System
Chin Ho Lee	LCH Group, Inc.
Kristin Lee	League of Conservation Voters
Richard F. Lee	Media General News Service
Jinsook Lee	Munhwa Broadcasting Corp.
Jessica Lee	USA Today
Robert B. LeGrand	U.S. Department of Education
Mildred K. Lehman	Freelance
Ray Lehmann	A.M. Best Co.
Evan Lehmann	MediaNews Group/Lowell Sun
Marvin Leibstone	Global Security & Trade Journal
Katherine Leiken	Kingsland Productions
Donna Leinwand	USA Today
Jean LeMasurier	Gorman Health Group
Harry A. Lenhart	
Jeffrey Lenorovitz	InfoWest Group
Jacqueline Leo	Reader's Digest
Richard A. Leonard	Gannett Co., Inc.
George Leopold	CMP Media LLC
Wil Lepkowski	Freelance
Jessica Leshnoff	Freelance
Robert Lesino	U.S. Department of the Treasury
Michael Lesparre	Roll Call Report Syndicate
Michael Lessin	ConnectLive Communications Inc.
Barnett B. Lester	
William Lester	Associated Press
Carl P. Leubsdorf	Dallas Morning News
Jim Leusner	Orlando Sentinel
Fay Leviero	
Herbert M. Levine	
Jeff Levine	Hill & Knowlton
Nathan Levinson	Congressional Quarterly
Riva Levinson	KRL International LLC
Frances L. Lewine	CNN
Joyce P. Lewis	Freelance
Katherine Lewis	Freelance
Robert D.G. Lewis	
Craig Lewis	
Robert G. Lewis	Agra News
Finlay Lewis	Copley News Service
Charles Lewis	Fund for Independence in Journalism
Robert K. Lewis	Global Advancement, LLC
Charles J. Lewis	Hearst Newspapers
Nancy Lewis	SAE International
Edward I. Lewis	Toyota Motor Co.
Gilbert A. Lewthwaite	Baltimore Sun
Bernard Liebes	
David Lightman	Hartford Courant
Tony Likins	Institute of World Politics
Richard A. Lillquist	
Elena Lilly	
Ian Limbach	Financial Times

Rae Lindsay	R & R Writers/Agents
Janet Bodnar Linnehan	Kiplinger Washington Editors, Inc.
Richard Linowes	American University
Harold H. Lion	
Larry Lipman	Cox Newspapers
Donald M. Lipton	American Farm Bureau Federation
Meredith Lisagor	New York Methodist Hospital
Richard Littell	Law Offices of Richard Littell
Basil R. Littin	
Laura M. Litvan	Bloomberg News
Ding Yih Liu	
Kuen-Yuan Jorge Liu	Central News Agency
Robin Lloyd	Reuters
James Lobe	Inter Press Service
Samuel R. Loboda	
Carolyn Lochhead	San Francisco Chronicle
Paul H. Lockwood	
Martha J. Lockwood	American Association of Political Consultants
Raimund Loew	ORF- Austrian Radio & TV
Sheila Loftus	Sheila's Information Network
Robert Logan	University of Missouri
Ralph Loglisci, Jr.	NCIFAP
Gina Kerra Logue	Middle Tennessee State University
Ann Hume Loikow	
Simon Lomax	Argus Media Group
C. Thomas Long	
Richard Long	Eagle Newspapers
Cúlver J. Long	Multinational Media
Mindy Rae Long	NATSO
Benjamin H. Long	Travaille
Penelope Longbottom	Longbottom Communications, LLC
Nick Longworth	AFM Group
James D. Looper	
Lesley Lopez	America's Most Wanted
Maureen Lorenzetti	Reuters
Francis J. Lorson	Supreme Court (Retired)
Jean Louviere	
William E. Loveless	McGraw-Hill
Doree Lovell	Freelance
W. Rush Loving	Loving Associates, Ltd.
James F. Low	
William A. Lowther	
Jeffrey S. Lubar	Mortgage Insurance Companies of America
David D. Lucci	
Joseph A. Luchok	March of Dimes
Caro Elise Luhrs	
Ilene Lumpkin	Berkeley College
Michael Lurie	
Patricia Lusk	
Cody Lusk	
Edward J. Lynett	Scranton Times-Tribune
Robert J. Lynett	Times Shamrock Communication
Monique M. Lyons	Discovery Communications, Inc.
Tamara Lytle	Orlando Sentinel
Rafic K. Maalouf	Freelance
Courtney B. Mabeus	The Examiner
Larry Macauley	COL
David MacDonald	

Neil MacDonald	Canadian Broadcasting Corp.
Lynn MacDonald-Westrope	AFL-CIO Solidarity Center
Don Mace	FEDweek LLC
Colin Macilwain	Nature America, Inc.
Duncan MacInnes	U.S. Department of State
Ian R. MacKenzie	MacKenzie McCheyne Inc.
Ross Mackenzie	Richmond Times-Dispatch
Paul Mackie	World Resources Institute
Matthew Mackowiak	
Michael MacMurray	U.S. Department of Defense
Neil MacNeil	Time. Inc.
Helen Drury Macsherry	Stone Ridge School
Ian MacSpadden	NBC News
Mike Madden	Gannett News Service
Thomas J. Madden	Venable LLP
Bob Madigan	WTOP Radio
Wayne Madsen	WayneMadsenReport
Howard M. Mager	McGraw-Hill
Fairley W. Mahlum	AAA Foundation for Traffic Safety
Arshad Mahmud	Daily Prothom Alo
Carol A. Mahoney	
Staci Maiers	National Education Association
Michal Wynn Mainwaring	Freelance
Frank Maisano	Bracewell & Giuliani
Edward Maixner	Kiplinger Washington Editors, Inc.
R. Roger Majak	
Anthony S. Makris	Mercury Group
Michael J. Malbin	Campaign Finance Institute
Joy Malbon	CTV Canadian TV
Herbert K. Mallard	
Richard J. Maloy	Thomson Newspapers (Retired)
Timothy K. Maloy	United Press International
Suzanne Malveaux	CNN
Ralph Malvik	
Joe Mancias	
Saverio Mancina	
Katie Mandes	Pew Center on Global Climate Change
Harry Mandil	MPR Associates, Inc.
Arnold Mann	Time, Inc.
Stacey Mannari	National Geographic
Elizabeth H. Manning	The Fine Line
B. Thomas Mansbach	Overseas Private Investment Corp.
Ruth Mantell	Dow Jones Marketwatch
H. Alexander Manuel	U.S. Dept. of Housing & Urban Development
Diane L. Maple	American Lung Association
Phyllis R. Marcuccio	
Barbara Hoch Marcus	Kiplinger Washington Editors, Inc.
Judith C. Marden	
Samuel Marein-Efron	
Doris Margolis	Editorial Associates
Eric S. Margolis	Toronto Sun Newspapers
Bernard Margueritte	Tygoonik Solidarnose
Herbert E. Marks	Squire Sanders & Dempsey LLP
Judith Marlane	Marlane Media Consultants
Michael J. Marlow	King Publishing Group
Katy Marquardt	Kiplinger Washington Editors, Inc.
Joe Marquette	
Maria D. Marquez	U.S. Information Agency

Eric Marquis	Quebec Government Office of Tourism
Diana Marrero	Gannett News Service
Emma Marris	Nature Magazine
Jessica Marron	McGraw-Hill
Christoph V. Marschall	Der Tagesspiegel
Charmayne Marsh	American Chemical Society
Jack Marsh	Freedom Forum
James J. Marshall	Bradinal Associates
Ivan D. Martchev	KCI Communications
David K. Martin	Freelance
Mia Martin	
Abby McCardell Martin	
M. Lynne Martin	
J. Sperling Martin	
John J. Martin	Columbia University
Chelsey Martin	Embassy of Australia
Conrad Martin	Fund for Constitutional Government
Gregory A. Martin	General Motors
Michael J. Martin	HELDREF Publications
Gary R. Martin	San Antonio Express News
George A. Martin	U.S. Department of Agriculture
Harold H. Martin	United Press International
Fred J. Martin	University of California
Jose Roberto Martinez	Luis Munoz-Marin Foundation
Charles S. Marwick	Medical News Reports
Alan L. Marx	King & Ballow
Lisa Mascaro	Las Vegas Sun
Georg Mascolo	Der Spiegel
Martin D. Masiuk	IMR Group Inc.
Robert S. Mason	
Glen D. Mason	American Physical Therapy Association
Mindy Masters	ICEO, Ltd.
Judy Mathewson	Freelance
C. Tyler Mathisen	CNBC
Jelena Cukic Matic	Embassy of Serbia
Patrick C. Matrisciana	Jeremiah Films/I.P.A.
Nathalie Mattheiem	Le Soir
Curt Matthews	Care First Blue Cross Blue Shield
Nancy H. Matthews	Meridian International Center
Dana Matthews	
Karen Matusic	American Petroleum Institute
Sherry Peters Matz	Freelance
Anthony E. Mauro	Legal Times
Albert L. May	George Washington University
Sue Mayborn	Temple Daily Telegram
Joseph L. Mayer	Copper & Brass Fabricators Council
David R. Mayhood	Mayhood Co.
Tshepo Mazibuko	Embassy of the Republic of South Afica
Timothy Mazzucca	American Banker
Jerome F. Mazzuchi	King Publishing Group
Susanna McBee	
Gregory McCaffery	BNA, Inc.
John G. McCandless	Toyota Motor Sales, USA, Inc.
Jean McCann	Medical News Inc.
William C. McCarren	Medialink
Andrea McCarren	WJLA-TV
Pender M. McCarter	IEEE-USA
S. Kelly McCarthy	Freelance

James McCartney	Knight Ridder (Retired)
Michael McCaughan	
Eileen T. McClay	
Rebecca L. McClellan	
Karel McClellan	Karel McClellan, Inc.
Bill McCloskey	
William B. McCloskey	Highliners Associates
Brooks McClure	Imar Corp.
Donovan V. McClure	The Carmen Group
Lauren McCollough	Crimes of War Project
Alan McConagha	
Bruce McConnell	McConnell International LLC
David F. McConnell	WTOP Radio
Richard McCormack	Publishers & Producers
Kevin McCormally	Kiplinger Washington Editors, Inc.
Stephen McCormick	
John McCormick	
Jane Moss McCune	
Michael D. McCurry	Public Strategies Washington Inc.
Chuck McCutcheon	Newhouse News Service
Lee McDonald	A. M. Best Co.
William F. McDonald	Emery Worldwide (Retired)
John McDonnell	Washington Post
Timothy J. McDonough	American Council on Education
Hobart K. McDowell	Bart McDowell
Charles R. McDowell	Richmond Times-Dispatch
Sandra McElwaine	Freelance
Sally C. McElwreath	
Ann Carey McFeatters	
Dale B. McFeatters	Scripps Howard News Service
Thomas J. McGee	
John F. McGee	McGee Enterprises
Robert M. McGee	Occidental International Corp.
Roy L. McGhee	
Elliott M. McGinnies	American University
Sheila A. McGough	
Michael P. McGough	Pittsburgh Post-Gazette
Victoria McGrane	Congressional Quarterly
George E. McGrath	
Patrick E. McGrath	WTTG-TV
Patrick B. McGuigan	Independent Writer
Barrett McGurn	Author
Sharon McHale	Freddie Mac
Susan Hume McIntosh	Federal Reserve System
Margaret Ann McKay	
Patricia Marina McKee	International Child Art Foundation
Robert J. McKee	Watson Wyatt Worldwide
Paul M. McKellips	U.S. Department of Agriculture
Edward McKenna	
James L. McKenna	
Bobbi McKenna	Freelance
Barrie McKenna	Globe & Mail
Kerry B. McKenney	Office of U.S. Rep. Donald |Payne
Phyllis Corbitt McKenzie	Capital Speakers Inc.
Joan McKinney	U.S. Senate Press Gallery
James A. McKoy	
Ruth E. McLaine	
John McLaughlin	Oliver Productions

Demian McLean	Bloomberg News
Winzola McLendon	
Jason McLure	Legal Times
Dorothy McManus	U.S. Environmental Protection Agency
Theresa McMasters	
Paul McMorris	Freelance
Douglas C. McNabb	McNabb Associates, P.C.
Patricia G. McNeely	University of South Carolina
Anjetta McQueen	Brookings Institution
Loren R. McQueen	Communications & Control Inc.
James McQueeny	Winning Strategies Washington
Larry McQuillan	American Institutes for Research
Mark McQuillan	Bloomberg News
William McQuillen	Bloomberg News
Vivienne McRoberts	The Examiner
William F. McSweeny	
James A. McTague	Barron's Magazine
Jane Meacham	
Marianne Means	Hearst Newspapers
Kathy Means	Produce Marketing Association
Daniel Medinger	Catholic Review
John Mehaffey	Selective Marketing & Mehaffey
Lisa Meier	Washington National Opera
Dori Meinert	Freelance
Mark Melcher	
David R. Melendy	Associated Press
Kenneth Mellgren	Associated Press Broadcast
Ari Meltzer	ABC News
Helene L. Melzer	
Marilynn Deane	Mendell Win Spin CIC, Inc.
Micheline Mendelsohn	Mendelsohn & Associates
Carlos Mendo	El Pais
Nonoy Mendoza	Filipono Image
Michael J. Meneer	Council on Competitiveness
Thomas Mentzer	Urban Institute
Marsha Mercer	Media General News Service
Anne Morrissy Merick	
James E. Merna	
Jesse H. Merrell	Merrell Enterprises
Paul R. Merrion	Crain Communications, Inc.
Robert W. Merry	Congressional Quarterly
Donald P. Merwin	Cahners Publishing. Inc.
Harold T. Meryman	Biomedical Research Institute
John M. Metelsky	Freelance
Eugene H. Methvin	
Mark Meudt	Anteon Corp.
Philip C. Meyer	
Roland H. Meyer	Enterprise Consultants
Kenneth Meyer	U.S. Census Bureau
Philip E. Meyer	University of North Carolina
Richard A. Meyer	VIP Group Travel Ltd.
Jim Michaels	USA Today
Mike Michaelson	
Jennifer Lynn	Michels Travel Agent Magazine
Joan Bryna Michelson	JB Michelson & Associates
Andrea R. Mihailescu	United Press International
Hoda Tawfik Mikhail	Al Ahram Newspaper
Noel J. Milan	National Edowment for Humanities

Richard A. Milburn	Northrop Grumman Corp.
Rosemary Mild	Magic Island Literary Works
Mark K. Miller	Freelance
Yvonne Lee Miller	
David E. Miller	
Kevin Miller	Bloomberg News
Arthur P. Miller	Bylines
William H. Miller	Industry Week Magazine
Bonnie Miller	Intermountain Commercial Record
James A. Miller	JA Miller & Associates
Eleanor C. Miller	National Rural Electric Cooperative
Kristie Miller	News Tribune
Andrew C. Miller	Prism Public Affairs
Julie Ann Miller	Science News
Lane F. Miller	Transnational Development Consortium
Patricia O. Miller	U.S. Coast Guard
Linda B. Miller	Volunteer Trustees Foundation
Brendan Miniter	Wall Street Journal
Gloria Minott	WHUR-FM Radio
Nell Minow	Freelance
John Minting	United Press International
Robert N. Miranda	Cognizant Communication Corp.
Robert N. Mirelson	NASA
Patrick A. Mirza	Society for Human Resources
Anthony A. Mitchell	
Kirsten B. Mitchell	Reporters Committee for Freedom of the Press
Helen Mitternight	Mitternight Communications
Francine Modderno	Bellmont Buzz
Kenneth Moffett	Labon Arbitrator
Matthew Mogul	Kiplinger Washington Editors, Inc.
Saad Mohammad	Kuwait News Agency
Elizabeth A. Moize	
Samuel T. Mok	
Russell Mokhiber	Corporate Crime Reporter
Andrew R. Mollison	Freelance
Gwendolyn E. Mollison	
Linda Molnar	Hincs Capital Research & Management Co.
Mark Monday	Titan Corp.
Melissa Monk	Energy Policy TV
Bill Monroe	
Marion Montague-Metcalfe	
Sara B. Montanari	
William J. Montgomery	
Anne Montgomery	Alliance for Health Reform
Hale Montgomery	Capstone Communications, Inc.
Karen Moody	Washington Media Associates
Joan Mooney	Auto Exec Magazine
Alexander X. Mooney	National Journalism Center
Johnnie A. Moore	
Bob Stahly Moore	
Donald T. Moore	American University
Miles David Moore	Crain Communications, Inc.
Iverson Moore	National Association of Realtors
William W. Moore	Olentangy Associates
Richard A. Moore	Richard A. Moore, LLC
Adonai Morales	NAHPF
Mike Moran	Ford Motor Co.
Celeste Morga	Bellizzi International Narcotic Enforcement

John R. Morgan	Textile Rental Magazine
Carol L. Morgan	U.S. Environmental Protection Agency
Lucie Morillon	Reporters Without Borders
Christopher Morin	Thompson Publishing Group, Inc.
Robert F. Morison	Journal of Commerce (Retired)
Joe Morocon	Kuwait News Agency
Frank Morring	Aviation Week & Space Technology
Richard Morris	
Robert Kellogg Morris	Global Business Dialogue, Inc.
Amy Morris	WTOP/WFED
John Fass Morton	DomesticPreparedness.com
Peter Morton	Financial Post
Joseph Morton	Omaha World-Herald
J. Robert Moskin	Freelance
Daniel B. Moskowitz	Freelance
Laurence Moskowitz	Medialink Worldwide Inc
Matt Mosley	Fuju Television
Mary Mosquera	Federal Computer Week - 1105 Media
Yiannis G. Mostrous	KCI Communications
Joe G. Motheral	Freelance
Gregory W. Mott	Bloomberg News
Thomas J. Mowbray	Journal of Enterprise Architecture
Yvette Moy	Stars & Stripes
Thelma S. Mrazek	
Amal Mudallali	Quretim Palace
Sherry L. Mueller	National Council for International Visitors
Nigel D. Muir	
George M. Mulhern	
Thomas R. Mullen	News Letter Journal
Richard Mullens	Silverstein & Mullens
John Mulligan	Providence Journal
Alicia Mundy	Seattle Times
Mary Norris Munroe	
Michael R. Muraszko	VantagePoint Strategies, LLC
Diane Murphy	Federal City Communications
C. Westbrook Murphy	PricewaterhouseCoopers
Dennis H. Murphy	Ruder-Finn, Inc.
Kenneth B. Murphy	Universal Air Travel Plan Inc.
Betty Southard Murphy, Esq.	Baker & Hostetler, LLP
Emily Murray	Freelance
Lee Winslow Murray	Beverage Journal
Samuel H. Murray	Profit Sharing/401(k) Council of America
Ghulam Murtaza	Voice of America
Talha Gibriel Musa	Asharq Al-Awsat Newspaper
Sean Mussenden	Media General News Service
Sam Ferguson Musser	Conestoga Title Insurance Co.
Charles D. Myers	McClatchy Newspapers
Larry E. Naake	National Association of Counties
Laurie Nadel	Freelance
Ruth G. Nadel	
Natasha Rosenstock Nadel	American Jewish Press Association
Allison Nadelhaft	National Association of Social Workers
Aki Naganuma	Tokyo Shimbun
Dawson B. Nail	Warren Publishing. Inc. (Retired)
P.C. Nair	Montgomery College
Helen Nash	
Bradley Nash	
Claus M. Naske	Naske & Associates

Daniel Nassif	Middle East Radio Network
James R. Naughton	
Krishnan P. Nayar	Telegraph
George Franklin Neavoll	
William Neikirk	Chicago Tribune
Andris Neimanis	
Brian Nelson	Boeing Co.
Katherine Shaw Nelson F	ood & Travel Writer
Salameh B. Nematt	Al Hayat Newspaper
Jeff Nesmith	Cox Newspapers
Allen H. Neuharth	Freedom Forum
Jodie Newell	Freelance
Christopher J. Newkumet	McGraw-Hill
Hugh C. Newton	Hugh C. Newton & Associates
Eric Newton	John & James Knight Foundation
Jay Newton-Small	Bloomberg News
Anh N. Nguyen	Pho Nho Vietnamese Newspaper
Lee Nichols	
Michael Nicholson	North Atlantic Treaty Organization
Jonathan Nicholson	Reuters
Katerina Nikolova	City College of San Francisco
Diane S. Nine	Nine Speaker's, Inc.
Carol A. Nippert	Hearst Newspapers
Ryoichi Nishida	Sankei Shimbun
Takuya Nishimura	Hokkaido Shimbun Press
Setsu Nishiumi	Fuji Television
Kaoru Nishizaki	Asahi Shimbun
William Nitze	Equinoz Energy Solutions Inc.
William H. Noack	Noack & Associates, LLC
Andrea Noble	Gazette Newspapers
Barbara Nocera	Mazda North American Operations
David S. Nolan	Nolan & Co.
Diana Nolan	STF Productions, Inc.
James A. Noone	The Washington Group
Knut-Einar Norberg	Dagen
Rod Nordland	Newsweek
David M. North	
Don North	Northstar Productions Inc.
C. JoAnne	Norton Bloomberg News
Susan Norton	National Geographic Society
Janet E. Novack	Forbes Magazine
Robert D. Novak	Evans & Novak
Jean McDuffie	Nowak Freelance
Gary K. Nurenberg	Freelance
Robert M. Nutting	Ogden Newspapers, Inc.
David Nydick	DANY News Service
Ursula Oaks	NAFSA: Association of International Education
Herman J. Obermayer	Publication Advisors Inc.
Cyril O'Brien	
Richard O'Brien	American Association of Advertising
Allie O'Connor	Attorney
Thomas Alfred O'Day	
Rice Odell	Freelance
Marjorie O'Donnell	Washington Times
Robert Ogburn	
Richard M. Ogden	NW Consulting
Yasuyuki Oguri	Tokyo-Chunichi Shimbun
Kenneth Ron O'Halloran	

Stephen L. O'Hearn	Sysorex Federal, Inc.
Gloria Ohliger	
Yuri Okuda	Time Warner, Inc.
Hebe Russo Olhagaray	T.V. Sodre
Cortright W. Oliphant	Oliphant News Service
Thomas Oliver	National Hispanic Press Foundation
Daniel J. Olmstead	United Press International
Pam Olson	Freelance
Thomas Olson	Pittsburgh Tribune-Review
William J. O'Neill	National Geographic News Service
Sally C. Opstein	
John R. Oravec	
Robert Orben	
Peggy M. Sands	Orchowski
Joseph Carrick O'Reilly	Bloomberg News
Anne P. Orleans	Washington New Observer
Thomas White Orme	Grandale Farm LLC
Lawrence O'Rourke	McClatchy Newspapers
Sarah Orrick	Congressional Digest Corp.
Ole Morten Orset	Radio Norway P4
Hafez Al Mirazi Osman	Al Jazeera
Virgil W. Ostrander	Energy Services Group
Jim Ostroff Kiplinger	Washington Editors, Inc.
Victor Ostrowidzki	Flagler College
Ryuichi Otsuka	Yomiuri Shimbun
Robert Ottenhoff	Guidestar
Patrick Ottenhoff	NationalJournal.com
Charles L. Overby	Freedom Forum
Geneva Overholser	University of Missouri
James Owen	Edison Electric Institute
Robert B. Owen	
Sheila Owens	Newspaper Association of America
Dion O'Wyatt	
Thomas Oxendine	EOP Group, Inc.
Kathryn Page	
Clarence Page	Chicago Tribune
Paul Page	Journal of Commerce
Gregory Page	U.S. Department of Justice
Susan Page	USA Today
Wendy Pagonis	American Red Cross
Walter C. Paine	
Janne K.C. Pak	USA Journal
John Pallasigue	Institute of World Politics
Ann Therese D. Palmer	Freelance
Sandra Palmer	
Craig A. Palmer	American Dental Association
Donna Larrabee Palmer	Congressional Quarterly
Anna Palmer	Legal Times
David R. Palombi	Freddie Mac
Juan R. Palomo	American Petroleum Institute
Tony Pals	National Association of Independent Colleges & Universitites
Benjamin L. Palumbo	Palumbo & Cerrell of Virginia
Harry K. Panjwani, MD, PhD	Medical Research & Communications
Ike Pappas	Icarus Asociates
Leonard V.	Parent Gas Price Report
John Parker	Freelance
Nancy Parker	
John Parker	Blue Cross Blue Shield Association

Elliott Parker	Central Michigan University
Richard Parker	New Republic
Michael Parks	University of Southern California
Amie Parnes	Scripps Howard News Service
Kelli Parsons	Hill & Knowlton
Hemai Parthasarathy	Public Library of Science
Marianne Pastor	
Jeff Patch	The Politico
David Patrician	Voice of America
Dee Pattee	
Eliza Patterson	Freelance
Dean J. Patterson	Reuters
Oliver B. Patton	Heavy Duty Trucking
Lawrence Paulson	Hoffman-Paulson Associates
Kenneth A. Paulson	USA Today
William Howard Payne	
Patricia Payne	
J. Leon Peace Jr.	Freelance
Robert Pear	New York Times
Susan Pearce	Consultant
Ronald W. Pearson	Pearson & Pipkin Inc.
Lisa McGrady Pellegrin	McPell Communications Co.
Richard Pellegrino	Central Arkansas Research
Patrick L. Pellerin	Patrick Pellerin Public Relations
Jeremy L. Pelofsky	Reuters
Annemarie Pender	Honda North America, Inc.
Edmund Pendleton	
Patricia Pengra	NASA
Jaime Perales	Organization of American States
Derwin Pereira	Straits Times
Rob Perks	Natural Resources Defense Council
David L. Perlman	
Herbert C. Perone	NASD Security
Matthew Perrone	Associated Press
James Perry	
Frank Perryman	Associated Press
Edward Pesce	U.S. Senate Periodical Gallery
Victor E. Pesqueira	
Claudia Peters	Food Marketing Institute
Frederick G. Peters	University of Michigan
Rosemary D. Petersen	Copley News Service
John E. Peterson	APCO Worldwide, Inc.
Scott Peterson	Nuclear Energy Institute
Jon Petrovich	Associated Press
Michael Petruzzello	Qorvis Communications
Richard Pfeiffer	Niagara Gazette
Robert Pflieger	National Association of Home Builders
Penny Phelps	Areva Inc.
Timothy Phelps	Newsday
Michael E. Phelps	The Examiner
Pat Phibbs	BNA, Inc.
Frank B. Phillippi	Lakeview Productions
Ronald B. Phillips	Animal Health Institute
Joe Phillips	Auto Exec Magazine
Beau Phillips	Beer Institute
Walter Phillips	Carteret Publishing Co.
Lockwood Phillips	Carteret Publishing Co.
Jeanne Phillips	Phillips-Van Buren Inc.

Cara Santos Pianesi	United Nations Development Program
Bruce Piasecki	
Dianne W. Pickar	District of Columbia
Philip Piemonte	Federal Employees News Digest
Gregory T. Pierce	Washington Times
Jim Pierobon Ogilvy	Public Relations Worldwide
Marilyn Piety	Montgomery County Public Health Services
Eberhard Piltz	ZDF German Television
Albert Wm. Jos. Pinder	U.S. House of Representatives
Natasha Pinol	
Christina Pino-Marina	Washingtonpost.com
Edmund Pinto	PA Consulting Group, Inc.
Wesley G. Pippert	University of Missouri
Alice C. Plaisted	
Judith Platt	Association of American Publishers
Paul R. Plawin	PlayWin Enterprises
Sue Pleming	Reuters
John P. Plum	
Jeff Plungis	Bloomberg News
Jane Podesta	Time, Inc.
Edgar A. Poe Jr.	U.S. Department of Agriculture
John Poirier	Reuters
Gene F. Policinski	First Amendment Center
Holly Pollinger	Deloitte & Touche
Brigette J Langmade Polmar	Cox Broadcasting
Norman Polmar	Maritime Publications, Ltd.
Judith D. Pomeranz	Freelance
Susan Pompian	Busan National University
Stanley Pond	BNA, Inc.
Albano Francis Ponte	DuPont Investment Bankers Inc.
W. Daniel Poole	
J. William Poole	
David Popper	Watson Wyatt Worldwide
Chuck Porcari	American Federation of Teachers
Betty (Lilly) Porter	
Margaret Pratt Porter	Vietnam Veterans of America
S. Eugene Poteat	
Steven F. Potisk	Dow Jones Marketwatch
Wendell B. Potter	Cigna Corp.
Danielle Potuto	American Society Clinical Oncology
Anne Elizabeth Powell	Civil Engineering
Stewart Powell	Hearst Newspapers
Joseph L. Powell	Powell Tate/Weber Shandwick
Francis Gary Powers	Cold War Museum
Martha C. Powers	International Reports: Early Warning
William C. Powers	Mercury Group
Charles H. Powers	Porter Novelli
Rebecca Noah Poynter	Poynter Communications
Carol Pozefsky	Northeast Broadcasting
William G. Prescott	Brook Lane Health Services
G. Jefferson Price	Freelance
Deborah Jane Price	Detroit News
Griffith B. Price, Jr.	Finnegan, Henderson, Farabow, Garrett & Dunner LLP
Louis Victor Priebe	Priebe PR
L. Edgar Prina	Copley News Service (Retired)
Giovanni Prosina	
Joan Pryde	Kiplinger Washington Editors, Inc.
Charles R. Pucie	Foundation of the National Institute of Health

Matt Pueschel	U.S. Medicine, Inc.
Gemma R. Puglisi	American University
Richard Pullen	Leader's Edge Magazine
Daniel E. Pulliam	Government Executive
Dr. Jack Pulwers	JP News
Todd S. Purdum	Vanity Fair
Nicholas Pyle	Pyle & Associates, Inc.
Sana Qadar	CTV News
James Quello	Wiley Rein & Fielding
Mark Quigley	National Council on Disability
Mary Kay Quinlan	University of Nebraska, Lincoln
Larry A. Quinn	U.S. Department of Agriculture
Joey Quinto	California Journal/Filipino America
Earl C. Quist	Toyota Motor North America, Inc.
Chuck Raasch	Gannett News Service
Md. Sayeed ur Rabb	Thikana
Eric W. Rabe	Verizon Communications
Jennifer Rabinowitz	White House Media LLC
Russell J. Rader	Insurance Institute for Highway Safety
Alex Radin	
Chitra Ragavan	U.S. News & World Report
John C. Rahming	
Gail A. Raiman	Associated Builders & Contractors
Marcelo Raimon	ANSA Italian News Agency
Mary H. Raitt	
Rodger Rak	University of California
Wafik Ramadan	L'Orient - Le Jour
Lourdes F. Ramann	Ramann & Graspo TV, Inc.
Richard R. Ramlall	RCN Corp.
Stewart W. Ramsey	
Ann Ramsey	Backstory Productions
Martha L. Ramsey	Ramsey Communications
Sheppard Ranbom	CommunicationWorks
Judith E. Randal	Mouse Trap Farm
Myron W. Randall	The Frederick News Post
Cortes W. Randell	Corporate Media Services
Jennings Randolph	St. Johns Mercy Skilled Center
Charles Rangel	U.S. House of Representatives
Angelique Ras	Nexstar Broadcasting/NBC25
Wayne Rash	Ziff-Davis Media
William Raspberry	Washington Post
Sidra Rausch	
Harold J. Raveche	Stevens Institute of Technology
Rachel Ray	Freelance
Mary Ann Rayner	Morning Call (Retired)
Cheryl A. Reagan	Federal News Service, Inc.
Viki Reath	U.S. General Services Administation
Bill Rechin	National Syndicated Cartoonist
Maria E. Recio	Fort Worth Star-Telegram
Thomas J. Reckford	World Affairs Council of Washington
Sudeep Reddy	
Dolores Redfearn	
John G. Reed	
Donna M. Reed	Media General News Service
Travis Dean Reed	T. Dean Reed Co.
Coleman Reed	Tuckson Consolidated News Pictures
John Rees	International Reports: Early Warning
David Gene Reese	

Robert R. Rehg	Edelman Public Relations
Barbara A. Rehm	American Banker
Diane Rehm	American University-WAMU-FM Radio
Jay H. Reid	
Patricia S. Reid	Internal Revenue Service
Tim Reid	Times of London
Daniel W. Reilly	Capitol Leader
Sean Reilly	Mobile Press-Register
Patty Reinert	Houston Chronicle
Frederick S. Reis Jr.	
Susan M. Reiss	Freelance
Seymour Reitman	Freelance
Louise Austin Remmey	CBS News (Retired)
Mary J. Renaud	
Werner Renberg	(Syndicated Columnist/Author)
Wolfgang Renezeder	Embassy of Austria
Wally Renfro	NCAA
Leo Rennert	McClatchy Newspapers
Mary Repass	R & R Global Communications, Inc.
Jerry L. Reppert	Reppert Publications
Thomas B. Reston	
Gene Retske	Prepaid Press
Magin Revillo	Radio Nacional de Espana
Michael Reyes	Georgetown University
Judy T. Reynolds	
Lissa Reynolds	American Journalism Review
Barbara Reynolds	Howard University
Michael Rhea	Wesley College
Donald Laird Rheem	RheemMedia
Reginald W. Rhein	Scrips World Pharmaceutical News
Geraldine E. Rhoads	
Barton R. Ribakow	Arthur Diamond Associates
F. Joseph Ricci	Ricci Communication, LLC
Charles Spencer Rice	Associated Press
Frank H. Rich	DC Vote
Spencer Rich	National Journal
Rita Rich Rita	Rich Media Services
Carol R. Richards	Newsday
Robert Richards	Pennsylvania State University
John Richardson	
Brian Richardson	Washington & Lee University
Jay Richter	Freelance
Lisa Richwine	Reuters
Ruth Rickard	
Edward M. Rider	
Miriam Rider	U.S. Department of State
Rem Rieder	American Journalism Review
Kurt W. Riegel	
Dana L. Riel	Business Solutions. Inc.
Sandra L. Riggs	
Erling Rimestad	Royal Norweigian Embassy
Tena Lowe Rips	Thoughts Facts & Comments
Jonathan Riskind	Columbus Dispatch
Andrea M. Riso	ARM (Audience Reach Media)
C. Jackson Ritchie	
Pedro Rivera-Casiano	Washington Advisory Group
Emilio-Adolfo Rivero	
Lee Rizzuto, Jr.	Harco Publishing

Peggy Roberson	Freelance
Carey Roberts	Freelance
Betty W. Roberts	
Carolyn G. Roberts	
William L. Roberts	Bloomberg News
Gail Roberts	McGraw-Hill
Eugene L. Roberts	University of Maryland
Lori Robertson	Annenberg Public Policy Center
Laura Robertson	CBN News
William L. Robertson	Robertson Consulting LLC
Gil Robertson Robertson	Treatment, Syndicated
Chris Robichaux	American Academy of Actuaries
Yolanda Robinson	
Ray M. Robinson	
Jeffrey Robinson	Author
Amy Robinson	Direct Selling Association
Faye Robinson	U.S. Department of Commerce
Julie A. Rochman	American Insurance Association
Theodore Rockwell	Author
Lee Roderick	Utah State University
Arlene Gould Rodman	Time-Life News Service
Paul M. Rodriguez	Burson-Marsteller
Randall B. Roe	Burns & Roe Enterprises
Daniel A. Roem	Gainesville Times
Keith Rogers	
William B. Rogers	
Alla Rogers	Alla Rogers Gallery
Carol L. Rogers	University of Maryland
Ginna Rogers-Gould	
Joshua Rogin	Federal Computer Week
Jacques Rogozinski	Inter-American Investment Corp.
Jannie Roher	
Mark F. Rohner	
Warren Rojas	Northern Virginia Magazine
Neil Roland	Bloomberg News
Paul B. Rolfes	Louisville Courier Journal
Ivan Roman	National Association of Hispanic Journalists
Lisa Romero	University of Illinois
Julie E. Rones	Rones
Emily Rooney	WGBH-TV
Selwa S. Roosevelt	
Ann A. Roosevelt	Defense Daily
Gordon Rose	Flight Concepts
Jacqueline Carole Rose	U.S. Environmental Protection Agency
James McKinley Rose, Jr.	
James R. Roseberry	Write Stuff
Gerald R. Rosen	
Jill Rosen	American Journalism Review
James Rosen	McClatchy Newspapers
Greg A. Rosenbaum	Palisades Associates, Inc
John Rosenberg	EEI Communications
Eric Rosenberg	Hearst Newspapers
Marc H. Rosenberg	Washington Post
Robert A. Rosenblatt	Freelance
Sherwood Ross	League for Nonviolent Solutions
Patrick C. Ross	The Progress & Freedom Foundation
Rae Rossen	Rossen Associates, Inc.
Virginia L. Rossiter	

Sheri E. Rothman	Freelance
Joe Rothstein	USPoliticstoday.com
Ruben O. Rotondaro	
Fred Rotondaro	Tiber Potomac
Frances Rotwein	
Mary Lucey Rowan	
Thomas F. Rowan	Catholic Standard (Retired)
Charles S. Rowe	
Elizabeth Rowe	Rutgers University
Sylvia Rowe	SR Strategy
Priscilla Rowe	Stars & Stripes
Alice S. Rowen	
Storer Rowley	Chicago Tribune
Arthur E. Rowse	U.S. News & World Report
William R. Royce	Voice of America
Linda G. Rozett	U.S. Chamber of Commerce
Brian Ruberry	Allhealth Public Relations
Elvera Ruby	
Patrick Rucker	American Banker
Joan Rudman	AWS Newsletter
Carol L. Rudman	U.S. Department of Commerce
Shirley Rudney	
Dr. Sharon Rudy	Public Health Institute
Frederick Gale Ruffner	Omnigraphics, Inc.
Conrad Rugart	
David Ruleman	Salem Communications Corp.
Malia Rulon	Gannett News Service
Daniel Rumelt	Federal Communications Commission
Nicholas Rummell	Crain Communications, Inc.
Rex A. Runyon	American Feed Industry Association
Tonda F. Rush	American Press Works, Inc.
Linda Russano	
John K. Russell	
James C. Russell	Lord Jim Productions
Carolyn Russell	Russell Public Relations
D.D. Russell	Washington Post (Retired)
Lori Ann Russo	Stanton Communications, Inc.
Diane Russomanno	
Dan W. Rutherford	International Brotherhood of Teamsters
Kertu Ruus	Estonian Business Daily Aripaev
Richard A. Ryan	Detroit News (Retired)
Frank T. Ryan	
Elliot Alden Ryan	Accelerated & Brain Based Learning in the News
April Ryan	American Urban Radio Network
Jan Ryan	Corporate Video, Inc.
Margaret Ryan	McGraw-Hill
Timothy G. Ryan	Reuters
William P. Ryder	
Geraldine Ryerson-Cruz	World Vision
Richard Sachs	Ron Sachs Communications
Scott Sacknoff	Quest Magazine
Takashi Sadahiro	Yomiuri Shimbun
Antoinette R. Saddler	
Jeanne Saddler	Metropolitan Washington Council of Governments
Aaron Sadler	Stephens Media
Riaz J.P. Saehu	Embassy of Indonesia
Dianne Saenz	EMS/Science Communication Network
Leslie Sage	Nature America, Inc.

Takashi Sakamoto	Yomiuri Shimbun
Inez Saki-Tay	University of the District of Columbia
Roberto Saladin	International Consultant
Jonathan D. Salant	Bloomberg News
Fayez I. Saleeb	Al Ahram Newspaper
Lee Salem	Universal Press Syndicate
Mohammad Ali Salih	Asharq Alawsat, Newspaper of London
Kathleen E. Salimena	Freelance
Franklin C. Salisbury, Jr.	National Foundation for Cancer
Patricia Saltonstall	Freelance
Carlo Salzano	Traffic World (Retired)
Arthur W. Samansky	The Samansky Group
Steve Sami	Military & Diplomats World News
Dr. Abbas William Samii	Radio Free Europe/Radio Liberty
Richard T. Sammon	Kiplinger Washington Editors, Inc.
Dave Samson	Chevron Corp.
Sheldon W. Samuels	Ramazzini Institute
Darren Samuelsohn	Environment & Energy Publishing
Orion C. Samuelson	WGN Radio
Theresa Catherine Sanchez	George Washington University
Pablo E. Sanchez-Obando	Univision News
Marc Sandalow	San Francisco Chronicle
Catherine Edwards Sanders	Freelance
Geraldine Sanderson	Sanderson Associates
Marideth Sandler	Office of U.S. Trade Representative
Laetitia T. Sands	
Brian Sansoni	Soap & Detergent Association
Tim Sargeant	Dominion Co.
Carole Sargent	Georgetown University
James Saris	U.S. Senate Press Gallery
Ron Sarro	Ron Sarro Productions
Kenneth S. Satterfield	Americans For Medical Progress
Patricia Saunders	
Teresa Savage	University of Illinois
Jon McCotter Sawyer	Pulitzer Center for Crisis Reporting
Sirena Scales	Thomson Financial Publication
Thomas R. Scanlan	
D. Duvrese Marr Scarlett	McGraw-Hill
Kathie Scarrah	Freelance
Edward A. Schaefer	St. Louis Informer
Charles P. Schaeffer	
Joan Pomprowitz Schaupp	Manna Co.
Joshua Scheer	truthdig.org
Kenneth M. Scheibel	
Barry F. Scher	Giant Food. LLC
Bob Schieffer	CBS News
David Schillerstrom	
Max Schindler	NBC News
Alan Norris Schlaifer	Wharton School Club of DC
Aileen Roberta Schlef	Creative Alliance Communications
Al R. Schleicher	Yomiuri Shimbun
Abdallah Marc Schleifer	Al Arabiya News Channel
Robert E.K. Schlesinger	Freelance
Courtney Schlisserman	Bloomberg News
Ann D. Schmidt	
Robert Schmidt	Bloomberg News
Peter G. Schmidt	Chronicle of Higher Education
Wayne W. Schmidt	Fire & Police Personnel Reporter

Michael Schmidt	McGraw-Hill
Tracy Samantha	Schmidt Time Magazine
Karen Schneider	Amnesty International USA
William Schneider	CNN
Andrew C. Schneider	Kiplinger Washington Editors, Inc.
Martin L. Schnider	Fred Schnider Co., LLC
Mark Schoeff	Crain Communications, Inc.
Michael J. Schoenfeld	Vanderbilt University
Patricia Q. Schoeni	Communications Consultation Network
Joseph B. Scholnick	Capitol News Service
Paul Schomer	Viacom
Daniel Schorr	National Public Radio
Roger Paul Schrum	Sonoco
David G. Schuchat	Freelance
Theodor Schuchat	
Sally Schuff	Feedsstuffs, Weekly Newspaper Agriculture
Harry D. Schultz	Business Aides Associates
Ralph R. Schulz	
William Schulz	Amtrak
John D. Schulz	Associated Press Broadcast
Franklin D. Schurz	Schurz Communications. Inc.
Priscilla Anne Schwab	U.S. Department of Labor
Milena Schwager	Media Silver
Leland Schwartz	
Stephen Schwartz	
Harvey Schwartz	
Marie Smith Schwartz	
Diane Schwartz	Access Intelligence
Emma Schwartz	Legal Times
Victor E. Schwartz	Shook Hardy & Bacon
Joan Schweitz	
Carole Schweitzer	National Association of College & Universities
Belinda Sciandra	NACON Consulting, LLC
Philip C. Scibilia	
Betsy Scolnik	National Geographic Society
Richard Scorza	
John Murphy Scott	
David N. Scott	815 Communications
Garland Scott	Folger Shakespeare Library
Ivan Scott	WTOP Radio
Edwin A. Scott, Jr.	Scott Group
Charles E. Scripps	Miramar Services Inc.
Walter H.T. Seager	Penny Hill Press
William Seamans	ABC News (Retired)
Andrew Seamans	Answer Man
Marika E. Sebsow	
Tod Sedgwick	Sedgwick Publishing Co.
Mark Seibel	McClatchy Newspapers
John P. Seidenberg	Federal Compensation Publications
John L. Seigenthaler	First Amendment Center
Naaman Seigle	
Jean S. Seitz	
Scott D. Seligman	United Technologies Corp.
Daniel Seligson	Election Reform Information Project
David A. Sellers	Administrative Office
Daniel Selnick	Business Wire
William C. Selover	Chaparral Working Group
Cynthia Semon	CS Communications

Joseph M. Sendry	Catholic University of America
William C. Senior	
Jennifer Sergent	HGTV Ideas Magazine
Dorothy U. Seyler	Northern Virginia Community College
Mark L. Sfiligoj	Kiplinger Washington Editors, Inc.
Bob Shabazian	American Stock Exchange
Ronald G. Shafer	
Mary M. Shaffrey	Winston-Salem Journal
Dean V. Shahinian	U.S. Senate Committee on Banking, Housing & Urban Affairs
Michael Shank	3D Security
Donald H. Shannon	
Benjamin Shapiro	Creators Syndicate
Martin R. Shapiro	Wachovia Securities
Leonard Shapiro	Washington Post
Deborah Shapley	
Adam Sharon	King Publishing Group
Adam Sharp	U.S. Senator Mary L Landrieu (D-La)
Daniel A. Shaw	Freelance
Ena B. Shaw	
Thomas M. Shaw	Healthcare Management Television
John T. Shaw	Market News International, Inc.
Richard L. Shea	
Terence Shea	HR Magazine
Claire M. Sheahan	TIAA-CREF
Natalie P. Shear	Natalie P. Shear Associates Inc.
Mary Ellen Shearer	Medill News Service
J. Craig Shearman	National Retail Federation
Rachel Sheedy	Kiplinger Washington Editors, Inc.
Mark T. Sheehan	
Molly O'Meara Sheehan	World Watch Magazine
Carrie Sheffield	The Politico
Fawzia Sheikh	Inside Washington Publishers
Charlotte Pilley Shepard	Freelance
C. Scott Shepard	Cox Newspapers
David Shepardson	Detroit News
Jerry Sherman	
Paul Sherman	Potomac Tech Wire (CapWire Inc.)
Patricia Sherr	Revista Credencial
Retha Sherrod	Association of American Medical Colleges
Mary Sherwood	
Susan Sherwood	Pennsylvania Public Television
Marciarose Shestack	
Nancy L. Shia	Shia Photos
Mark S. Shields	Syndicated Columnist
Carole Shifrin	
Jaegu Shim	MBC TV & Radio, South Korea
Kyung Youl Shin	Seoul Broadcasting System
Myrna Shinbaum	Anti-Defamation League
Bernard F. Shinkman	U.S. Department of State
Daniel K. Shipp	International Safety Equipment Association
Claude R. Shirai	Washington Nichibei Consultants
Gail L. Shivel	
Richard J. Shmaruk	Priest Magazine
Cheryl Ann A. Shoemaker	
Alan M. Shoemaker	MITRE Corp.
Ginger Shore	Bard College
T. Michael Shortal	
Mary Anne Shreve	Auto Exec Magazine

Margaret Shreve	Tax Analysts
Dmitry Sidorov	Kommersant Publishing House
Robert J. Siegel	
Martha N. Sigg	
Debra J. Silimeo	Hager Sharp
Jeffrey Scott Silva	Crain Communications, Inc.
Sam Silverstein	Graduate Management Admission Council
Paula Simmons	
Beverly Simmons	
Roynn Lisa Simmons	Fingerpost Productions
Amy Simmons	National Association of Community Health Centers
Rabbi Matthew H. Simon	B'nai Israel Congregation
William G. Simon	California Space Authority
Samuel A. Simon	Issue Dynamics. Inc.
Leslie D. Simon	Woodrow Wilson International Center
Peggy Simpson	Freelance
Kim M. Simpson	For the Record Photography & Public Affairs, Inc.
Alan Simpson	LTNN/Intel Briefine/Spies Magazine
Amarjit Singh	Chardhi Kala
Heidi K. Sinick	Freelance
Frank A. Sis	
Peter Sisler	Deutsche Presse-Agentur
Pastor B. Sison	
Andrei K. Sitov	Itar-Tass News Agency
Anne Sittmann	AICPA (Certified Public Accountant)
Margaret P. Skallerup	
Katherine M. Skiba	Milwaukee Journal Sentinel
Robert Skole	Freelance
Gary W. Slaats	
Francis Slakey	American Physical Society
Julie Slattery	Bloomberg News
Denise B. Slaughter	Institute Educational Leadership
Barbara Slavin	USA Today
Mounzer A. Sleiman	Almustaqbal Al Arabi
Katherine Day Slevin	
Jonathan Slevin	Washington Times
Steven Sloan	American Banker
Pamela Small	
Matt Small	Associated Press Broadcast
Edward Small	Tompkins Builders, Inc.
Diane Smiroldo	Business Software Alliance
Lee Smith	Freelance
Mignon C. Smith	
Benfred Clement Smith	Benfred Clement Smith Networks
Alison Smith	CBC
Philip S. Smith	CAPTEL
Nancy Smith	Contributing Columnist
Guy L. Smith	Diageo
Michael J. Smith	Dispatch Broadcast Group
Sylvia A. Smith	Fort Wayne Journal Gazette
Gordon L. Smith	Gordon L. Smith Co.
Stephen Grant Smith	The Examiner
Mark W. Smith	Kasowitz Benson Torres & Friedman
Brendan Smith	Legal Times
Charles B. Smith	Media 24, South Africa
Michael J. Smith	Michael Smith Business Development
Starr Smith	Montgomery Advertiser
Guy Francis Smith	U.S. Conference of Mayors

Frances M. Smoak	Aiken Standard & Review
Rachel Smolkin	American Journalism Review
Frank M Smyth	Committee to Protect Journalists
Betty Snead	
Rachel Snyder	Freelance
Betty G. Snyder	
Wallace S. Snyder	American Advertising Federation
John M. Snyder	Citizens Commitee for the Right to Keep & Bear Arms
Jane Peters Snyder	Independent Filmmaker
Edith Holmes Snyder	Journal of Orthopaedic & Sports Physical Therapy
Alice Sofield	Chandler Chicco Agency
Elena Sokolova	Russian RTR-TV
Richard Ray Solem	American Rowers Almanac
Steven Solomon	Freelance
Steve Solomon	National Museum of Health & Medicine
Norman H. Solon	
Glenn F. Somerville	Reuters
Michael Song	RTNDA
Mike Soraghan	Denver Post
John H. Sorrells	Altria Corporate Services Inc.
Roberto Soto	Imaginus
Jeannette C. Sowers	
Matt Spangler	McGraw-Hill
Sarah Sparks	Education Daily
Larry M. Speakes	U.S. Postal Service
William H. Speakman	Best-Met Publishing Co. Inc.
Gregory L. Spears	Vanguard Group
Mary Specht	American University
Anthony J. Spence	Catholic News Service
Timothy Spence	Transitions Online
Solveig B. Spielmann	Washington International Business
Miranda Spivack	Washington Post
Alvin A. Spivak	General Dynamics Corp.
Scott Spoerry	CNN
Andi Sporkin	National Public Radio
Tom Squitieri	Dittus Communications
James L. Srodes	James Srodes News Service
Florence Parrish	St. John Freelance
Noel R. St. John	Freelance
Jeff St. Onge	Bloomberg News
Suzanne St. Pierre	Freelance
Eleanor Stables	Congressional Quarterly
Stephanie Stahl	CMP Media
Diane Stamm	
Dustin Stamper	Tax Analysts
Sylvia Stanard	Church of Scientology International
Ruth Stanat	SIS International Research
Bella Stander	
Jeanne M. Stanek	U.S. Department of Justice
Mitchell K. Stanley	
Scott Stanley	Insight Magazine (Retired)
Peter V. Stanton	Stanton Communications
Meredith Stanton	The Magazine Group
John William Starke	
Timothy Alan Starks	Congressional Quarterly
Frank Starr	
H. Brooke Stauffer	Nationall Electrical Contractors Association
Denis Staunton	Irish Times

Laurel Stavis — Dartmouth College

Samuel E. Stavisky

Carla Stea — War & Peace Digest

William Stebbins — Al Jazeera

Diane Stebbins — Capitol Hill Magazine

Robert N. Steck — Steck Associates

Sally Steele — Freelance

Dennis Steele — Army Magazine

Laura Steele — Kiplinger Washington Editors, Inc.

Brian L. Steffens — National Newspaper Association

Daniel A. Stein — Federation for American Immigration

Scott Steinke — Elsevier Reports

Jon Steinman — Bloomberg News

Ellen B. Steis — Intelligence Press

Philip W. Steitz — Artists & Writers Syndicate

David E. Steitz — NASA

Irwin M. Stelzer — Irwin M. Stelzer Associates, Inc.

Neil Stempleman — Reuters

Oddvar Stenstrom — TV 2 Norway

Andrew Stephen — New Statesman (UK)

Saul I. Stern

Samson B. Stern

Christopher Stern — Bloomberg News

Marcus Stern — Copley News Service

William A. Stern — Neustar Inc.

Marc H. Stertz — Auto Exec Magazine

E.J. Gary Stevens — U.S. Postal Service

Allison Stevens — Womens eNews

Hal D. Steward — Freelance

Robert W. Stewart — Crossfire Communications

Mary Marshall Stewart — WETA-TV/FM

Gordon M. F. Stick

Grant M. Stockdale — Energy Policy Television

Brooke C. Stoddard — Freelance

Rob Stoddard — National Cable & Telecommunications Association

Russell Scott Stoermer — University of Virginia

Harry B. Stoffer — Crain Communications, Inc.

Richard B. Stolley — Time Inc.

Jack I. Stone — JSEconomic Consulting

Chuck Stone — University of North Carolina

Andrea Stone — USA Today

William C. Storey — Teal Group Corp.

Ralph Stow

Nina Straight — Freelance

William E. Strasburg

Linda Strating — Institute of World Politics

Richard Strauss — Strauss Radio Strategies, Inc.

David A. Straz — David A. Straz. Jr. Foundation

Jessica Strelitz — SmartBrief

Maria Streshinsky — U.S. Department of the Interior

John G. Stringer

Anna Stroman — Times of London

Arild Strommen — Royal Norwegian Embassy

Leigh Strope — International Brotherhood of Teamsters

Stephan Strothe — N24 TV

Suzanne Struglinski — Deseret Morning News

Pamela Stuart

Elizabeth M. Stuckle — USEC Inc.

Rex Allen Stucky
George Stuteville — National Rural Co-op Association
Katsuhiko Suetsugu — Asia-Pacific Energy Forum
Hiroki Sugita — Kyodo News America Inc.
Alan Suhonen — CBS News
Brian E. Sullam — T. Rowe Price Associates
Frances Sullinger
Marguerite H. Sullivan
Will Sullivan — ASI Marketing
William Sullivan — CSIS
Rebecca M. Sullivan
Andrew Sullivan — Reuters
Sam Summerlin — SAGA Agency
Mattias Sundholm — European Union
Curt Suplee — National Science Foundation
Justin J. Supon — U.S. House of Representatives Press Gallery
Joseph Sutherland — Burness Communications
Kirsten Suto — Special Olympics
Susan M. Sutter — Scrip World Pharmaceutical News
Gary Douglas Sutton — WSBA Radio
Susan Swain — C-SPAN
H. Kirk Swann — SAP Public Services. Inc.
Thomas W. Sweeney — Indian Health Services
Lynn Sweet — Chicago Sun-Times
Bethanie Swendsen — Family Research Council
Christian Swezey — Washington Post
Matthew Swibel — Forbes Magazine
Calnen I. Swingen — American Foreign Policy Council
Clayton E. Swisher — Middle East Institute
Henry M. Switkay
Peter A. Szekely — Reuters
Andrew E. Szucs — U.S. Air Force Materiel Command
Ryoji Tachio — Tokyo-Chunichi Shimbun
R. Michael Tackett — Chicago Tribune
Judith F. Taggart — JT& A, Inc.
Thomas J. Tague
Pamela Tainter-Causey — National Committee to Preserve Social Security & Medicare
Mamoru Takahara — Japan U.S. Concert & Cultural
Scott Talan — NASPAA
Richard Taliaferro — Wall Street Journal
Mark Tapscott — The Examiner
Ruth M. Tate — U.S. House of Representatives Radio & TV Gallery
Lisa M. Tate — National Association of Children's Hospitals
Santiago Tavara — Notimex
April Taylor
Laura L. Taylor — A&R Edelman Inc.
Stephen Taylor — ABC News
William Taylor — Action Image
Kendall Taylor — Artbank
Marjorie Taylor — Milliman, Inc.
Darlene Taylor — Pfizer, Inc.
Leslie Taylor — Roanoke Times
Truman B. Taylor — Rolyat News Service
Brian Taylor — U.S. Newswire
Albert Teich — AAAS
Ira Teinowitz — Advertising Age
Richard Tejan — CANUSA Publications, Inc.
Thomas R. Temin

Stanley L. Temko	Covington & Burling
Barbara Diane Tempchin	National Gallery of Art
Jerald F. terHorst	Ford Motor Co./ Detroit News (Retired)
John G. Terino	Freelance
Joseph Terrell	Terrell Communications, Inc.
Branko Terzic	Deloitte Services LP
Richard Teske	Strategic Advocacy
Joseph M. Tessmer	Tessmer of Fairfax
Stephan R. Tetreault	Stephens Media Group
Paul J. Thanos	U.S. Department of Commerce
Marjorie Tharp	American Academy of Pediatrics
Virginia A. Theis	
Nancy Theis	The White House
Jeanne Theismann	Alexandria Times
William V. Theobald	Gannett News Service
Ronald W. Thomas	Freelance
Milton Thomas	
Helen Thomas	Hearst Newspapers
Marjorie B. Thomas	Ivanhoe Broadcast News, Inc.
Richard King Thomas	Newsweek
Richard G. Thomas	Roll Call Report Syndicate
Dan Thomasson	Scripps Howard News Service
Cynthia Lynde Thompson	
Nancy E. Thompson	
Mary M. Thompson	Farm Foundation
Marilyn Thompson	Los Angeles Times
Jake Thompson	Omaha World Herald
Elvia Thompson	Stellar Presentations
Richard Thompson	Thompson Trails, Inc.
Pauline Thompson	Tysons Realty, Inc.
Monica Thompson	Fragale Reporter, The
Landon K. Thorne	Midas Advisory Group, Inc.
C. Patrick Thorne	Washington Bureau News Service
Jeannye Thornton	
Karen Thuermer	Freelance
Angus M. Thuermer	A & A Associates
William B.J. Tibbits	
Carolyn Tieger	Porter Novelli
Gene Tighe	Rockwell Collins
Christine Till	Howrey, Simon, Arnold & White LLP
Karen Timmons	Scripps Howard News Service
Richard W. Tippett	Washington Post
Gerald N. Tirozzi	National Association of Secondary School Principals
Charles Tobin	Holland & Knight, LLP
Maurice B. Tobin	Tobin French & Dillon
Vincent R. Tocci	American University
James Toedtman	AARP Bulletin
Shira R. Toeplitz	National Journal
Richard S. Toikka	Metropolitan Legal Services, LLC
Martin Tolchin	
Robert Michael Tomasko	Author
Diane Tomb	Tomb & Associates LLC
W. D. Tomlinson	
Leo S. Tonkin	Washington Workshops Foundation
Ellen F. Toomey	Freelance
Jack E. Tootson	eTelecare Golbal Solutions
Constantine Toregas	Public Technology, Inc.
Richard Torrenzano	Torrenzano Group

Jack Torry	Columbus Dispatch
Connie Totten-Oldham	U.S. Postal Service
Jonathan B. Tourtellot	National Geographic Traveler
Stephen J. Trachtenberg	George Washington University
Edward C. Tracy	Tawani Foundation
Rebecca Trager	Research USA, LLC
Laszlo Trankovits	Deutsche Presse-Agentur
John M. Trask	First Carolina Corp.
Ruth R. Traurig	
Mary Ann Treger	Freelance
Phyllis Treusch	
Tali Trigg McClatchy-Tribune	Regional News
Patti Tripathi	TriPath Media
Alvin W. Trivelpiece	Consultant
Gordon Trowbridge	Detroit News
Charles L. Trozzo	
Thomas L. Trueblood	International Truck & Engine Corp.
Susan Truitt	WUSA-TV
Chung Li Tsai	TECRO (Press Division)
James T.H. Tsao	Journal of Asian Economics
Nadia Yu-Fen Tsao	Liberty Times
Howard McK. Tucker	Consultant
James P. Tucker	Freelance
Jean E. Tucker	
Paul A. Turk	Federal Aviation Administration
John M. Turner	
Douglas L. Turner	Buffalo News
Diane M. Turner-Hurns	American Society of Safety Engineers
Katherine R Turpin	
Katherine Tynberg	Tynberg Group
Emily Tynes	American Civil Liberties Union
Elaine Tyrrell	U.S. Consumer Product Safety
James L. Tyson	Bloomberg News
Toshihide Ueda	Asahi Shimbun
Satoshi Ukai	Asahi Shimbun
Omar Ullah	University of Texas at Austin
Sanford M. Ullman	
David J. Umansky	The Umansky Network
Toshiya Umehara	Asahi Shimbun
April Umminger	Washington Post
Peter Urban	Connecticut Post
Jennifer C. Urquhart	
Joe Urschel	Freedom Forum
Steve Usdin	BioCentury
Jon B. Utley	Ludwig von Mises Institute
Matthew Vadum	Bond Buyer
Vivian Vahlberg	
Rodrigo Valderrama	Long & Foster Commerical Division
Ann Valuchek	Andrew J. Valuchek Scholarship
Peter van Aartrijk	The van Aartrijk Group
Kristen van de Graff	
Michael Van Den Branden	Porcupine Press, Inc.
Simon Van Der Burg	Embassy of the Netherlands
Gerry Van Der Heuvel	
Benjamin van der Horst	Emory University
Darryl Van Duch	Jenner & Block
Marty van Duyne	
Peter Van Haverbeke	

Jane Van Ryan	American Petroleum Institute
Doorn Dominique Van Steyn	Photo Bank International
Greta Van Susteren	Fox News Channel
Barbara Vandegrift	
Nicholas P. Vaslef	
Mary Lowry Vaughan	
Hal W. Vaughan	Freelance
Anthony Vaz	Insight Engineering Inc.
Aerica Veazey	The Heritage Foundation
Alison Vekshin	Bloomberg News
George Vercessi	Freelance
Carlos Verdecia	Washington Times
Michael Verespej	Crain Communications, Inc.
Wes Vernon Freelance	
Stephen Villano	Cable Positive, Inc.
Robert E. Vitarelli	Capitol Media Management LLC
Claire Vitucci	Belo Broadcasting
Daniel C. Vock	Stateline.org
Drew Von Bergen	National Association of Letter Carriers
David von Sothen	
Phil Von Tom	Hendon Publishing
Elisabeth Vondracek	
Virginia VonFremd	Professionally Speaking Association
Julie Vorman	Reuters
William O. Vose	
Kathryn Kahler	Vose Porter Novelli
Martha Voss	Toyota Motor Sales USA, Inc.
Ginger Vuich	
Melvin L. Vulgamore	
Richard H. Wade	American Hospital Association
Terry Wade	The WadeGroup, Inc.
Leon R. Wagener	
Susan Wagner	Freelance
Patricia M. Wait	
Alden C. Waite	
Nancy H. Waitz	Reuters
Patricia R. Wakeling	
George M. Wakiji	
Thomas Walde	ZDF German Television
Tom Walek	Walek & Associates Inc.
Chandra Walker	
Savannah Walker	
Norman O. Walker	Associated Press (Retired)
Antony Howard Walker	Australian Financial
Tom Walker	Dispatch Broadcast Group
Janice Daue Walker	Fannie Mae
Richard W. Walker	Post Newsweek Tech Media/Government Computer News
William N. Walker	Rensselaer Polytech Institute
A.E.P. Wall	Freelance
James H. Wallace	
William C. Wallack	
Maeve Walls	Northern Ireland Bureau
Edward James Walsh	
Louise D. Walsh	AFL-CIO Solidarity Center
Trudy Walsh	Post Newsweek Tech Media/Government Computer News
Lynne Walsh	SUNY New Paltz
Bill Walsh	The Times-Picayune
Nolan Walters	National Press Foundation

Mia Walton	Rolls Royce North America, Inc.
Vickie L. Walton-James	Chicago Tribune
Barbara S. Wamsley	LMA International
James Wang	Community TV Network
Sheila Ward	American Society of International Law
Barbara Ware	AdvaMed
W. Robert Warne	W. Robert Warne Consultant
John W. Warner	
Christine Warnke	Hogan & Hartson
Paul Warren	Warren Communications News
Ellen A. Wartella	University of California/Riverside
Lelia K. Washburn	
P. Neely Washington	Middlesex Newspaper
Larry W. Waterfield	Vance Publishing Corp.
Jane Watrel	Freelance
George H. Watson	
George J. Watson	
William H. Watson	Fairplay Publications
William L. Watts	Dow Jones Marketwatch
David A. Waugh	
Alex Wayne	Congressional Quarterly
Peter Weaver	
Robert E. Webb	
Robert Webster	North American Securities
William R. Weeks	Fort Collins Consolidated Royalties
Sumner S. Weener	NBC News (Retired)
Ellie Wegener	Employment Support Center
Robert P. Weil	
Jenny Weil	McGraw-Hill
Sharon Weinberger	
Lawrence Weiner	Executive Realty Services
Bonnie H. Weinstein	Attorney at Law
Harris Weinstein	Covington & Burling
Stan Weinstock	NBC News
Jeffrey W. Weir	National Semiconductor Corp.
Steve Weisman	New York Times
Steven H. Weiss	McGraw-Hill
Rozanne Weissman	Alliance to Save Energy
Norma Weitz Zager	Los Angeles Jewish Journal
John E. Welch	Jones Day LLC
Rupert Welch	Rupert Welch News Service
Gary Wells	Dix & Eaton
Chris Wells	Freedom Forum
L. Dana Wells	The Politico
James L. Wells	University of the District of Columbia
Betsey Welton	Freelance
David Wenkert	Michigan State University
Kevin M. Wensing	U.S. Navy
Cole Palmer Werble	RPM Report
Ed Wergeles	
Erica Werner	Associated Press
Theresa Werner	Associated Press Broadcast
Isabel West	
Benjamin C. West	
Robert D. Westgate	
Richard Wexler	CNN
Anne Wexler	Wexler & Walker Public Policy Associates
Thomas Weyr	

Teodora Dominique	Weyr Voice of America
Gerald Wheeler	National Science Teachers Association
Esther Whieldon	McGraw-Hill
Kirk Whisler	Latino Print Network
Joel Whitaker	Whitaker Newsletters Inc.
David N. Whitcombe	Niles & Associates, Inc.
Susann Lee White	Freelance
Helen R. White	
Elizabeth White	
Robert A. White	
Jean White	
Thomas C. White	Association of American Railroads
Brad White	Financial Planning Association
Peter T. White	National Geographic Society
Robert M. White	
Heather White	U.S. Newswire
Tim White	WKYC TV
Quentin C. Whiteree	IDEEA Inc.
John Whitesides	Reuters
Theresa C. Whitfield	Salvation Army
Summer Whitford	Maison Chanterclerc
Pamela J. Whitted	National Stone Sand Gravel Association
Joan Lewis Whittington	
Bonnie S. Whyte	
Stacey H. Widdicombe	
Scott D. Widmeyer	Widmeyer Communications Inc.
Brett Widness	America Online
Heidi Wiedenbauer	Cox Broadcasting
Arthur E. F. Wiese	Entergy Corp.
Valentine M.N Wilber	Wilber Republican
Jane Ann S. Wilder	
Marion Bell Wilhelm	U.S. Department of State
Margaret C. Wilhide	Association of American Railroads
Dana M. Wilkie	Copley News Service
William M. Wilkins	Road Information Program (TRIP)
Julia Wilkinson	
Mark Willen	Kiplinger Washington Editors, Inc.
Kim Willenson	
Arthur K. Willey	
Aretha Williams	
Mary Lois Williams	
John D. Williams	
Jack C. Williams	American Meteorological Society
Mantill J. Williams	American Public Transportation Association
John M. Williams	Assistive Technology News
D.E. Williams	Hampton News Service
Robert H. Williams	National Defense Magazine
Wade S. Williams	Political Action Committee Services
Ralph Williams	The Titan Corp.
Sarah Williams	Voice of America
Deirdre Willits	Medialink
Ann R. Willner	
Frank Wilner	
Jane S. Wilson	
Arthur H. Wilson	Disabled American Veterans
David M. Wilson	EZ Consulting
Kimberly Wilson	Georgetown University Press
John W. Wilson	J.W. Wilson & Associates, Inc.

Julia A. Wilson	Wilson Global Communications LLC
Walter S. Wingo	
Frances Winkler	
Matt Winkler	Bloomberg News
Deborah Winn	National Institutes of Health
Joycelyn Winnecke	Chicago Tribune
Joe Winski	Bloomberg News
Joyce Winslow	Freelance
Colette J. Winston	U.S. Department of Justice
Thomas S. Winter	Human Events
Gretchen M. Wintermantel	Office of U.S. Rep. Paul Kanjorski
Grethe Winther	Scandanavian Broadcast/News Center
Alan E. Wirzbicki	Freelance
Christy Wise	Freelance
Lawrence A. Withers	Consultant
William L. Withuhn	Smithsonian Institution
Richard Wittenberg	Act for Health
Koko Wittenburg	Current Newspapers
Alexandra Witze	Nature
Lorraine Woellert	Business Week
Marc Wojno	INPUT
Larry Wojno	Larry Wojno Consulting
Jim Wolf	Reuters
Elizabeth Jackie Wolfe	
John F. Wolfe	Columbus Dispatch
Mark R. Wolff	Credit Union National Association
Venlo J. Wolfsohn	
Charles A. Womack	Womack Publishing
Daniel Woo	ABC News
Winston S. Wood	Freelance
Gwendolyn C. Wood	Public Broadcasting Service
Arthur Wood	
Kenneth Wooden	Wooden Publishing House
H. Graham Woodlief	Media General News Service
Fred A. Woodress	
David K. Woodroof	
Michael Woods	Toledo Blade/Pittsburgh Post Gazette
Anne H. Woodworth	Freelance
Ellery B. Woodworth	
Mary Woolley	Research America
Amy C. Worden	Philadelphia Inquirer
Colleen McDonough	Wordock Bloomberg News
Ronald David Worth	Society for Marketing Professionals
Barry Worthington	U. S. Energy Association
Kelly Wright	Fox News Channel
Charlotte L. Wright	McGraw-Hill
Kim Wright	National Committee to Preserve Social Security & Medicare
Gretchen Wright	PR Solutions
Layla Wright	WETA
Walter L. Wright III	
Terri Wu Epoch	Times
William J. Wyatt	National Conference of State Legislatures
Ben Wyche	Cato Institute
Qinduo Xu	China Radio International
Don Yacoe	U.S. News Ventures
Marjorie A. Yahreas	
Nick Yaksich	Association of Equipment Manufacturers
George L. Yaksick, Jr.	CCH Inc.

Hideya Yamamoto	Sankei Shimbun
Chunfang Yang	New Tang Dynasty Television
Priscilla Yap	Northern Virginia Magazine
Mary Helen Yarborough	Medical University of South Carolina
Russell Yarrow	Chevron Corp.
Seifeldin Omar Yasin	Embassy of Sudan
Ken Yates Jefferson	Waterman International
Cynthia D. Yeast	Fannie Mae Foundation
Peter Yessne	Staffing Industry Analysts, Inc.
Patrick Yoest	Congressional Quarterly
Robert Yoon	CNN
Sock-Joong Yoon	Embassy of the Republic of Korea
Yong Chul Yoon	MBC TV & Radio
Milena Yordanova	McGraw-Hill
Ryota Yoshimura	Sumitomo Corp. of America
Jeane R. Young	Freelance
Maria Young	Bloomberg News
Kerry Young	Bloomberg News
Albert W. Young	Boston Globe
Maryann S. Young	District of Columbia Office of Chief Finance Officer
Bruce K. Young	Evans-McCan Group
Patrick Young	Oncology News International
Rachelle Younglai	Reuters
Wayne A. Youngquist	WISN-TV
Sidney Lawrence Yudain	Roll Call
Meghan Yudes	Portovert Magazine
Rob Yunich National	Small Business Association
Nicholas M. Zacchea	
Narda C. Zacchino	San Francisco Chronicle
Janine Zacharia	Bloomberg News
Walter Zachariasiewicz	
Jeffrey Zack	International Association of Fire Fighters
Lisa Zagaroli	McClatchy Newspapers
Katharine Zambon	Pew Charitable Trust
Jose Lopez Zamorano	Notimex, Mexican News Agency
Bruce J. Zanca	Bankrate, Inc.
Nicholas Zapple	
Joe Leroy Zaring	
Rob Zatkowski	U.S. House of Representatives Periodical Press Gallery
Bern H. Zeavin	
Denice E. Zeck	American Forum
Mayssaa Zeidan	MBN/Al Hurra Television
David Zenian	Anteon Corp.
Kasper Zeuthen	Yomiuri Shimbun
Lisa-Joy Zgorski	LJZ Strategic Commnications
Elaine Ziemba	ez's Solutions, Inc.
Jan Ziff	Sound*Bytes Radio
Steve Ziffer	Focus
Lester Ziffren	
Marvin Zim	Freelance
Richard G. Zimmerman	Freelance
Sacha Zimmerman	Reader's Digest
Richard Zmuda	Severn School
Jerry Zremski	Buffalo News
Todd Zwillich	

Index

INDEX